Freedom Under Siege

Freedom Under Siege

The Impact of Organized Religion on Your Liberty and Your Pocketbook

Madalyn Murray O'Hair

PUBLISHED BY J.P. TARCHER, INC., LOS ANGELES
Distributed by Dell Distributing Inc. New York

THIS BOOK IS DEDICATED TO PUP

Table of Contents

Preface

The information that I offer in this book has been drawn from thousands of sources. Occasionally in these chapters I have tried to note the sources of the information that I am presenting. In many other instances, however, I have not, nor do I feel that it would serve the purposes of a general book of this kind to provide citations or notations for each statement. Many readers will regard some of the information as examples of Madalyn Murray O'Hair's Believe It or Not and will choose to doubt the facts and statistics no matter what their source. For these people, my citing specific references would prove nothing. However, I invite readers who are concerned about any given facts and wish to learn their sources to write me directly at the Society of Separationists, Inc., Post Office Box 2117, Austin, Texas 78767. I will try to reply to their questions.

It will be quickly evident to anyone who reads this book that the arguments presented do not rest upon any single pieces of information or statistics any more than an ocean depends for its existence on a drop of water. My statements and positions are the result of distilling and interpreting masses of facts, stories, and statistics.

The interpreting of information from these multifarious sources is much like the work of a government intelligence officer who sifts the miscellaneous data flowing out of foreign bureaucracies and agencies and then tries to piece it all together into some meaningful whole.

In doing this I have relied, for instance, on such "primary sources" as the *Congressional Record,* the reported court decisions in numerous legal journals, Gallup polls, many U.S. government publications, many legal journals, and records and speeches printed in contemporary magazines and newspapers. I have gone through the records of many congressional hearings and the reports submitted to the U.S. Congress by various executive departments and agencies, including the Internal Revenue Service, and I have also used compiled information found in U.S. census reports and in other government reports on hospitals, tax-exempt entities, and the like.

I have relied also on "bulletins" and "reports" issued by the National Council of Churches of Christ, the (Roman Catholic) National Association of Laymen, the (Protestant) Americans United, Roman Catholic Right-to-Life groups, and Roman Catholic pro-parochiaid groups, such as the Citizens for Educational Freedom. I have examined published annual reports of various philanthropic foundations and church groups as well as in-house bulletins of some such organizations sent to me by persons employed on their staffs. I have used the records of the hearings of the Federal Communications Commission, as well as its determinations reports, and have read the transcripts of television shows furnished by networks and individual stations.

The best newspapers for information on religious issues are the *Christian Science Monitor, Wall Street Journal, New York Times, Los Angeles Times, Washington Post, Philadelphia Inquirer, Deseret News, St. Louis Post-Dispatch, Chicago Tribune, Boston Globe, Cleveland Plain Dealer, Detroit Free Press, San Francisco Chronicle,* and *Miami Herald.* Religious editors are found on the staffs of the Copley News Service, the King Features Syndicate, the Associated Press, and the United Press International. There is one reporting service just for religion: the Religious News Service.

Among magazines, those that cover religious issues with some degree of regularity are *Forbes, Harper's Magazine, U.S. News and World Report, Masonic Magazine, Nation's Cities, Atlantic Monthly, Newsweek, Time, National Observer,* and the *American Bar Association Journal.*

The religious world has magazines and newspapers that also have been instructive from time to time. They include, *Jesuit's America; Catholic Reporter; Catholic Weekly; Catholic Bulletin;* the Baptists' *Report from the Capital;* the Protestants' *Church and State;* the Seventh-Day Adventists' *Liberty;* the Jehovah's Witnesses' *Awake* and *Watchtower;* the fundamentalists' *Changing Times* and *Christianity Today;* Baylor University's *Journal of Church and State; Jewish Free Press;* the Episcopal *Churchman,* and the Unitarian-Universalist *World.*

The *Annals of America,* a twenty-volume set of historical documents and readings published by the Encyclopaedia Britannica, is invaluable for primary source material and includes a great deal of the true history of religion in the United States.

Many of the statistics in this book have derived from random papers issued by the churches themselves; and such advertising and public relations information had to be studied with caution. Stories have come from newspaper and magazine clippings that have been sent to me by people who are aware of my efforts and concerns in the area of church-state separation. In some cases I have written directly to religious organizations involved in specific activities, but such organizations have usually evaded or simply ignored my inquiries. Government organizations, too, have sometimes answered my inquiries, sometimes not. Anyone who has attempted to research even the least controversial of subjects will attest to the fact that obtaining accurate information from private or governmental organizations is, at best, difficult; and, if one is seeking information on politically controversial subjects, even press representatives and public information officers are apt to clam up. My name is anything but an "open sesame" to the organizations to whom I must direct my inquiries.

There have been some interesting writers in the field of religion about whom the public should know something.

They include Paul Blanshard, Gaston Cogdell, Martin Larson, C. Stanley Lowell, Avro Manhattan, and Leo Pfeffer. Some very good individual books are E. Digby Baltzell, *The Protestant Establishment: Aristocracy and Caste in America* (1964); C. Thomas Dienes, *Law, Politics, and Birth Control* (1972); Matilda Gage, *Woman, Church and State* (1972); Frank Swancara, *The Separation of Religion and Government* (1950); Margaret Sanger, *An Autobiography* (1938); and Andrew D. White, *History of Warfare of Science with Theology in Christendom* (1896).

I wish to thank all the people, known and anonymous, who have helped in the development of this book. The editors at J. P. Tarcher, Inc., have been especially helpful and patient, and I am grateful to them. I wish also to express my gratitude to Jon Garth Murray, Ben Akerley, Samuel Miller, Mary Hartay, and Robin Lloyd, all of whom have been especially kind and helpful over the years. Finally, I wish to express affection and gratitude to my husband, Richard F. O'Hair.

Madalyn Murray O'Hair
Austin, Texas

Freedom Under Siege

The American people have always been captured by the idea of freedom. The supposition that "this is a free country" or that "I can do whatever I please" has permeated American thought to such an extent that many Americans have been unable to see the true measures of freedom and authority under which we live.

Americans, looking abroad, tend to show a mixture of pity and contempt for the many underprivileged nations whose peoples suffer under a variety of tyrannies. Few Americans, however, recognize that they too are under bondage to many authorities and that, if the bondage seems less apparent than the foreign tyrannies, it is because the controls are more covert and more subtly manipulative.

Every society has a system of social control, whereby individual members learn to adjust to the social behavior of which the society approves. This training proceeds from infancy; and the values and goals that it instills may become so internalized in the mind that one may scarcely question or even think about how one is being controlled by them. When, however, a person of independent mind should happen to appear—that is, one who questions certain standards or who departs from certain expectations of society—society has means of repression or discrimination to eliminate the person or put him in his place. In openly tyrannical countries, the means may often be especially direct and physical. In a "free" nation like America they can often be just as coercive but consist of less obvious but still almost irresistible economic and psychological pressures, or social reeducation. All such American methods can be summed up in the phrases "You can't beat the system" or "You can't fight city hall" or "What can a person do?" The system becomes a way of life.

Government, or the state, is not the only agent of control. There are many others, among them the family, one's peer group, business and industry, various clubs and associations, and so on. One of the most powerful institutions involved in this massive psychological and social conditioning is organized religion—that is, singly or as a whole, the various churches, sects, orders, and congregations governed by clergy and other officials and governing under systems of formal, frequently rigid rules and procedures. The major representatives of organized religion in the United States are collected under the names of Protestants, Roman Catholics, and Jews. The degree to which the state has its policies influenced by such institutions of organized religion is one of the subjects of this book.

Organized religion in America is formidable in its ability to make disadvantageous and often distasteful controls seem palatable and even desirable for the individual and to weaken his will to act as an individual and to combat injustice. This prominent institution, hallowed by tradition, has the power to align masses of people in a socially and politically "acceptable" direction under a complex system of doctrinal controls. The church doctrines of obedience to authority, repentance, fear of punishment, self-abnegation, acceptance of outer direction rather than inner assurance, elevation of faith over reason, and intolerance make institutionalized religion an ideal instrument of social constraint. In an unconstitutional partnership with the state, the church can impose the most irresistible, if covert, controls conceivable. Linked together, these two organizations constitute one of the most ominous threats to individual liberties.

VIOLATIONS OF THE SEPARATION OF CHURCH AND STATE

In the several chapters of this book I try to survey the grand range of major issues centering on the principle of the separation of church and state. One sees organized religion's inroads on government policy and practice. One sees its intrusion on secular public education and its successful inveigling of public moneys for parochial schools. One sees its suppression of books and films and its drives against birth control and abortion. One sees its accumulation of vast wealth through profit-making businesses and investments, gifts, grants, and subsidies, all tax-free. Throughout this book I try to sample the myriad areas in which organized religion has intruded its powerful influence, and I sample many other areas from which it draws its economic power. Primarily, however, I have tried to stick with the major issues and not attempted to catalog the literally thousands of violations of church-state separation that happen every day all over the country. This is not to suggest that the single violations are unimportant. On the contrary, cumulatively they offer a vast picture of evidence of the corruption of First Amendment freedoms, even though they receive scant public notice. Unless the violations involve a lawsuit of high constitutional significance, they receive minimal local press notice and, even then, are apt to be dropped by the press in a day or so for more interesting news. Editorials rarely appear on the subject of church-state separation; and the national press, radio, and television media are by and large totally unconcerned with the issues. Nevertheless, it would be possible to publish volumes of such violations, which often are permitted and even encouraged by every branch of government. The following sampling should give the reader a fair notion of the variety of single violations.

ITEM: In December 1971 Congress passed a private law extending for seventy-five years the existing copyright on Mary Baker Eddy's principal Christian Science work, *Science* and Health with Key to the Scriptures, and rescuing from the public domain all the editions whose copyright had already expired. This was the first time that the federal government had favored any book of any kind with such a sweeping special copyright (only about a ten-year extension has, on rare occasions, been granted certain publications). The precedence, now established, opens up fearful possibilities of all kinds of special religious copyrights.

ITEM: The U.S. Office of Education distributes a booklet entitled The Declaration of Independence and Its Story. On page 30, in a series of questions and answers, appears the following: "What are the basic rights of all people? All people are created equal; they are equal before God. God has given them certain rights which lawfully cannot be taken away." Under the constitutional doctrine of separation of church and state, the U.S. government should not be catechizing and proselytizing in this manner.

ITEM: Religious services are held in the White House, and Prayer Breakfasts are held in government buildings on various levels of federal, state, and local government.

ITEM: Congress has proclaimed April 30 the National Day for Humiliation, Fasting, and Prayer. The first "Whereas" in the resolution reads:

> Whereas, it is the duty of nations, as well as of men to owe their dependence upon the overruling power of God, to confess their sins and transgressions, in humble sorrow, yet with assured hope that genuine repentance will lead to mercy and pardon, and to recognize the sublime truth, announced in the Holy Scriptures and proven by all history, that those nations are blessed whose God is the Lord; . . .

This resolution goes on to declare that "we have forgotten God" and have become "too proud to pray to the God that made us" and that "only God can be the ultimate guardian of our true livelihood and safety." Because we have "blinded ourselves to God's standard of justice and righteousness for this society," it "therefore behooves us to humble ourselves before Almighty God, to confess our national sins, and to pray for clemency and forgiveness." The First Amendment to the U.S. Constitution expressly prohibits Congress from legislating for the "establishment of religion." The prescriptions for the National Day for Humiliation, Fasting, and Prayer clearly constitute efforts to establish religion.

ITEM: Many tax-exempt organizations that have been incorporated by Congress on the condition that they remain nonsectarian have nevertheless made belief in God a qualification for membership. The Boy Scouts and the Veterans of Foreign Wars are two such organizations.

ITEM: Military chaplains who perform a wide variety of religious functions are salaried by the U.S. government, not by the specific religious groups from which they come.

ITEM: The phrases "In God We Trust," "Under God," and "So help me God" have been legislated into official governmental language, despite the prohibitions of the First Amendment. "In God We Trust" was made the national motto in 1956; it appears on all currency and coins. "Under God" was added to the Pledge of Allegiance in 1954. "So help me God" is required in several oaths and affirmations, including the oaths of all elected and appointed federal legislative and executive officers (except the President), the oaths of all individuals seeking passports or naturalization papers, and the oaths of witnesses in most courts of law. Applicants for naturalization or passports have been rejected for refusing to affirm, "So help me God."

ITEM: Catholic hospitals receiving federal funds have refused to perform legal abortions for taxpayers who have provided the funds for the operation of the hospitals.

ITEM: The state of California gives state employees three hours off with pay for the observance of Good Friday. It denies non-Christians equivalent free time with pay for observance of other holidays or events.

ITEM: The U.S. Department of the Interior and the U.S. Department of Agriculture permit church groups to hold religious services in national parks and recreation areas without having to pay federal recreation fees. All other groups and individuals must pay—and thus in effect subsidize the church groups.

ITEM: Throughout Texas the diverse school boards have applications for teachers that invariably contain the following question:

Do you believe in a Supreme Being?

This religious test is actually supported by the Bill of Rights of the Texas Constitution, which says, in Section 3, that, although there shall be no religious test for public office, office seekers must acknowledge "the existence of a Supreme Being." This requirement violates the U.S. Constitution's prohibition against religious tests for office (Article VI), a prohibition that extends to the states by the Fourteenth Amendment.

The examples could go on and on. Some of the violations may not appear to be of great moment; but all the violations, the small ones as well as the ones of great constitutional issue, place our individual freedoms and rights under constant siege. They are a part of the whole invasion of organized religions on American secular life today—in fields of free enterprise, taxation, freedom of speech, education, abortion and divorce laws, and personal rights of citizens.

All the violations are vital symptoms of a disease so serious that the wise men who were present at the birth of our nation wrote out a prescription to deal with it. That document named The Constitution of the United States of America calls for an absolute and total separation of church and state. Slowly over the past century and rapidly over the past decade, the churches have begun to break out of this quarantine and infect the body politic. That process has to be stopped now if the nation is to live to a ripe old age as a democracy.

THE CHURCHES' REJECTION OF SEPARATION
OF CHURCH AND STATE

My publisher asked me when we discussed the contents of this book, "Why worry" about the separation of church and state? "Isn't it an academic problem with little or no significance in our daily lives?" History answers that. But, in addition, so does the Methodist church in America, which has an official interpretation of church-state relations that is not at all unique. It says:

Man has evolved both religious and political institutions —churches and government. Christians view these and all other institutions as instruments to be used under the sovereignty and judgment of God. Man's religious and political institutions, therefore, must find their justification as means to ends that accord with the will and purpose of God. . . .

The true nature of relations between churches and governments in the United States becomes clear only when it is realized that the actual and inescapable fact of our time is not their separation but their interaction and their correlation.

In the past fifty years, a number of social forces have combined to multiply the points of contact between churches and government, and significantly increase the frequency of interaction at any given point of contact. Among the social forces that have contributed to this transformation have been the extensive institutional development of churches, the tremendous expansion of the functions of governments, and the rapid industrialization and urbanization of American society.

Churches have acquired a large amount of economic and social power. They employ labor, provide social services, and operate educational institutions; they sponsor recreation, entertainment, and cultural enterprises; they are landlords as well as tenants; and they collect, expend, and invest money, as well as administer retirement and pension systems. Clearly churches now have the power to make economic and social decisions that vitally affect the lives and welfare of millions of people. No government can completely ignore the manner in which this economic and social power is exercised by church officials.

A "new breed" of church leaders and members has asserted, both in words and in social action activities, that religious interests are not simply matters of personal belief, worship, and piety, but that they are also relevant to public policy and the world of daily affairs. Congregations, denominations, and administrative agencies of interdenominational religious bodies have joined *in efforts to reconstruct the economic and political systems of American society along lines that will insure a greater realization of ethical and religious values. One result of this development has been the establishment of new and more sophisticated patterns of relations between churches and governments.*

This was a position statement of the Methodist church in 1968, and it is still operative. It frightens me. It should frighten everyone. The Methodist church, like other churches in our land, however, is so blinded to the system of discrimination working in its favor that it fails to see the enormity of the social injustice that can issue from such a commitment to public action and moralistic domination.

The churches' commitment to public action, moreover, is being made easier by the increasing consent and compliance of the state. Not only is organized religion seeking involvement in affairs of state, but government itself is inviting that involvement. The evidence of this interaction and counsel grows daily. Leaders of organized religion now speak of it freely and relish it. On May 6, 1974, in the *Los Angeles Times,* for instance, Rabbi Balfour Brickner of the New York Federation of Reformed Synagogues editorialized in this outspoken fashion:

America's organized religions are replete with a treasury of paradoxes, especially when it comes to their relationship with the state. Two of these paradoxes are particularly curious:

—At a time when many Americans doubt the credibility of institutional faiths, more and more religionists demand to be heard as witnesses by governmental bodies.

—In a society ostensibly committed to the ideal of church-state separation, government constantly seeks the views of organized religion.

Hardly a day passes when those who represent organized denominations are not asked to testify before Congress, presenting their considered opinions on subjects that range from civil rights to proposed legislation on divorce, gambling, fair housing or abortion.

Some think this is a terrible state of affairs. . . .

> *That . . . strikes me as nonsense. In practice,*
> *organized religion has never stayed out of politics; in*
> *principle, it dare not stand outside.*
>
> *I suggest that a major task of religion ought to be*
> *greater engagement in the gears of government.*

The rabbi is right about one thing. "Some think this is a
terrible state of affairs." I am one of those who think it is a
terrible state of affairs, and I have written this book to
demonstrate the dangerously expanding power of organized
religion in American life and politics.

The rabbi is dead wrong about one thing. He says that
"in principle" organized religion "dare not stand outside"
politics and government. On the contrary, the Founding
Fathers of our country, as well as their illustrious successors
down through time, all supported *the principle of the
separation of church and state,* of keeping religion out of
the affairs of government. The First Amendment to the
Constitution—which embraces the dictum "Congress shall
make no law respecting an establishment of religion, or
prohibiting the free exercise thereof"—has always been
interpreted as the guaranty of church-state separation.

Furthermore, lesser law also denies the rabbi's claims.
Religious groups have always eagerly sought exemption
from taxation; and the Internal Revenue Code liberally
grants them exemption but does so on the express condition
that they engage in no "political or legislative activity."
Section 501(c)(3) reads in part:

> *An exempt organization may not engage in certain
> political activities, or attempt to influence legislation as
> a substantial part of its total activities. Briefly, forbidden
> political activities include direct or indirect intervention
> in any political campaign on behalf of, or in opposition
> to, any political candidate. Attempts to influence legis-
> lation include: (1) contacting or urging the public to
> contact legislators in order to support, propose or
> oppose legislation, or (2) advocating the adoption or
> rejection of legislation.*

The reader must ultimately decide why an organization like
the Sierra Club should lose its tax-exempt status because of

its efforts on behalf of conservation legislation, while religious organizations remain tax-exempt despite their constant lobbying and petitioning in legislative debates on taxation, parochial aid, abortion, sex education, censorship, and everything else.

PROVISOS

Here and there throughout the book I may refer to situations or conditions that have receded into the past and no longer hold true. The reader is mistaken, however, if he assumes that such histories merely show how organized religion once upon a time tried to curtail individual freedoms in violation of the Constitution or tried to obtain illegal benefits in violation of the Constitution. The fact that organized religion may once have succeeded but was eventually stopped in one effort or another does not mean that its efforts do not continue or do not show a continuous pattern of intent. More important, past events warn us of what can happen to our freedoms when we are no longer willing to pay the price of vigilance.

Furthermore, although some sections of this book are strongly focused on the activities of the Roman Catholic church, this book should not be construed as anti-Catholic. The Roman Catholic church simply happens to be the biggest, most powerful, and most organized of the denominations in Christendom. With its vast and imperial organization, it has a persuasive voice that acts on both communicants and disbelievers alike, urging them to follow the moral prescriptions of the church. The Roman Catholic church is not alone by any means, however, in its attempts to constrict individual options and freedom of choice and to tinker with the law of the land.

FREEDOM UNDER SIEGE

This book is about freedom under siege—freedom that is constantly under siege from one of the most massive and powerful forces known to history: organized religion. Its several assaults and incursions on our freedoms, its prolonged erosion and wearing down of our defenses, may singly or individually seem small or unapparent; but when its political and economic aggrandizements are viewed overall, they become awesome. The purpose of this book is to supply, in some measure, this overall view, which is so necessary if we are to preserve our freedom from religious dictates.

Although I am an Atheist, this is not a book about Atheism. It is a book about the hallowed principle of the separation of church and state, of denying organized religion the prerogative to interfere in the affairs of government and the affairs of the average citizen. Anyone who freely joins an organized religious group may place himself under the obligation to observe its rules and prescriptions so long as he remains a member. I have no argument with such acts of free personal choice. I deny, however, that any organized religion can, with right or honor, impose its judgments and financial burdens on the rest of us. I plead the unalienable right to freedom *from* religion as well as freedom *of* religion.

1 The Book of Numbers

A Statistical Portrait of the Churches in the United States

One of organized religion's greatest propaganda triumphs has been to convince most Americans that they live in a Christian country. Of all the myths propagated by the churches, this one has probably been the most successful. It is also, from the churches' point of view, one of the most essential, for it forms the basis of organized religion's claim to special, unconstitutional treatment by the government. Therefore, before going on to consider the various ways in which the churches have increasingly been permitted to violate the Constitution and infringe on the individual freedoms of Americans, we must examine the foundations of this myth so that we can place Christianity, the predominant American religion, in its proper global, statistical, and historical perspective.

THE WORLD'S RELIGIOUS COMMUNITY

There are roughly 3.5 billion people in the world. It is very difficult to obtain accurate statistics on religious affiliations, and the figures vary depending on which agency does the reporting, but it is generally conceded that at least 28 percent of the world population has no religion at all—that is, about 1,025,000,000 persons, almost five times the population of the United States.

Of the rest, the Eastern religions—Muslim, Zoroastrian, Shintoist, Taoist, Confucian, Buddhist, and Hindu—account for about 45 percent of the world population and about 60 percent of the religious population. The Hindu religion, originating in India, is the oldest of these, dating back at least 5,000 years. Today it has 475 million adherents, over twice as many people as the total population of the United States. The next oldest are perhaps the Zoroastrian and the Taoist religions. The Zoroastrian faith stemmed from the teachings of Zarathustra in Persia in the early sixth century B.C. Much of this religion has been absorbed into others, and there are presently about 125,000 adherents. The Taoist religion developed in China around the philosophy of Lao-tzu (604?–?531 B.C.) and now claims 52 million adherents. The Buddhist religion began in India with Prince Siddhartha of the family Gautama, who was later called the Buddha or the "enlightened one" and who lived about 563 to 483 B.C. There are now approximately 302 million Buddhists, mostly outside of India, in southeast and east Asia. In China, Confucius, or K'ung Fu-tzu (c.551–479 B.C.) developed what has come to be known as the Confucian religion, which now claims approximately 305 million adherents. The Shinto religion of Japan was first formally recognized in A.D. 585, to distinguish it by name from the newly introduced Buddhism, but it actually developed long before in the dim past. Centered in Japan, Shintoism has 60 million believers. Islam, which is the only major religion to have appeared after Christianity, was formulated by the prophet Muhammed (A.D. 570–632) in the holy book of the Qur'an at the beginning of the seventh century A.D. There are today 472 million Muslims.

Christianity is thus a relative latecomer to the world community of religions. Deriving from the teachings of the New Testament writers of the first and second centuries A.D. and officially sanctioned by the Roman Emperor Constantine in A.D. 325 at the Council of Nicaea, it eventually divided into three major groups: the Eastern Orthodox, the Roman Catholic, and the Protestant. The

Eastern Orthodox comprise 3 percent of the world's population and 4 percent of the religious population. The Protestants, with an estimated 295 million adherents, make up 8 percent of the world population and 11 percent of the religious population.

The Roman Catholic church must be separately considered, because it claims as a member everyone who has ever been baptized into the faith. This leads to certain anomalies. For example, although most French people belong nominally to the Roman Catholic church, the number of practicing Catholics in France is estimated at not more than 15 percent of the Roman Catholic population. Of the 190,000,000 people in South America, the Roman Catholic church claims 164,500,000, or 86.5 percent, although the average church attendance on Sunday is only 9 percent among women and 3 percent among men. With head-counting methods like these, the Roman Catholic church claims 567 million faithful throughout the world. This is 15 percent of the world population and 21 percent of the religious population.

Other Christian denominations have a similar tendency to make unrealistic claims. Most Greeks are nominally Greek Orthodox, but church attendance is less than 2 percent on any normal Sunday. And in England, where two out of three have been baptized into the Church of England, the largest turnout for church is once a year, at Easter, when about 6 percent attend.

CHURCH MEMBERSHIP IN THE UNITED STATES

The United States is unique in that statistical records indicate church attendance to be higher here per capita than in any other country in the world. Yet, even according to these statistics, there are more than 77 million Americans who are *not* church members and who have never gone to any church, anywhere, at any time. Religious leaders call these people the "unchurched." In total there are about 112.3 million Americans who currently do not attend church at all.

Let us look at these recorded statistics in a little more detail, however. Each year the religious community of the

United States publishes reports of its membership. These reports are then sent to the federal government, where they are recorded and later reported to the American people by the U.S. Bureau of the Census. The U.S. government itself makes no survey of religion, officially or unofficially. The figures all come from the churches. But it was not always so. Under the Permanent Census Act, approved March 6, 1902, the Bureau of the Census became a permanent organization within the Department of Commerce, and one of its functions was to gather statistics concerned with organized religion in the United States. The reporting was to be on the individual history of each sect: its organization, its communicants, its overall membership, and its places of worship (churches, halls, other edifices). Each state of the nation and all sections of the country were to be differentiated. The value of church property and of parsonages was to be sought, as well as a report on the debts outstanding against each property. Reports were to be gathered on Sunday schools, on the number of officers and teachers involved, and on the number of "scholars" in those schools. A church was to be counted both as to "communicants" (all those persons currently in regular attendance) and as to "members" (all persons who had ever been baptized or enrolled), who were to be further distinguished both by age and by sex. In short, every statistical aspect of every religious group was to be noted by the church concerned and forwarded to the Census Bureau.

In the very first survey, made in 1906, the Bureau began to encounter problems. There was a lack of accurate and complete lists, since churches that had become dead or dormant were still carried on the rolls. Also, the Bureau was constantly hampered by the failure of pastors, clerks, and denominational officers to reply promptly or clearly. In many cases there was a definite unwillingness to reply to inquiries. Many churches, in fact, protested against the inquiries, claiming that the U.S. government had no constitutional authority to make any investigation in regard to religious matters. In most cases, however, there were responses, though they required considerable correspondence and occasioned no little delay. Finally, on the 1936 instruction sheet, the Bureau decided to add this warning:

AUTHORITY FOR COLLECTION OF INFORMATION: The information to be used as a basis of religious statistics is collected by the Census Bureau under authority of Acts of Congress approved June 7, 1906 and June 18, 1929. These acts make it the duty of every person in charge of any religious body to answer all questions on the printed schedule, applicable to the religious body, church or organization; and upon refusal or neglect to comply, such person is subject to a fine not exceeding $500 or to imprisonment not exceeding 60 days, or both; and if any such person willfully gives false answers, he is subject to a fine not exceeding $10,000 or to imprisonment not exceeding one year, or both.

In its analysis of the reporting prior to 1936, the Bureau had conservatively calculated that the churches were enlarging their figures by at least 15 percent. Under the new guidelines, the 1936 returns showed a dramatic drop in numbers. Whereas, earlier, for example, 232,154 church edifices had been reported, now, with the threat of punitive actions for erroneous reporting, there were 173,574.

The victory for true reporting, however, was short-lived. In 1938, the Alabama Baptist State Convention, the largest religious body in that state, adopted a resolution that its ministers not cooperate further in the federal census. When the next survey was coming due, Congress passed a law that a religious body need not report its statistics if its "doctrine" prohibited disclosure of such information. When the time came for the 1946 census, no religious reporting of any kind was included. In 1956 and again in 1966 the government was so cowed by organized religion that no further count was made.

Instead, the procedure was adopted that the religious community itself would do its own counting and publish its findings. This was undertaken by the National Council of Churches of Christ, and the figures were given quasi-official status by inclusion in the federal statistics issued yearly by the Census Bureau. That even the government is slightly skeptical of these figures is indicated by the explanatory note that appears at the front of the Bureau's report dealing with church membership. It warns, in part:

. . . not all groups follow the same calendar year, nor count membership in the same way; some groups give only approximate figures. Roman Catholics count all baptized persons, including infants; Jews regard as members all Jews in communities having congregations; Eastern Orthodox churches include all persons in their nationality or cultural groups; . . . many Lutheran bodies and the Protestant Episcopal Church now report all baptized persons. . . .

Because the government does not supervise the reporting, nor make any count of its own, the churches can make any claim they want. And of course it is in their interest to make exaggerated claims. Large numbers reported are evidence of power, prestige, and importance. Moreover, in recent years, as large federal funds have become available for preschoolers, for homes for the aged, for low-income dwellings, and for hospitals and nursing homes, it has been increasingly necessary for the churches to make large claims of membership in order to capture these funds for a given community. The church with the most membership shown tends to be the recipient of pork barrel funds.

Many among the new generation of churchmen, however, are embarrassed by this system of exaggerating membership rolls. One young minister who recently quit his church was quoted in the press as saying:

It had long troubled me that we listed 800 members and only half ever came to church, even periodically. . . . At least 100 "members" no longer even lived in that suburb. Why should we continue to carry this dead-wood? It cluttered up the rolls, demeaned the image of the church. . . .

THE METHODS OF COUNTING—AND THE RESULTS

Churches, like insurance companies, use actuarial methods based on statistical probabilities to estimate the number of persons in a particular category—in this case, membership in each church. They rely on the listings of persons who were once received into the church, by whatever means. But even if these people never show up again during their adult lives, the churches still are apt to count them. To take one example, the Presbyterian church continues to count me—an avowed Atheist—in its statistics because I was baptized into that church and attended its services until the age of about twelve. Using actuarial methods, I may be considered as having a life expectancy of sixty-seven years, and thus the church will continue to count me as a part of its membership until 1986! By now the Girl Scouts have let me go, but not the Presbyterian church.

Quite apart from the obvious unreliability of figures based on vague calculations of "life expectancy," there is the added problem of duplication. For instance, it is common knowledge that many persons switch church allegiances, notably at the time of puberty, marriage, or chance conversion. Thus a person could be counted in one church as having been baptized there, in another church as being a communicant, in a third church as having been converted at marriage, and perhaps in a fourth church as an actual, attending member.

Turning to 1973, which is the last year for which church statistics were available as this book went to print, we find that the *Yearbook of American and Canadian Churches* lists 329,672 churches in the United States with 131,389,642 reported members. Because organized religion has not exactly earned a reputation for statistical accuracy, however, it is worth considering how these statistics are compiled.

One huge problem results from counting both "current" and "noncurrent" members. "Current" statistics are those gathered from two years prior to reporting. This means that in 1973, various figures from 1971 to 1972 were accepted as valid for 1973. The "noncurrent" statistics are those obtained as far back as 1951, and they yield some truly amazing information. The Protestants, for instance, claim 114,369,013 current church members, but actually only 55,020,752 of these are full communicants, or recently confirmed members. The rest are doubtful members. In other words, the Protestant churches claim at least 59,348,261 persons as members whom they do not really know whether they have.

As we turn from Protestant reporting we encounter another problem. The National Council of Churches of Christ, which is the reporting group, cannot verify the claims of either the Roman Catholics or the Jews. These two groups report only "inclusive" members; that is, the Roman Catholic church reports everyone ever born into a Roman Catholic family, and the Jewish rabbinate counts all members of that ethnic group wherever they are found if there is a synagogue in the community. As a result, in 1973 the Roman Catholics, in the *Official Catholic Directory,* were able to claim 48,460,427 members; and the Jews, in the *American Jewish Year Book,* 6,115,000 members.

To fully appreciate the absurdity to which this kind of census taking leads, consider the case of New York City. According to the *Official Catholic Directory* for 1973, the New York archdiocese (which consists of Manhattan, the Bronx, Staten Island, and seven nearby counties) claimed church membership for 1,800,000 persons. The report further states that its members are served by 406 parish churches and 535 "chapels." This is an average of 1,913 active members in each parish church or chapel, a figure that would test the credulity of any investigator, considering that many of the churches and chapels were not built to seat more than 200 people.

In its long history of analyzing church statistics, the U.S. Census Bureau has found that the average membership of a church is small. In 1926 it was 235 persons—115 for each church in rural areas and 546 for each church in urban areas. By 1936 the number had slightly increased to an average of 280 for each church, with 133 members in a rural church and 541 in an urban church. Yet the churches continue to list among their memberships more people than could possibly be accommodated in the church buildings.

Although it is difficult to avoid these obviously inflated figures and get at the real truth, we can try at least to recognize only "confirmed" members, when possible. If we do so, we find these totals:

Protestant	55,020,752
Jewish	6,115,000
Roman Catholic	48,460,427

In this manner organized religion can claim, at most, 109,596,179 true members. Moreover, if we take the Census Bureau's advice and deduct 15 percent from these totals, we would get these perhaps more realistic membership figures:

Protestant	46,767,639
Jewish	5,197,750
Roman Catholic	41,191,363

This gives us a total of 93,156,752 church members in the United States, out of a population of 209,851,000 (July 1, 1973, Census Bureau estimate).

The figures may be even further diminished if we try to consider the question of true adherence to a faith. It is impossible not to admit, for instance, that church attendance or professed religious affiliation in the United States today is often a matter of indirect coercion—the result of social pressure, personal obligations, good business, and even political considerations—rather than of deep spiritual conviction concerning the unique truth of specific religious ideology. Furthermore, it is virtually impossible to determine how many persons listed as church members are infants and children—that is, youth under thirteen years of age who cannot generally be considered to have the mature capacity to choose church membership on their own. (In its thirty-year study, the Bureau estimated that between 15 and 18.4 percent of reported church members were thirteen years of age or under.)

WHO GOES TO CHURCH?

From time to time the American Institute of Public Opinion has made inquiries about church attendance. The persons queried were asked if they had attended church during the prior week; and the results, tabulated over a twenty-five-year period from 1940 to 1965, look like this:

Date	Percentage of Adults Attending Church
1940	37
1950	39
1960	47
1965	44

On the other hand, a 1965 Harris Poll revealed a somewhat different pattern of attendance. It showed that 22 percent of American adults attended church once or more a month, that 33 percent attended only three times a year, and that 43 percent never went to church at all. Where the truth lies is unclear, but we can be fairly certain that the totals include not only those persons who actually did attend but also persons who claimed to have attended but in truth did not.

It is unfortunate that it is necessary to rely on church statistics. Continuous, impartial, and reliable investigation and reporting undertaken by the federal government itself might give a much clearer picture. Nonetheless, organized religion is being forced to admit what is already obvious to everyone. There is a decline. The latest chart issued by the National Council of Churches of Christ shows that church attendance in any given week in a year has steadily declined since 1957, until even by its own count now attendance is down about 41 percent. And only a large Roman Catholic attendance keeps the national average high. The Protestant attendance has been fairly constant at around 38 percent since 1964, and the Jewish attendance has been about 18 percent in the same period, whereas church going among Roman Catholics has been around 60 percent.

The point to be made from all these potentially confusing and perhaps contradictory statistics is that there has never been a report of even 50 percent church attendance among Americans at any time in the history of our nation. If anything, the statistics—even the churches' statistics—

indicate that nonattendance at church, indeed nonmembership in church, is an unbroken American tradition. Even in the colonial period, for example, the number of church members was almost everywhere small. The voluminous literature left by pious churchmen and theologians should not cause us to overestimate the religious devotion of the general populace. At the close of the colonial period (1780), for example, there were only 3,105 congregations of all churches out of a population of 2,781,000. This is to say that there was one church—and a small one at that—for every 895 persons in the population. And those early churches often sat only twenty-five persons. Even in New England, allegedly the most devout section of the original colonies, there was not more than one church member out of every eight persons in the total population. Church affiliation at the founding of the Republic was limited to 4 percent of the population.

Today the churches are desperately trying to attract more members. They put on hard rock music for the young, hot jazz programs for the nostalgic middle-aged, and thumping hymns for the elderly. They have coffee breaks, cushioned pews, air conditioning, and avant-garde architecture. They have summer camps, seminars, retreats, picnics, luaus, barbecues, and even swimming pools. There are agonizing appraisals of our drug culture, our lost youth, the problems of the aged, and "swinging" housewives. The churches tailgate on such social issues as the war in Vietnam, integration, ecology, and oppressed minorities. Radio and television carry a large number of religious services and special programs. There are drive-in churches, and even the credit card has now been accepted as a device to "charge" tithing.

THE CHURCHES' DECLINING INFLUENCE

Out of all this, how is religion faring? In continuing surveys, year after year, the polls have found that increasing numbers of people feel that religion is losing its influence. This graph, published by the National Council of Churches of Christ, illustrates the extent of this decline:

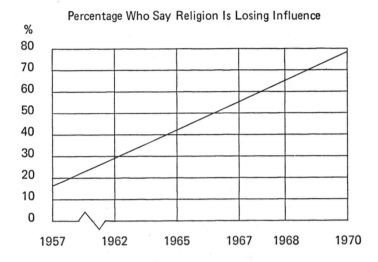

Percentage Who Say Religion Is Losing Influence

The situation looks even bleaker for the churches when one considers the attitudes of the younger generation. In a recent poll of youth in every part of the country and from every socioeconomic group, young people were asked, "How important is organized religion to you personally in your own life?" Only 34 percent answered that it was "very important," and the figure would have been much lower still if it had not been for the 53-percent affirmative response from the Bible Belt of the South. Also, the numbers of young people who said that organized religion was "very important" to them decreased sharply—with a parallel increase in those who said it was "not important"— as the respondents moved up the ladder chronologically, economically, and educationally. Between the ages of fifteen and twenty-one, for example, those who thought organized religion "very important" dropped from 38 percent to 26 percent. Of the youngsters whose families made less than $10,000 a year, 39 percent said that it was "very important," whereas only 30 percent of those whose families earned more than $10,000 gave the same answer. Similarly, whereas 37 percent of the high school students considered organized religion "very important," the figure plunged to 24 percent among college students. Thus it would appear that the greater an individual's age, education, and financial well-being, the more the churches' appeal is diminished.

The same pattern emerged in the figures on church attendance. Although the churchgoers and the abstainers were equally divided, the distribution of churchgoers was anything but equal. The ranks of the faithful were drawn from the youngest (58 percent of those under sixteen), the poorest (53 percent), the least-educated (58 percent), the women (58 percent), the South (60 percent), the rural communities (60 percent), and the Roman Catholics (66 percent).

Finally, a majority of the nation's youth said that they found "greater spiritual benefit in nature or in fellowship with each other than in going to church." However, when asked whether the churches' importance in their lives would be enhanced by greater church unification or by liberalizing and modernizing the churches, only 35 percent thought that the churches would be strengthened by unification and a mere 27 percent felt that more liberal, modern attitudes would help the church "a lot."

THE LESSON OF HISTORY

These are not exactly good tidings for organized religion, which already finds itself losing its hold over its former constituency. Nor, paradoxically, are they good tidings for the rest of us, because the history of every civilization shows that it is precisely when organized religion feels threatened by its declining influence that it makes its most strenuous efforts to force compliance with its ideology. We are in such a period now. Church attendance is on the wane, the moral authority of the churches is being challenged, ecclesiastical rituals are being scrapped, and ancient doctrines are being discredited. Yet organized religion has never had so much power and so much money as it has in the United States today. This is neither a contradiction nor a coincidence. It is a fact—and one that I shall document in detail in this book.

That probably sounds alarmist. After all, we hear in the United States that religion is a private affair. We are told that the idea of separation of church and state is an inviolable principle. There is much talk of pluralism, of a multiplicity of religious sects, and of the freedom of choice. But this book will show just what the leaders of perhaps 44 percent of the population who go to church are permitted to inflict on the 56 percent who do not. It will show that we need not only freedom *of* religion but also freedom *from* religion for those who desire it. The choice is there to be made, but it will not be there much longer unless we wake up to what is happening in this country.

We have already come close to losing one of the basic principles upon which the United States was founded: the principle of the separation of church and state. Indeed, not only have we lost the ideal of separation, but also we seem to have lost the energy for pursuing it as well. That would create an unfortunate situation in any society, but for us it would be tragic because the principle of church-state separation was the very cornerstone on which this nation was built. It was what distinguished us from the history of previous nation building. As that cornerstone goes, so goes the whole building of America.

2 Chronicles of Sanctity
The Role of the Churches in American History

In every American history course, at all levels of education, we are taught that the United States was founded by persons longing to be free of political and religious oppression. These stalwarts arrived in the early colonies bringing with them, so the story goes, the concept of a free man whose ideals of freedom derived from his Protestant faith.

Nothing, alas, could be further from the truth. The petty bickering and factional strife of the colonial transplants continually bewilders any researcher. Every prejudice, every fanatical idea, every narrow interpretation of doctrine was brought with the colonists and firmly implanted in our soil. Many settlements supported an established church and were often riddled with repressions and fanaticism. Consider just a few examples.

In Virginia, the "Lawes, Divine, Moral and Martial" provided the death penalty for speaking impiously of the Trinity, the death penalty for speaking impiously of one of the Divine Persons, the death penalty for speaking against any known article of the Christian faith. Conviction of a third offense of breaking the Sabbath was punishable by death, as was a third offense of "cursing."

Massachusetts would permit no Roman Catholic to enter the state, and a General Court there decreed that any person not freeing himself of suspicion of being a Roman Catholic "shall be jailed, then banished. If taken a second time, he shall be put to death."

In Rhode Island, as late as 1762, the Superior Court refused the application of two Jews for citizenship. The laws limited citizenship and eligibility for public office to Protestants.

In Pennsylvania, the Great Law, enacted in 1682, required the acknowledgment of "one God." Profanity was penalized. Sunday observance was required. Neither Catholics nor Jews enjoyed freedom of worship.

In New York, a law was enacted in 1700 to banish "any Jesuit, priest or other ecclesiastic ordained by the Pope."

Delaware barred from holding public office any person who did not subscribe to "Trinitarian Christianity."

South Carolina adopted a constitution in 1778 which said, "The Christian Protestant religion shall be deemed, and is hereby constituted and declared to be, the established religion of this State." This remarkable document went on to declare:

> That there is one eternal God, and a future state of rewards and punishments.
>
> That God is publicly to be worshipped.
>
> That the Christian religion is the true religion.
>
> That the holy scriptures of the Old and New Testament are of divine inspiration, and are the rule of faith and practice.
>
> That it is lawful and the duty of every man being thereunto called by those that govern, to bear witness to the truth.

Perhaps the most famous law alleged to grant religious freedom in the colonies was the one passed in Maryland. Every school child in the United States reads about that law, for it is given as the supreme example of real ecumenism in nascent America. Religious historians often cite it as the first American law granting complete religious liberty. Passed in 1649, it is generally known as the Toleration Act, since it is supposedly representative of religious toleration. In actuality it was entitled "An Act Concerning Religion." I recommend that you look it up and read it in its entirety instead of being told about it. It reads in part:

> . . . that whatsoever person or persons within this province and the island thereunto belonging shall henceforth blaspheme God, that is, curse Him, or deny our Savior Jesus Christ to be the Son of God, or shall deny the Holy Trinity—the Father, Son, and Holy Ghost—or the Godhead or any of the said three Persons of the Trinity or the unity of the Godhead, or shall use or utter any reproachful speeches, words or language concerning the said Holy Trinity, or any of the said three Persons thereof, shall be punished with death and confiscation or forfeiture of all his or her lands and goods. . . .

THE FOUNDING FATHERS AND DEISM

Organized religion in the Colonies, before the nation was founded and the Constitution adopted in 1788, had over a century and a half in which to exhibit some kind of concern for human brotherhood and to respect the principle of freedom of conscience. It never happened. On the contrary, the intolerance, the repressions, the factional strife over doctrinal differences were so bad that by the time of the Revolution many of the more educated of our leaders had left Christianity and opted for Deism. Unfortunately, adequate information about this is never made available to those who acquire their education in our public schools. There the impression is given that this is a nation founded on Christianity. Deism is only briefly mentioned, although intellectual leaders of the Revolution were committed to the concept.

Deism was the system of thought that advocated a natural religion, divorced from the Judeo-Christian Bible, based on reason rather than revelation, emphasizing nature's harmony and intelligibility, and rejecting the idea that the Creator could interfere with the laws of nature and the matters of mankind on earth. Simply put, the Founding Fathers believed in nature and nature's God. Among those who disapproved of Christianity as it manifested itself in the Colonies were Colonel Ethan Allen, Thomas Paine, George Mason, Benjamin Franklin, George Washington, John Adams, Thomas Jefferson, James Madison, and John Quincy Adams.

Colonel Ethan Allen, the revolutionary hero of the capture of Fort Ticonderoga, wrote a full-scale attack against the Christian religion, entitled *Reason the Only Oracle of Man*. In the book's preface he declared, "I am no Christian, except infant baptism make me one." And on the subject of prayer: "Prayer to God is no part of a rational religion, nor did reason ever dictate it."

Thomas Paine—of whom John Adams said, "Without the pen of Paine the sword of Washington would have been wielded in vain"—wrote *Age of Reason,* a bitter attack on the Christian church and its theology. His central credo: "I do not believe in the creed professed by the Jewish church, by the Roman church, by the Greek church, by the Turkish church, by the Protestant church, nor by any church that I know of. My own mind is my own church." He added, "All national institutions of churches, whether Jewish, Christian, or Turkish, appear to me no other than human inventions, set up to terrify and enslave mankind, and monopolize power and profit."

Benjamin Franklin, in his *Autobiography,* explained how he "became a thorough Deist." Of Christianity he wrote: "I wish it were more productive of good works. I mean really good works, not holyday keeping, sermon hearing, or making long prayers filled with flatteries and compliments desired by wise men."

George Washington said, "The government of the United States is in no sense founded upon the Christian religion "

John Adams declared, "This would be the best of all possible worlds if there were no religion in it."

James Madison wrote, "Experience witnesseth that ecclesiastical establishments, instead of maintaining the purity and efficacy of religion, have had a contrary operation. During almost fifteen centuries has the legal establishment of Christianity been on trial. What has been its fruits? More or less, in all places, pride and indolence in the clergy; ignorance and servility in the laity; in both, superstition, bigotry and persecution."

Thomas Jefferson went even further: "I have recently been examining all the known superstitions of the world, and I do not find in our particular superstition (Christianity) one redeeming feature. They are all alike founded upon fables and mythologies. The Christian God is a being of terrific character—cruel, vindictive, capricious, and unjust." Few people know that Jefferson was so disenchanted with organized Christian religion that he attempted to create his own Bible. He introduced it as a "wee little book" and called it *The Philosophy of Jesus Christ*. "It is," he wrote, "a paradigm of his doctrines, made by cutting the texts out of the book and arranging them on the pages of a blank book, in a certain order. . . . In extracting the pure principles which he taught, we should have to strip off the artificial vestments in which they have been muffled by priests, who have travestied them into various forms as instruments of riches and power for themselves." An inspection of the book reveals that Jefferson weeded out the illogicalities and the absurdities in such a way as to give Jesus a new dignity and stature.

As for the great national documents relating to the founding of our nation, not one of them recognized either Jesus Christ or Christianity. The Articles of Confederation, proposed in 1777, did have one reference to Deism in the phrase "great God of the universe"; and the Declaration of Independence included such deistic terms as "Nature and Nature's God" and "Divine Providence." In the Constitution, however, even such vague references were quite deliberately avoided by the Founding Fathers. It is important to remember that the Constitution was written more than a decade after the signing of the Declaration of

Independence, and that by this time religious groups were demanding that some reference to the Christian God, to Christianity, or to Jesus Christ be included in that instrument. Yet not only were such references not included, but safeguards against such religious intrusions were established.

One of the first guarantees established in the Constitution was that there be no religious test for office. On August 30,1787, Article VI was adopted, and it read, ". . . no religious Test shall ever be required as a Qualification to any Office or public Trust under the United States."

The Constitution in this respect was an echo of Virginia's Act for Establishing Religious Freedom, drafted by Jefferson in 1779 and passed by the state legislature in 1786, just a year before the Constitution was drafted. It also held that a man's religious beliefs could not be made a condition for holding public office. Writing about the law in his autobiography, Jefferson said:

> *Where the preamble declares that coercion is a departure from the plan of the holy author of our religion, an amendment was proposed, by inserting the words Jesus Christ, so that it should read a departure from the plan of Jesus Christ, the holy author of our religion. The insertion was rejected by a great majority, in proof that they meant to comprehend, within the mantle of its protection, the Jew and Gentile, the Christian and the Mohometan, the Hindu, and infidel of every denomination.*

Indeed, much of the literate world known to the West was beginning to accept this attitude. Not long after, it so happens that the fledgling nation attempted to conclude treaties with other nations, and some of these were of the Muslim faith. Some indication of our religious posture was felt to be needed in the treaties, and so this clause was inserted:

> *As the government of the United States is not, in any sense, founded on the Christian religion; as it has in itself no character of enmity against the law, religion, or tranquility of Musselmen; and as the States never have entered into any way or act of hostility against any Mohometan nation, it is declared by the parties that no*

pretext arising from religious opinion shall ever produce an interruption of harmony existing between the two countries.

The most famous treaty citing this provision is the Treaty of Tripoli concluded on February 10, 1797. The same statement was made in separate treaties with Algiers and with Tunis.

The churches fought back. Even after the Constitution had been ratified, the religious leaders of the Christian community began to press for some acknowledgment of their religion by the predominantly deistic national leaders. On October 27, 1789, the First Presbytery Eastward in Massachusetts and New Hampshire made a protest to George Washington because there was no "explicit acknowledgment of the only true God and Jesus Christ whom He has sent, somewhere in the Magna Carta of our country." In 1793, the year Philadelphia was stricken by the yellow fever, the Reverend John Mason preached a sermon in which he declared that the plague was being sent as a visitation from God (the Christian one) because He had not been recognized in the supreme law of the land (at this time Philadelphia was the capital of the United States). In 1803 the Reverend Samuel B. Wylie, Doctor of Divinity of the University of Pennsylvania, preached a sermon in which he asked rhetorically, "Did not the framers of this instrument [the Constitution] in this . . . resemble the fool mentioned in Psalms 14:1–3 who said in his heart, 'There is no God'?" In 1811 Samuel Austin, Doctor of Divinity and later president of the University of Vermont, preached a sermon in Worcester, Massachusetts, in which he said that lack of recognition of God was the "capital defect" in the Constitution, which "will issue inevitably in the destruction of the nation." These few examples should be sufficient to indicate the unhappy reaction among the clergy.

DISESTABLISHING THE CHURCHES

Reading colonial history immediately prior to the Revolution, specifically the theological clashes between the states, one finds that the Founding Fathers had become completely disenchanted with each colony's insistence upon a particular sect established and supported financially by tax funds and the body politic. Thus arose the idea called "disestablishment," which held that each sect should support itself and not be legally, politically, and financially "established" as the only official religion in a particular state. This move was well received by minority religious groups, which desired to see pluralism or a number of diverse sectarian groups legally acceptable in each state. The Baptists, for example, fought long and hard to dissuade the new state legislatures from continuing to recognize legally only the Anglican (or Episcopal) church, the Congregationalists, or any other established church of the colonial era. The federal leaders supported such efforts.

Virginia, the home of presidents, led the way. Its Declaration of Rights, drafted in part by James Madison and enacted June 12, 1776, advocated "free exercise of religion." An act later the same year, which suspended payment of tithes or church taxes, effectively disestablished the Church of England, although final confirmation of this disestablishment awaited passage in 1786 of Jefferson's Act for Establishing Religious Freedom. Jefferson's act, already noted, declared that, in Virginia, "no man shall be compelled to frequent or support any religious worship, place, or ministry whatsoever, nor shall be enforced, restrained, molested, or burdened in his body or goods, nor shall otherwise suffer on account of his religious opinions of belief; but that all men shall be free to profess . . . their opinion in matters of religion."

Similarly, the churches were disestablished in Pennsylvania, Delaware, and New Jersey in 1776 and in New York, North Carolina, and Georgia in 1777. South Carolina waited until 1790. In New York and in most of the New England states, however, assistance to the churches in the form of land endowments did persist until 1800. Connecticut's church, moreover, did not yield its grip until 1818, when the new constitution there decreed separation of church and state. In Massachusetts the constitutional amending did not come until 1833.

The legislature of Virginia ventured beyond disestablishment. In the colonial period it had granted lands to the towns in the state for the support of religious worship. After the Revolution, reaction against the old established church eventually reached such a pitch that in 1799 and 1802 the legislature repealed the earlier grants. The state seized not only the original lands but also all their appurtenances— buildings, church furnishings, books and even communion silver. It took everything that had belonged to the "Established Church of Virginia" as of July 5, 1776. All properties were sold, and the proceeds used for public purposes.

The Virginia churches' bitter fight to have their land restored is one of the most famous in legal annals, and it led to a direct confrontation between Supreme Court Justice Joseph Story and ex-President Thomas Jefferson. Story, speaking for the Supreme Court in decisions handed down in 1815, held that Virginia's repealing acts were contrary to the Constitution and hence void. "If the legislature posessed the authority to make such a grant and confirmation," he said, "it is very clear to our minds that it vested an . . . irrevocable title. We have no knowledge of any authority or principle which could support the doctrine that a legislative grant is revocable. . . . Such a doctrine would uproot the very foundations of almost all the land titles in Virginia, and is utterly inconsistent with . . . the right of the citizens to the free enjoyment of their property legally acquired." This part of Story's argument—affirming the rights and security of property and contract—is perhaps sound, but Story went dangerously on to declare that the First Amendment, citing freedom of religion, was actually proposed and adopted for the encouragement of Christianity. His famous argument reads:

> Every American colony, from its foundation to the revolution, . . . did openly, by the whole course of its law and institutions, support and sustain in some form the Christian religion; and almost invariably gave a peculiar sanction to some of its fundamental doctrines. . . . Probably at the time of the adoption of the Constitution, and of the [first] amendment to it . . . the general if not the universal sentiment in America was, that Christianity ought to receive encouragement from the state. . . . The real object of the amendment was not

to countenance, much less to advance, Mohometanism, or Judaism, or infidelity by prostrating Christianity, but to exclude all rivalry among Christian sects, and to prevent any national ecclesiastical establishment which would give to a hierarchy the exclusive patronage of the national government.

Story later reaffirmed this opinion in another case, in which he wrote: "It is also said, and truly, that the Christian religion is a part of the common law of Pennsylvania."

Jefferson was incensed by the interpretation given by Story, and he wrote a memorandum strongly disputing the accuracy of the maxim that Christianity was a part of the common law. His study is a careful historical and legal one. Later, in a letter to John Cartwright dated June 5, 1824, on the subject of a book that Cartwright had written, Jefferson wrote:

I was glad to find in your book a formal contradiction at length, of the judicial usurpation of legislative powers; for such the judges have usurped in their repeated decisions that Christianity is a part of the common law. The proof of the contrary, which you have adduced, is incontrovertible. . . . What a conspiracy this, between Church and State!

The disestablished churches did not give up in any of the colonies and tried to rally their people wherever they could. Soon a fight developed around their "incorporation" in the new nation. Incorporated institutions then were given unusual rights, notably the power to levy a tax on the members of their communities. This provision was an extension to the colonies (and thus the states) of a right that had had its beginning in the ecclesiastical corporations of England. In order to finance itself, the Episcopal church in Alexandria, Virginia, tried to incorporate through the U.S. House of Representatives. James Madison, strongly believing that churches should be self-supporting through free contributions, vetoed the bill that would have incorporated the church, because he conceived it as a violation of the concept of separation of church and state.

Some years later, for the same reason, the Virginia state constitutional convention of 1829 forbade the incorporation of a theological seminary by the state legislature. Today the constitutions of both Virginia and West Virginia still contain the restriction that "the General Assembly shall not grant a charter of incorporation to any church or religious denomination." Not all states, however, provided these safeguards; and in some states, the churches under the corporate status granted to them continued to exercise the power to tax their own adherents well into the 1860s, when such power was finally withdrawn everywhere.

REVIVAL AND GROWTH OF THE CHURCHES

The Protestant religious leaders learned a costly lesson in the Revolutionary and post-Revolutionary period, as they were slowly divested of exclusive powers and tax support. The Church of England, of course, was shattered by the American Revolution, because many of its clergymen had been loyalists and, after the war, had to flee to Canada or England; its successor in the new United States, the Protestant Episcopal church, was not organized until 1789. The Methodist church organized along independent national lines in 1784, the Presbyterians in 1788, and the Dutch Reformed in 1792. In 1790, in a nation whose total population was about 4 million, the churches could claim only 195,000 active members, less than 5 percent of the populace. The churches' gathering together was slow and painful. "In the religious ebb tide of the immediate post-war years," wrote church historian Winthrop S. Hudson, "it was by no means obvious that the churches would be able to survive."

They did survive, however, and multiplied, as I shall indicate later. And, while they lost important battles, such as those for establishment and incorporation, they were beginning to win others, the results of which are still with us.

As an example, as the churches slowly became more powerful again and more wealthy, they began to request special legislation granting them tax exemptions. They put what pressure they could on the politicians then as now

Pennsylvania gave in first, in 1835, and adopted a state constitutional amendment specifically granting tax exemption to church property—that is, to the land on which the church edifice actually sat. At first, exemptions for churches, synagogues, and cathedrals were won. Then came the push to have the parsonage, the parish house, and the retreat headquarters tax-exempt. When that battle had been won, the next fight was for the administration buildings to be tax-exempt, then the adjoining lands, then church-owned buildings that housed profit-making businesses, and then, finally, the businesses themselves. From 1859 to 1911, churches fought for and won tax exemptions in thirty-eight states. Today they have these exemptions in all states.

The religious leaders still believed that they could not get all the special privileges that they wanted unless they could first get Christianity declared the religion of the land, either officially through specific laws or unofficially through acceptance of religious cultural mores. Their initial success in this area came with U.S. Senator James Buchanan, later President of the United States, who on January 18, 1844, introduced a resolution in the Senate that we should become a Christian nation and acknowledge Jesus Christ as our savior. Although the Senate did not act favorably on the resolution, the fact that an august personage had promoted and an august legislative body had considered such an idea did not augur well for the future. From 1874 to 1910, almost seventy bills favoring religion were introduced in the Congress, though luckily none passed. The most famous of these was the effort to add a "Christian amendment" to the Constitution. This had to do with the Preamble to that instrument, which begins:

> We, the People of the United States, in order to form a more perfect union, establish justice, insure domestic tranquility, . . .

Organized religion wanted to change this to read:

> We, the People of the United States, in order to acknowledge Almighty God as the source of all authority and power in civil government, the Lord Jesus Christ

as the ruler among the nations, and His will, revealed in the Holy Scriptures, as the Supreme Authority, in order to constitute a Christian government, form a more perfect union, establish justice, insure domestic tranquility, . . .

Despite the fact that a Supreme Court Justice (William Strong) was a leading figure in this movement to amend our Constitution, the committee on the judiciary of the House of Representatives, on February 18, 1874, reported out to the Congress that the framers of the Constitution had seen fit not to enter such Christian wording and that the determination of the Founding Fathers should be sustained.

What could not be won openly by legislative action could sometimes be won unofficially and deceptively. Religious individuals as well as organizations could erode the principle of separation of church and state. From 1831 to 1835, for instance, John Marshall, Chief Justice of the U.S. Supreme Court, instituted the practice of opening the court with the call, "Oyez, oyez, God save our nation and this honorable court." This is a patently unconstitutional exercise, but most of our Founding Fathers were dead when this kind of religious affirmation was introduced into the federal Court. The practice was later to be extended to federal district courts also.

In 1861 the Reverend M. R. Watkinson persuaded the Secretary of the Treasury to try to introduce "In God We Trust" as a motto on the coins of the land, arguing on the theological premise that in a Judeo-Christian nation "There is but one God." Congress, then beginning to be responsive to the religious community and the votes that it was presumed to control, passed the Coinage Act of April 22, 1864, which designated that "In God We Trust" be put on coins "when and where sufficient space in the balance of the design" would permit it.

There was considerable opposition to moves such as these, and in 1867 the Free Religious Association was founded to counteract such activities. The idea was to propound a religion of humanity, guided by reason, and also to provide an organizational home for those who did not wish to remain within the confines of diverse sectarian

Christian groups. On January 1, 1874, the association published its demands, which survey quite well the various areas in which organized religion was intruding upon government and politics and sacrificing the rights of free citizens:

1. *We demand that churches and other ecclesiastical property shall no longer be exempt from taxation.*
2. *We demand that the employment of chaplains in Congress, in state legislatures, in the navy and militia, and in prisons, asylums, and all other institutions supported by public money shall be discontinued.*
3. *We demand that all public appropriations for sectarian educational and charitable institutions shall cease.*
4. *We demand that all religious services now sustained by government shall be abolished; and especially that the use of the Bible in the public schools, whether ostensibly as a textbook or avowedly as a book of religious worship, shall be prohibited.*
5. *We demand that the appointment by the President of the United States or by the governors of the various states of all religious festivals and fasts shall wholly cease.*
6. *We demand that the judicial oath in the courts and in all other departments of the government shall be abolished, and that simple affirmation under the pains and penalties of perjury shall be established in its stead.*
7. *We demand that all laws directly or indirectly enforcing the observance of Sunday as the Sabbath shall be repealed.*
8. *We demand that all laws looking to the enforcement of "Christian" morality shall be abrogated, and that all laws shall be conformed to the requirements of natural morality, equal rights, and impartial liberty.*
9. *We demand that, not only in the constitutions of the United States and of the several states but also in the practical administration of the same, no privilege or*

advantage shall be conceded to Christianity or any other special religion; that our entire political system shall be founded and administered on a purely secular basis; and that whatever changes shall prove necessary to this end shall be consistently, unflinchingly, and promptly made.

Against this, organized religion fought for a continuing emphasis on public prayer and prayer at state functions, reverence for the Bible and its continued use in the educational system, oathtaking both for public office and in the court system, tax support of ministers in public institutions, official observation of holy days, and an official proclamation that this is a nation "under God."

THE NEW IMMIGRATION AND THE WASP REACTION

In the first fifty years after the nation's founding, European immigrants did not arrive in very large numbers; their annual total never surpassed 10,000 until 1825, or exceeded 100,000 until 1842. By 1854, however, the annual number had risen to over 400,000, and—after a decline just before, during, and following the Civil War—again reached 400,000 by 1872. There were yearly fluctuations thereafter, but the overall trend continued upward, until annual peaks of 1 million or more immigrants were reached six times between 1905 and 1914.

The national origins of the new immigrants would deeply concern the old Protestant establishment, now usually referred to as White Anglo-Saxon Protestants, or WASPs (though not all of them were, strictly speaking, Anglo-Saxon, or British). The old tide, up to 1842, had consisted largely of welcomed immigrants from northern and western Europe, especially from Great Britain, Germany, and, to a lesser extent, Scandinavia, all predominantly Protestant and many of them with some education and small savings. Irish also came in good numbers during the early years, but the great influx of poor Irish Catholics would not be experienced until the late 1840s and early

1850s, as a result of the famines in Ireland. They would represent the first great wave of the so-called new immigration, largely unlike the old native Protestants in religion and culture. Especially after the Civil War era, the new immigrants began swarming from eastern and southern Europe, mostly from Italy, Poland, the Balkans, and Russia. To a large extent these were peasant folk, poor and illiterate—in religion usually Roman Catholic or Jewish—who contrasted sharply with the old Protestant Yankee stock. Their numbers were to cluster largely in the cities of the Northeast; by 1900, 54 percent of the population in New England and 50 percent of the population in the middle Atlantic states were either foreign-born or of foreign-born parentage (fifty years earlier both proportions had been only 15 percent).

The Protestants or WASPs were concerned about the new immigration, naturally; and as early as the 1850s there had developed organized groups opposed to foreigners and Catholics. In the late nineteenth and early twentieth centuries, however, the tremendous expansion of American industry and the need for cheap labor thwarted attempts to restrict such immigration. Industrialists and steamship companies recruited foreign labor wherever they could, without ethnic considerations. Not until the First World War and its aftermath, when antiforeign feeling in America rose to fever pitch, did Protestant efforts to limit immigration finally achieve a thoroughgoing victory.

The first efforts at restriction began in the late nineteenth century and were directly primarily at non-Christians. In 1882, after 160,000 Chinese had been imported as laborers to build the transcontinental railroads and work on other projects, congressional passage of a Chinese Exclusion Act began a national policy of prohibiting their entry further. When similar numbers of Japanese began arriving around the turn of the century, a series of "Gentlemen's Agreements" (especially in 1907 and 1908) were worked out with Japan whereby that nation agreed to withhold passports from laborers proposing to go to America. In reality, this kind of religious "protectionism" did not stop with allegedly strange aliens. The various American Indians, of

highly diverse beliefs and faiths, were also brutally eliminated from the mainstream of American life.

In 1917, at the time of World War I, the first restriction
on European immigration was pushed through the U.S.
Congress. It embodied a literacy test for admission, mani-
festly aimed at closing the door to the impoverished
illiterates of southern and eastern Europe who lacked
Protestant persuasions. In 1921 the first "quota law" was
passed, decreeing that the number of immigrants to be
admitted would be 3 percent of each nationality actually
resident in the United States in 1910, the maximum overall
quota being 357,000. In 1924 a new quota law limited
immigration to 2 percent of each nationality resident in the
year 1890, the earlier year being selected in order to reduce
sharply the quotas of southern and eastern Europeans. (The
great majority of such Europeans had arrived after 1890.)
The law also totally excluded Orientals, and the maximum
annual quota of immigrants was also reduced—to 150,000.
The quotas were revised in 1929 and again in 1952, but the
restrictions had generally the same aim. Liberalization of
the laws did not begin until the 1960s.

This public policy against the new immigrants was
narrow and bigoted, but the general atmosphere of prejudice was equally oppressive from the very beginning.
American Protestantism, with its ancient memory of bloody
conflict and persecution at the hands of the Roman
Catholic church in Europe and with its Old Testament scorn
for faiths unlike its own, was by no means a tolerant
institution. If, at the nation's founding, it yielded to
constitutional ideas of separation of church and state, the
motive was more largely fear of other religions than respect
for them. In fact, the fear of Roman Catholics eventually
became so great that in the 1830s and 1840s there were
violent armed clashes between Protestants and Catholics in
such places as New England and Philadelphia. In the early
1840s there arose a movement of nativist Americans who
wanted to keep the country politically pure of the new
arrivals. Meeting in convention in Philadelphia in 1845, the
group soon had a membership of 100,000. Then in 1849 in
New York a secret society was formed known as the Order
of the Star-Spangled Banner. This became the backbone of

the Know-Nothing Party. The oath required of members included a promise to support for public office only American-born Protestants.

The name of the party derived from the secrecy with which its members operated. The common answer to questions from outsiders concerning their convictions was "I don't know." By the time of the elections of 1854, with scarcely any public campaigning, this party controlled over one-fourth of the votes in New York and two-fifths of the votes in Pennsylvania, and it carried the state of Delaware. In Massachusetts it elected the governor and all state officers, every member of the state Senate, and all but 2 of the 378 members of the state House of Representatives. By 1855 it carried Rhode Island, New Hampshire, Connecticut, Maryland, and Kentucky. In some other states it held a balance of power. In the U.S. Congress it elected forty-three members of the House and five members of the Senate. At its peak it reported over a million members. Other issues—especially the fiery slavery issue—soon led to internal dissensions, however, which resulted in the party's collapse between 1856 and 1860.

Although the party disappeared, the social and religious bigotry that it reflected were intense as ever and flared up again in the 1880s. The American Protective Association, spawned in that decade, actively sought to have laws passed to curb immigration and to strengthen Protestant influence in the public schools, all the while giving vocal opposition to Roman Catholicism. The Catholic issue even touched national politics in the presidential election of 1884, when a supporter of James G. Blaine referred to Grover Cleveland's Democrats as the party of "Rum, Romanism, and Rebellion."

Although the original Ku Klux Klan was organized after the Civil War to maintain "white supremacy" in the South, a second Ku Klux Klan was founded in 1915, adding to the violent policy of anti-Negro white supremacy a virulent antiforeign, anti-Catholic, and anti-Semitic wave of propaganda and mob action. Its appeal was not sectional, and it spread through the North as well as the South, even controlling the politics of many communities, electing state officials as well as U.S. congressmen. In the mid-1920s its membership was estimated at nearly 5 million; and the anti-Catholic feeling that it helped to inspire contributed to Al Smith's defeat in his bid for the White House in 1928.

In the general story of WASP prejudice, the prejudice against Jews is noteworthy. In the early days their numbers were few, only 2,000 in 1790 and still only about 150,000 seventy years later. Coming in on the new immigration, however, their numbers increased to 4 million by 1920, clustered primarily in the eastern seaboard cities of New York, Philadelphia, Boston, and Baltimore, with some going as far west as Chicago. Like others of the new immigrants, they were forced into residential segregation comprising ghettos or slums and into labor exploitation, especially in the sweatshops of the garment industry. New Yorkers, notably, made no attempt to assist them to assimilate into an American culture, which was basically anti-Semitic as well as anti-Catholic.

Anti-Catholics in America at least had to contend with a highly organized and determined minority in the Roman Catholic church. The discrimination against the less numerous Jews could be more thorough—and more invidious and discreet. The Jew was excluded from clubs, hotels, resorts. He was refused membership in country clubs, golf clubs, businessmen's leagues. Certain residential areas were prohibited to him, and discreet notices in advertising indicated that "Gentiles only" should apply. It was unthinkable that a Jew would be appointed or elected to a high office of public trust, or to top management of a non-Jewish business firm. There were anti-Semitic hiring practices built into applications for employment and the selection of job applicants. Many colleges and universities had a quota system, which finally came to be openly acknowledged as such in the 1920s. Most of the fraternities and sororities did not offer membership to Jews. Now and then a prominent member of the Jewish community might be accepted in a special club, but slights to his family and friends often caused him to quietly resign from membership. Most of this was done in a covert and "gentlemanly" way.

This can perhaps best be illustrated by the case of Louis D. Brandeis. Born in Louisville, Kentucky, in 1856, the son of a prosperous merchant who had immigrated from Czechoslovakia, Brandeis grew up in a cosmopolitan atmosphere, finding part of his education in Europe, and went on to graduate in 1877 from Harvard Law School, where he had been top student in his class. He became very successful in his law practice in Boston and accumulated substantial wealth. He then abandoned this work to become a "people's attorney," a champion of public causes. Coming into contact with Jews as a group around 1910, he soon turned to Zionism and became a leader of that movement in America. He was well known throughout the land as a Progressive Democrat, a reformer, and a Zionist, when on January 28, 1916, President Woodrow Wilson nominated him for the seat on the U.S. Supreme Court.

The reaction was immediate. In New York, the *Times,* the *Sun,* and the *Press* all opposed him, as did the American Bar Association. A petition published against Brandeis's appointment included the signature of President A. Lawrence Lowell of Harvard. Editors, lawyers, columnists, politicians, and social reformers joined the national debate over his confirmation. The bizarre affair continued for almost five months. His nomination was finally confirmed in the U.S. Senate by a 47 to 22 vote, but the episode illustrated the workings of anti-Semitism in the United States. Although no *public* reference was ever made to the fact that Brandeis was a Jew, there was no doubt in anyone's mind that anti-Semitism was the major factor in the opposition to his appointment.

CHANGES IN THE RELIGIOUS MAKEUP OF AMERICA

The new immigration was giving a new look to the religious pattern of America, enlarging the numbers of Roman Catholics, Jews, Greek Orthodox, Buddhists, and others. But the religious picture was changing in another fashion—in the multiplication of faiths and cults in the nation. During the colonial period, virtually all the sects had been imported from Europe; but with the coming of the Revolution, native churches began to sprout as a result of dissatisfaction with conventional organized religions. Some of the first, like the United Brethren in Christ and the Rappists, were evangelistic, arising during a period of frontier revivalism in the first decades of the nineteenth century. Others, like the Unitarians, founded by William Ellery Channing about 1819 and denying the Trinity, centered mainly among the social and intellectual upper classes of New England. Some, like the Latter-Day Saints, or Mormons, resulted from personal visions, in this case by Joseph Smith. Persecuted for their beliefs, he and his followers were pressed successively westward, and when he was seized and lynched by a mob in Illinois in 1846, the Saints trekked on to the Great Salt Lake, under the leadership of Brigham Young.

Another sect arising in the 1840s was the Adventists, or its best-known branch, the Seventh-Day Adventists, who believed in the imminent end of the world and the advent of Christ (first predicted by the sect for 1843, but repeatedly postponed). Also believing in the imminent Armageddon and coming of Christ were the Jehovah's Witnesses, originally called the Russellites when first organized in the 1870s. In another part of the religious spectrum was Christian Science, first formulated by Mary Baker Eddy about 1866. Also during the nineteenth century, many of the old churches—such as Presbyterians, Baptists, Methodists, Quakers, and Lutherans—each split into two or more rival synods or organizations, proliferating the number of national groups. Enslaved—and, after emancipation, segregated—blacks also formed their own independent churches under such traditional labels as Methodists and Baptists.

Many people raised in a faith did not continue to adhere to it. The *Catholic Mirror,* in its first issue, dated September 17, 1904, for example, observed, "If all the descendants of our Catholic forefathers had remained in the faith, there would be more than 40,000,000 Catholics in the United States today." In that year, however, the Roman Catholic church claimed only 11,887,317 communicants (including children), of whom probably less than half were active in the church. Also abroad in the land were the new scientific discoveries relating to Darwinism, which undoubtedly persuaded large numbers to rethink their religious and secular ideas and to discard old baggages of superstition and myth. Twentieth-century Freudian psychology helped to demolish older theological doctrine even more.

Adding to the religious confusion was the development of a fundamentalist reaction, especially from the 1870s to the 1930s. It was spearheaded by such traveling evangelists as Dwight Moody, Billy Sunday, John Alexander Dowie, and Aimee Semple McPherson, who preached a thundering, theatrical kind of evangelism, inspired more by zeal than by education. This ministry embodied the competitive spirit of capitalism. The evangelist had to show results. He had to go out and get his customers as did everyone else. His success was judged by the crowds he could attract or the effect that he had upon the persons assembled. In later times, he has been replaced by a usually better schooled but nevertheless basically similar revivalist, in the person of such preachers as Billy Graham and Oral Roberts.

In the twentieth century, nevertheless, the proliferation of churches and sects did begin to subside, and in fact there developed what might be called a dangerous counter-trend—a unity movement both worldwide and national. From the late nineteenth century to the 1930s there were a number of world "ecumenical" conferences; by 1938 there had developed plans for a World Council of Churches, to be formally set up in 1941; the outbreak of World War II, however, postponed preparations, and the council was not officially formed until 1948. Reflecting a trend in church mergers in countries all over the world, the churches in the United States began to enter into unions and federations. The first interdenominational organization, the Federal Council of Churches of Christ in America, was founded as early as 1905, to be succeeded by the National Council of Churches of Christ in the U.S.A. in 1950, embracing twenty-five Protestant and five Eastern Orthodox bodies. In 1918 forty-five separate Lutheran synods combined into the United Lutheran Church. In 1939 the major Methodist churches reunited. In 1943 the National Association of Evangelicals was formed. Many other unions were accomplished in the 1950s and 1960s. The churches, in short, were consolidating their power—to be used persuasively on politicians and others of society's leaders, as well as on the American public generally.

CHRISTIANIZING AND THE COLD WAR

In the period from the Second World War to the present, freedom from the dictates of religion has perhaps undergone the severest trials in the history of our country. To the U.S. Supreme Court have gone a number of cases involving violations of the separation of church and state or involving discriminations against ethnic or religious minorities and others defending their right to believe as they wish. Sometimes the decisions have been unfortunate ones, in my view; but overall, I feel, the Court has tried to make a considered judgment and interpretation of the First and Fourteenth Amendments as related to religion. Congress and the executive branch of government, on the other hand, as well as the states, have promoted policies and acts dangerously inclining toward establishing virtually a civil religion. They have put through one act or order after another giving aid and assistance or preferred standing to religion. At the same time that the churches have been seeking to augment their own power and influence, the government has been abetting that expansion of influence.

The new mood was signaled as early as 1942, when, as a national security measure, the government rounded up 110,000 Japanese on the West Coast, two-thirds of them American citizens, and held them in interior relocation centers for most of the war. This action of the government—regrettably, later upheld by the Supreme Court—was an out-and-out act of ethnic discrimination. No comparable violation of civil liberties was ever undertaken against German and Italian Americans of "Christian" ancestry.

Concurrently, however, the Supreme Court was reestablishing a valuable principle of the separation of church and state—ironically while deciding in favor of a religious sect. The issue involved the Jehovah's Witnesses and their strict application of the Old Testament dictum, "Thou shalt not make unto thee any graven image, or . . . bow down thyself" to it. Believing that the American flag was such an image, the Witnesses were forbidding their children to salute the flag in the public schools. In three federal cases resulting from the issue, the Supreme Court in 1940, 1941, and 1943, with conflicting results as it reversed itself, took this matter under advisement. In the final decision the Court enunciated two key principles:

1. *The very purpose of a Bill of Rights was to withdraw certain subjects from the vicissitudes of political controversy, to place them beyond the reach of majorities and officials, and to establish them as legal principles to be applied by the courts. One's right to life, liberty, and property, to free speech, a free press, freedom of worship and assembly, and other fundamental rights may not be submitted to vote; they depend on the outcome of no elections.*

2. *If there is any fixed star in our constitutional constellation, it is that no official, high or petty, can prescribe what shall be orthodox in politics, nationalism, religion, or other matters of opinion, or force citizens to confess by word or act their faith therein.*

Immediately after the war the Court began to accept further cases that would create judicial guidelines for the effective separation of church and state. Two of these cases were to become landmarks. The first has remained the most famous and most often quoted and is called the *Everson* case, decided in 1947. It concerned a board of education in New Jersey, which had authorized financial assistance to parents who were obliged to pay for bus transportation for their children to and from Roman Catholic schools. A taxpayer protested. In its decision the Court emphasized that it was aware of "efforts to force loyalty to whatever religious group happened to be on top and in league with the government of a particular time and place." But, emphasizing that the government had no right to establish any religion, the Court stated:

The "establishment of religion" clause of the First Amendment means at least this: Neither a state nor the Federal Government can set up a church. Neither can pass laws which aid one religion, aid all religions, or prefer one religion over another. Neither can force nor influence a person to go to or to remain away from church against his will or force him to profess a belief or disbelief in any religion. No person can be punished for entertaining or professing religious beliefs or disbeliefs. No tax in any amount, large or small, can be levied to support any religious activities or institutions, whatever they may be called, or whatever form they may adopt to teach or practice religion. Neither a state nor the Federal Government can, openly or secretly, participate in the affairs of any religious organizations or groups and vice versa. In the words of Jefferson, the clause against establishment of religion by law was intended to erect "a wall of separation between Church and State."

In the following year, 1948, the *McCollum* case was decided. In this instance a taxpayer protested when a board of education permitted a religious teacher to come into a public school building during regular hours to teach classes on religion. The Court reaffirmed the *Everson* case, and Justice Felix Frankfurter added:

Separation means separation, not something else. Jefferson's metaphor in describing the relation between Church and State speaks of a "wall of separation," not a fine line easily overstepped.

While the U.S. Supreme Court was thus carefully and legally defining what was permissible and impermissible in church-state relations, however, the political leaders were on the march, embracing the symbols of the church in opposition to what they conceived as a grander menace to liberty and democracy. These were the initial years of the cold war, years in which Winston Churchill in his famous "Iron Curtain" speech would speak of the menace of Soviet policies, with "Communist fifth columns . . . established and at work in great numbers of countries," all constituting "a growing challenge and peril to Christian civilization." The "Christian" nations, Great Britain and the United States, he pleaded, had to unite as guardians of the peace. A few years later, Dwight D. Eisenhower, running for the presidency, defined the spirit of the times even more starkly, in his description of the war against "atheistic" communism in Korea:

> We know that — for all the might of our effort — victory can come only with the gift of God's help. . . . In this spirit — humble servants of a proud ideal — we do soberly say: This is a crusade.

All this was a harbinger of the Christian civil religion that was to be developed as an adjunct to our foreign policy. Moreover, between about 1947 and 1954 the nation was gripped by what has later been termed the Great Fear, the fear that the nation was about to be undermined by communism and communist agents. Anything traceable to communist ideology immediately became suspect, and a witch-hunt of persons with un-Christian ideas was carried out by government and by private groups. Several Americans, including Julius and Ethel Rosenberg, were tried and convicted of espionage; the Rosenbergs were executed in 1953. In such a context of hysteria, godless communism came to be thought of as aligned against Christian America.

Godliness thus became a test of national loyalty. On June 25, 1948, Congress passed a law requiring every federal justice or judge to take an oath concluding with "So help me God" before entering upon the duties of his office. This was the first legislative requirement of a religious test for office ever passed by a federal body. The religious spirit also entered the executive offices. As soon as Eisenhower assumed the office of President, he instituted prayer breakfasts for meetings with public officials. There were congressional prayer breakfasts, governors' prayer breakfasts, and the like; and these prayer breakfasts were imitated in many of the state capitals and in a thousand city halls. Although it might be granted that, as private citizens, these officials have a right to attend prayer breakfasts, it cannot be denied that these breakfasts constitute governmental policy meetings and, as such, mix religion and government.

Shortly after Eisenhower's first election, the Hearst newspaper chain began campaigning for the addition of the words "under God" to the Pledge of Allegiance. The American Legion endorsed the idea, as, of course, did the

Roman Catholic and Protestant churches. On June 14, 1954, the change of wording was passed into law by Congress without one dissenting vote; the pledge thus read:

I pledge allegiance to the United States and to the republic for which it stands, one nation, under God, indivisible, with liberty and justice for all.

In the same year Congress approved special mailing rates for all religious magazines, rates lower than those given to any other group of organizations; the rates remain in effect today. On July 11, 1955, President Eisenhower signed Public Law 140, making it mandatory that all currency and coins bear the motto "In God We Trust." A year later, on July 30, 1956, he signed Public Law 851, replacing our national motto *"E Pluribus Unum"* ("One Out of Many") with "In God We Trust."

Eight months later, in speaking to the Israelis on the Middle East crisis, President Eisenhower proclaimed:

There can, of course, be no equating of a nation like Israel with that of the Soviet Union. The peoples of Israel, like those of the United States, are imbued with a religious faith and a sense of moral values. We are entitled to expect, and do expect, from such peoples of the Free World a contribution to world order which unhappily we cannot expect from a nation controlled by atheistic despots.

In his years in office Eisenhower seldom missed an opportunity to contrast the "atheistic" foe with the freedom-loving people of America under God. Americans had become God's chosen people.

The trend did not change after Eisenhower left office. In 1964, when the civil rights bill was going through Congress, incredibly an amendment was attached to the effect that anyone discovered to be an Atheist could be discharged from his public employment for that reason alone, without right of appeal or compensation. Known as the Ashbrooke amendment, it actually passed the House of Representatives and was stopped only narrowly in the Senate. In 1966 the Federal Communications Commission, in the so-called

Murray decision, affirmed that the right to freedom of speech did not extend fully to Atheists, who were held to have no right to purchase radio or television air time in order to combat misrepresentation of their position, should a radio or television station wish to deny them air time. Instead of attending to the specific rights of the nonbeliever, the Commission hid behind a proclamation that "equal time" for controversial issues did not include religion because the question of religion and the existence of God was a settled matter in the United States, beyond the reach of anyone wishing to protest.

Later in the same year, on September 6, 1966, Congress passed Public Law 89-554, requiring that any individual elected or appointed to an office of honor or profit in the civil service or the uniformed services (with the exception of the President) must take an oath or affirmation of allegiance concluding with the phrase "So help me God." This requirement directly violates Article VI of the Constitution, which says:

> . . . *no religious Test shall ever be required as a Qualification to any Office or public Trust under the United States.*

I personally have attempted to challenge the law—but, so far, unsuccessfully. The chief reason, by the way, that the President was excused from the oath to God was that his oath is already spelled out in the Constitution, in Article II Section 1:

> *Before he enter on the Execution of his Office, he shall take the following Oath or Affirmation:—"I do solemnly swear (or affirm) that I will faithfully execute the Office of President of the United States, and will to the best of my Ability, preserve, protect and defend the Constitution of the United States."*

There is no mention of God. President Richard M. Nixon, however, in both of his swearing-in ceremonies, added the expression, "So help me God." The precedent is now there.

Nixon, of course, went further than this. He did not stop with godly oaths or occasional prayer breakfasts but instead brought full-scale religious services directly into the White House. This is the symbol of the new executive branch of government and of the new evangelism now comfortably quartered there. Nixon even gave aid to the evangelical Christian movement by appearing at a Billy Graham crusade in Tennessee. It is tragic that the Chief of State, sworn to uphold and defend the Constitution of the United States, should be a focal point and a chief aid for those who would establish a civil religion, with a nationalistic, evangelistic base. We are completing the circle. If this trend is not reversed, we will again have the situation described at the beginning of this chapter.

CHRISTIANIZING THE CITIZEN OF GOD'S COUNTRY

The whole Christianizing policy—including the characterization of foes as Atheists and of Atheists as foes—was not limited to the upper levels of government and to the public forum. The Christianizing was also directed at the private individual. And in this area the courts sometimes upheld and sometimes did not uphold the rights of individuals, as against the Christianizing efforts of legislators and other politicians.

The famous issue of prayers in the public schools is a case in point. In 1963, for instance, my own case came before the Supreme Court, which wisely held that Bible reading and prayer recitation, as a religious exercise, were impermissible in the public schools. (See Chapter 4 herein and also my book *Atheist Epic: Bill Murray, the Bible, and the Baltimore Board of Education.*) From then on, organized religion and its political allies have waged a relentless campaign to have religion restored in any form whatsoever, either as overt prayer or as covert religious studies. The onslaught on the Supreme Court and the Congress has been tremendous. By April 1964 no less than 150 amendments to the Constitution had been offered in the House of Representatives alone simply to overturn this one decision. The hue and cry was so great that the House judiciary committee held hearings for eighteen days during April, May, and June of that year while the religious community stormed the halls to be heard. The testimony is contained in 2,774 pages of government documents in small print.

Out of that struggle came the Becker amendment. Frank J. Becker was a representative from the state of New York, supported in his amendment effort primarily by the American Legion and the Roman Catholic church. Everyone thought that this amendment would put prayer back only in the schools. But it was more comprehensive than that. The actual wording of the amendment would have put the Bible and prayers into "any governmental or public school, *institution, or place"* (italics added).

Congress, in the view of the Christianizers, was not moving on this fast enough, so several suits were brought. In New York (*Stein* v. *Oshinsky*), a trial court upheld the right of schools to assist children in reciting voluntary prayers, but the U.S. Court of Appeals reversed this decision. In De Kalb, Illinois, a trial court held that a schoolteacher who wanted prayer could lead children in this exercise. Again, the U.S. Court of Appeals struck down the decision.

By this time, such a famous figure as Senator Everett Dirksen, Republican minority leader in the U.S. Senate, decided to push the matter and introduced the so-called Dirksen amendment to the Constitution, which would allow public prayer in the schools. He entered the fray when an effort to use a religious stanza of the "Star-Spangled Banner" as a prayer in the Hicksville, New York, schools was halted by the local commissioner of education, who ruled the action illegal. In Levittown, New York, a program to open school days with a religious song, "Our Fathers' God," was also declared illegal. The Dirksen amendment fortunately withered away in the Senate.

In Leyden, Massachusetts, one scheme was to have children report five minutes early for voluntary prayers. This too was ruled unconstitutional. In Netcong, New Jersey, another "voluntary plan" was worked out, whereby child's prayers specially composed by the chaplains of the U.S. House of Representatives and U.S. Senate were to be recited by school children. The intent of using such prayers was apparently to give national and federal sanction to local praying. The New Jersey state supreme court found this exercise unconstitutional.

In 1971 a new bill, called the Wylie amendment, was introduced into Congress. This amendment was for prayer "in any public building which is supported in whole or in part through the expenditure of public funds." Conceivably an aircraft manufacturer with a government contract could, under this law, require his employees to say prayers. The amendment failed narrowly of passage, but plans are now afoot to try again.

While perhaps guarding our liberties on the prayer front, the courts were not always doing so well on some other fronts. The issue of the conscientious objector is a good example.

The first naturalization act, passed in 1790, has been occasionally amended, but not until 1905 was there added the specific provision that any alien desiring to become a U.S. citizen must declare on oath that he will "support and defend the Constitution and laws of the United States against all foes foreign and domestic." In 1950 this provision was amended to the effect that he must "bear arms on behalf of the United States or perform non-combatant service in the Armed Services of the United States when required by law unless the applicant showed that he was opposed to bearing arms or to performing non-combatant service by reason of religious training and belief."

This was tested in April 1970 in the case of *In re Weitzman*. The petition for citizenship was from a twenty-seven-year-old woman, formerly of the Jewish faith, who refused to agree to bear arms simply because she was a humanitarian; she "did not believe in any supernatural power, Supreme Being or superior relationship." A lower court denied her citizenship, and the case went up on appeal. There a fluke developed. One judge held that she was reared as a Jew and hence had religious training and that her beliefs were in reality founded on that; therefore, he would give her citizenship. The second judge held that, because she believed sincerely in conscience against bearing arms anywhere, he would give her citizenship. The third judge wrote what I consider a vindictive and frightening opinion, which would have denied citizenship to her. This opinion is of great importance to us because the man who wrote it is now on the U.S. Supreme Court. He is Justice Harry A. Blackmun, an appointee of President Nixon. He held that the law requiring religious belief as the basis for objecting to killing was a "legislative accommodation to religious freedom"; it was an effort on the part of government to "remain neutral rather than to prefer religion." However, he went on, religion meant "belief in a supreme allegiance to the will of God," and anyone not so believing in a god—however humanitarian or deeply felt was his abhorrence of the idea of bearing arms—could not qualify ·as a conscientious objector. Blackmun frankly admitted rather cavalierly that in such instances he considered "the dilemma of the secular individual . . . of a different and lesser order than that of the religious individual." Fortunately, in this decision, Blackmun was outvoted by the other two federal judges. Nevertheless, the final outcome on this question of secular conscience is still dangerously in doubt.

Allied to this issue involving the applicant for citizenship is the issue of the citizen who as a conscientious objector opposes engagement in war. Here, a very crooked road has been followed in order to hold the conscientious objector to a belief in some higher power. In the case of *U.S.* v. *Schacter,* decided in 1968, the Court declared that the objector could not reach his objection as the result of a purely intellectual exercise, that is to say, by the application of reason and logic. It *must* be based on faith— because if it is based on faith it cannot be "falsely assumed as readily as can views based essentially on the exercise of the intellect, because recognizing a duty to a moral power higher than that owed to the state" is an inducement to honesty. Only a religionist, in other words, is capable of a true higher morality! The nonbeliever or Atheist thus does not have a prayer when he gets into a court of law in our land, seeking relief as a conscientious objector. The thrust of such cases and laws is to do what earlier court decisions held could not be done: "prescribe religion" and "force citizens to confess by word or act their faith therein."

Probably the most bizarre situation developed in the case of the West Point cadets who desired *not* to be pressed into compulsory church services each Sunday. The cadets brought suit. The defense that the government used in the case, which dragged on for three years, was ludicrous. It contended that the compulsory attendance was required as a "purely secular exercise carried out for purely secular reasons"—these reasons being to train officers to understand the religious sentiments of their men. If this were so, then one would think that the Roman Catholic cadets would be going to a synagogue, or the Protestants attending mass, in order to acquire this increased intercultural understanding. But not so. The religious "training" was to be conventionally sectarian, for the Jews went to the synagogue, the Roman Catholics to mass, and the Protestants to services. Ultimately, the government lost the case (1972), for the specious argument could not stand up in a final test, even in our new Christian theocracy.

While the courts were vacillating, the legislators and government administrators were determinedly at work. The great principle of separation of church and state on which the American republic was founded may not survive the torrent of regulations and laws designed to undermine it. In October 1971, for example, the U.S. Department of State decreed that all applicants for passports had to take an oath concluding with the phrase "So help me God"; subsequently many Atheists complained that they had been denied passports for refusing to take the oath. In December 1971 and again in January 1972 the Congress voted to circumvent all copyright laws in order to give the powerful Christian Science and Mormon churches perpetual copyrights on their religious books. In February 1972 the Equal Employment Opportunity law was amended so that all religious organizations became exempt from its provisions; thus henceforth, for example, any black man who cleans up at the local Roman Catholic church may have to be a Roman Catholic to get or retain his job.

Taken singly, laws and edicts such as these may seem minor instances of governmental favoritism toward organized religion. Taken together, however, these and other similar enactments form a familiar and ominous pattern by which the churches have historically gained power. Perhaps to really understand the significance of each new law, one would best consult an old law. The constitution of New Hampshire was written many years ago, but it is still operative. In the jargon of today's youth, we may say that it lets it all hang out:

> . . . *morality and piety, rightly grounded on evangelical principles, will give the best and greatest security to government, and will lay, in the hearts of men, the strongest obligations to due subjection.*

I have written this book because I do not believe that the American people are ready to accept "due subjection."

3 Believing Is Not Seeing

The Churches' Suppression of Knowledge

In school we are taught that the churches have long been in the forefront of the struggle to preserve the wisdom of the ancients and at the same time to advance the frontiers of knowledge. We learn from history courses, for example, that during the Dark Ages the monasteries were the centers of learning and, as such, were responsible for the survival of our civilization's scholarship and intellectual tradition despite the onslaughts of the barbarians.

Therefore, it comes as something of a shock—even to a skeptic—to discover the extent to which the churches have systematically, and often brutally, attacked the postulates and suppressed the findings of science and scholarship throughout history. Indeed, it would be no exaggeration to say that both the natural and the social sciences were set back many centuries by the hostility of organized religion. Even today, in these supposedly more enlightened times, the churches and their religionists reach out to restrain the progress of education and knowledge.

RELIGION AND THE SCHOOLS' CURRICULA

A curious development, spiraling out of a California political quarrel, led me to review the restraints of religion upon the progress of knowledge, and the results of that review stunned me.

Up until the early 1960s in the United States, biological textbooks for use in the public schools contained only random, timid references to evolution if they had any such references at all—even though research in biology and genetics had made spectacular strides in the twentieth century, soundly confirming and advancing evolutionary ideas and facts. By the 1960s France had long been teaching the concept in its schools, as had Germany and England, Japan and India, even Israel and Ethiopia. But in the United States the forces of organized religion had effectively hamstrung the teaching of evolution. Only after 1960, when the Biological Sciences Curriculum Study Group assembled to reform the contents of academic studies in the public schools, did there gradually appear new high school biology textbooks that carefully and thoroughly explained evolution.

This "crime" of science, however, did not elude the eyes of two mothers in Orange County, California, in 1962. In religious indignation, they went immediately to the California School Board. By May 1963 they were insisting that the matters of evolution be clearly designated as "theory," and thus in the following December the school board issued, unanimously, the following policy statement:

1. *Future state textbooks dealing with the subject of man's origins should refer to Darwinian evolution as an important scientific theory or hypothesis.*
2. *California teachers should be encouraged to teach Darwinian evolution as theory rather than as a permanent unchanging truth.*

This was only the first salvo in the fight. The next move was to have the "divine creation" theory of man's origin, as outlined in the Holy Bible, introduced on an equal basis with the evolutionary concept. The religionists' campaign began in 1966, but not until 1969, when state adoption of new science books was up for review, did the battle really flare. At that time the state curriculum commission protested that the only *scientific* theory for the origin of man was evolution. The evangelical fundamentalists lashed back and applied pressure successfully on the state board of education. Thus, in its guidelines to textbook publishers, issued in late 1969, the board added these insidious statements:

> *All scientific evidence to date concerning the origin of life implies at least dualism or the necessity to use several theories to fully explain relationships between established data points. This dualism is not unique to this study but is also appropriate in other scientific disciplines, such as the physics of light.*
>
> *While the Bible and other philosophic treatises also mention creation, science has independently postulated the various theories of creation. Therefore creation in scientific terms is not a religious or philosophic belief.*

Behind this verbiage was the firm suggestion that publishers had better include double versions of man's origins. However, when new books arrived in 1971, it was evident that only two of the dozens of standard publishers had attempted in any way to meet the demand for dual theories. By the beginning of the school term in 1972 the two housewives and their coreligionists went to battle again, and, curiously, this time the government of the United States was drawn into the controversy, if unofficially, when the famous Wernher von Braun of the National Aeronautics and Space Administration gratuitously wrote the state board of education in the religionists' favor:

> *For me, the idea of a creation is not conceivable without involving the necessity of design. One cannot be exposed to the law and order of the universe without concluding that there must be design and purpose behind it all.*
>
> *To be forced to believe only one conclusion—that everything in the universe happened by chance—would violate the very objectivity of science itself.*

Although Von Braun was trained an engineer and not as a scientist, much less a biologist, his relation to the space program unfortunately gave his words a "scientific" aura. In any event, the National Academy of Sciences judged otherwise and, in October 1972, adopted a resolution that the divine creation theory be kept out of California's science textbooks. Religion and science, it said, are

> *. . . separate and mutually exclusive realms of human thought whose presentation in the same context leads to misunderstanding of both scientific theory and religious beliefs.*

When the issue was finally debated at a public hearing in November 1972, there were overflow crowds and at least fifty speakers. Nineteen Nobel Prize winners released a letter asserting that

> *. . . the creation theory is not based on science and does not belong in science textbooks.*

The Academic Council of the University of California, representing 7,000 professors, issued a policy statement declaring,

> *Virtually all biological scientists are agreed on the broad features of the theory of evolution of life forms, the evidence for which is completely overwhelming.*

The council further noted that to accept as scientifically equal the idea of a "special creation" by a supernatural force would be a "gross misunderstanding" of the nature of science. The American Association for the Advancement of Science backed up these arguments.

So what was the result? The religionists' pressures were too strong. The California State Board of Education hedged and voted unanimously that the textbook series used in the public schools must downgrade evolutionary concepts by labeling them "speculation." Where a text originally said, for example, "It is known that life began in the seas," the rewording came out, "Most scientists believe that life may have begun in the sea." The statement, "All scientists do not agree on when and how the earth was formed," was changed into "Scientists are not sure when and how the earth was formed." One publisher had already anticipated the outcome and, in its book *Science, Environment and Man,* had entered several changes, including the deletion of a page-long biographical sketch of anthropologist Louis Leakey, who had discovered evidence of man's ancient origins in Africa, and the insertion in its stead of a photograph of Michelangelo's painting of the creation, with the caption (Genesis 1:44), "And God said, Let there be lights in the firmament of the heaven to divide day from night; and let them be for signs, and for seasons, and for days, and nights." Professor Thomas J. Jukes of Berkeley, California, condemned the book: "This is art, not science." Moreover, "The suggestion of a white creator giving life to a white man first is ethnically dubious."

The fundamentalists were attacking in other states as well, of course, and using a variety of strategies to invade the classroom with fundamentalist ideas. In 1964, for example, members of an organization misleadingly called the American Science Affiliates set up a Creation Science Research Center, which, in the ensuing years, issued a series of textbooks for all grade levels, incorporating religious precepts into several areas of science. With scarcely any publicity, these hybrid books were pressed on school board members in several areas and were actually adopted in thirteen states. A major coup was their introduction into the Columbus, Ohio, school system. The work of this very small, very vocal, very dedicated, and very well-financed religious group was supplemented, with great success, by the work of the Moody Institute of Science (associated with Chicago's Moody Bible Institute), which was distributing evangelizing "science" films that were being shown in schools through the country. It was big business; the institute had sixty distribution outlets in thirty-eight states.

Organized religion was also carrying its banners into the halls of the various state legislatures. A typical bill, introduced into the Michigan Senate in 1972 (though to date not enacted), declared:

> When the scientific theory of evolution is taught in any course in public school, a biblical story of creation shall

also be taught in the same course with an equal amount of time devoted thereto to an historical version of the subject.

In April 1973 a "creationist" bill was introduced into the Tennessee Senate. The lieutenant governor himself appeared to shepherd the bill through and asked that it be done quickly, with no debate, in order to preclude national attention being drawn on the state. Thus there were no formal debates, no committee hearings. The bill was quickly passed, 28 to 1, and sent to the House of Representatives, where debate lasted just one hour and the bill passed with a 54-15 vote. The bill required that any textbook offering any theory of evolution must give equal space and wordage to the Genesis account of creation.

Other state legislatures were beginning to consider such measures. A deliberate confusion of science and religion was emerging.

THE SUPPRESSION OF KNOWLEDGE

Of course from early times the Christian churches have always claimed a special monopoly on knowledge concerning the origin of our planet. The natural sciences were rather contemptuously disregarded in the formulation of theories of creation. Tertullian in the early third century asserted that fossils resulted from the flood of Noah. St. Jerome in the late fourth century insisted that the broken and twisted crust of the earth exhibited the wrath of God against sin. St. Augustine in the early fifth century went even further, writing, "Nothing is to be accepted save on the authority of the Scripture, since greater is that authority than all the powers of the human mind."

St. Augustine's method was to study the letter of the sacred text and then try to make it explain natural phenomena. In so doing he helped to give direction to the mainstream of thought in Western Europe and on the continents of North and South America for nearly thirteen centuries. In the time immediately after St. Augustine's, the vast majority of Christian scholars followed similar paths. Even so strong a man as Pope Gregory the Great yielded to his influence, and such leaders of thought as St. Isidore and the Venerable Bede reached their conclusions along the lines he had laid down.

The Christian churches thus substituted dogma for investigation. Even at the Reformation, the Protestant leaders were rejecting scientific theories. Martin Luther and Philip Melanchthon denounced any idea that appeared to be at variance with biblical accounts. The reformer Peter Martyr made clear why this was necessary. For if the story of creation in Genesis were to be discredited, he wrote, "all the promises of Christ fall into nothing, and all the life of our religion would be lost."

Up to about 1700, most of the great philosophers and thinkers insisted that the strictest devotion to the theory of creation as laid down in the Bible was essential and that no knowledge regarding the earth's origin and structure could be drawn from any other source. With the advancement of science, such dogmatic ideas became untenable. Still, today we have the great state of California reintroducing the biblical version of creation in the public schools. And if you ask any of your neighbors or friends about the origin of the solar system you will be amazed by the number who still believe that it was personally created by the particular god of the Christian religion. The idea that the story of Genesis could be revived in our own time, as it is in the schools of California, boggles the mind.

After 1700, and in scattered instances before that, independent thinking did achieve some breakthroughs. But the Christian religious community and the churches went to great lengths to suppress any scientific investigation. In the seventeenth century at the University of Paris, offending treatises were destroyed and their authors were banished from Paris and forbidden to live in any town or to enter places of public resort. In the middle of the eighteenth century the Comte de Buffon, the great French naturalist, tried to state a few basic scientific truths, and the faculty at the Sorbonne removed him from his high position and forced him to recant ignominiously and to print his recantation. It ran as follows:

I declare that I had no intention to contradict the text of Scripture; that I believe most firmly all therein related about the creation, both as to order of time and matter of fact. I abandon everything in my book respecting the formation of the earth, and generally all which may be contrary to the narrative of Moses.

The heretical idea that Buffon was forced to repudiate was that the earth rotates on its axis! Today the churches that fought such an idea call it a marvel of God that the rotation occurs.

Buffon's humiliating document is a painful reminder of what had happened to Galileo a hundred years before, when he abjured his belief that the sun, not the earth, was the center of our planetary system. Most people have heard of Galileo's recantation before the Inquisition, but generally assume that the trouble was with one man and that it generally ended there. It neither began nor ended there. Such active suppression of thought went on for more than 1,300 years.

Generally speaking, in every religious campaign against any science there have been three phases, each extending over long stretches of time:

The first phase is marked by *a general use of scriptural texts against the new scientific theory, accompanied by an attempt to suppress independent inquiry.*

The second phase is marked by *an appeal to some theological doctrine or apologia as proof of the error of the scientific discovery.*

The final phase is marked by *an attempt at compromise, by trying to reconcile proven facts with scriptural texts.* This sometimes results in the conclusion that the Holy Scriptures had revealed the scientific truth in the first place.

This embattled retreat can be illustrated by the argument over the antiquity of man and earth. St. Augustine had insisted that man on earth had existed 6,000 years and that any belief to the contrary was a deadly heresy. The number was derived through the computation of biblical genealogies and ages; and although the exact time and dating became a matter of scholastic quibbling, there was absolute certainty that human life and the earth existed no earlier. Later scientific efforts to demonstrate that the earth might be more than 6,000 years old were just too threatening to be contemplated by Christian theologians and therefore had to be suppressed, on the grounds that such researches led to infidelity and Atheism and represented nothing less than an effort to depose the Almighty from his throne.

The most influential study affecting modern times was that of James Ussher, archbishop of Armagh in Ireland. In 1650-1654 he published *Annals of the Old and New Testaments,* in which he propounded a remarkable system of dates which set the "Creation" at 4004 B.C.; and for some reason his verdict was widely received as final. His dates were inserted into the margins of the Authorized Version of the English Bible and soon came to be regarded as sacred as Scripture itself.

Yet there were still some brave and enlightened men prepared to challenge the accuracy of the church's time-table in these matters. Sir Walter Raleigh some years earlier, for example, had pointed out the problem of Egypt. He noted that Egypt had magnificent cities, and "these were not built with sticks, but of hewn stone . . . which magnificence neede a parent of more antiquity than those other men had supposed." Later, about the middle of the sixteenth century, a man named La Peyrere put out a book on "pre-Adamites," men allegedly living before Adam. Great theologians from all parts of Europe rushed forward to attack him. Within fifty years, some thirty-six learned refutations of his arguments appeared in book form, not to mention thousands of articles. The Parliament of Paris burned his original book. The grand vicar of the archdiocese of Mechlin threw him into prison and kept him there until he was forced not only to retract his statements but also to abjure his Protestantism and return to the Roman Catholic fold. And in England, Dr. John Lightfoot, vice-chancellor of Cambridge University and reputed to be one of the greatest rabbinical scholars of his time, demonstrated through meticulous examination of biblical and talmudic works "that heaven and earth, centre and circumference, were created together, in the same instant, and clouds full of water" and that "this work took place and man was created by the Trinity on the twenty third of October, 4,004 B.C., at nine o'clock in the morning."

As late as 1850, eminent egyptologists were still modifying the results of their work so that their chronology would not be inconsistent with the accepted date of the Deluge of Noah. But the papyrii, the monuments, the steles, and the tombs could not be so easily tampered with. And the evidence they yielded showed that an advanced civilization had flourished in Egypt with a high standard of manufacturing, commerce, engineering, architecture, sculpture, and astronomy. Still, this was the nation that had held the Jews in bondage, so nothing favorable about its history could be accepted or believed by the churches, steeped as they were in Judeo-Christianity. Then bones were found, and flint weapons, and other artifacts that indicated the existence of ancient, highly developed cultures. Later it was discovered that the four sides of the Great Pyramid were adjusted to the cardinal points of the compass with the utmost precision. One scientist marveled: "The day of the equinox can be taken by observing the sun set across the face of the pyramid, and the neighboring Arabs adjust their astronomical dates by its shadow."

The churches retaliated as best they could. In one amazing argument, the flint stones were depicted as being for the sacred ritual of circumcision. Another argument asserted that no civilization ever did or ever could emerge from a state of utter barbarism if unassisted by an external power, and that therefore all excavated traces of imperfect civilizations were but evidence of fallen descendants of those more fully civilized, as God had created them.

That no compromise would be tolerated can be illustrated by an incident in America. In 1872 a leading American industrialist endowed an institution in Nashville, Tennessee, which bore his name, Vanderbilt University. An eminent scholar, Alexander Winchell, was appointed to its chair of geology. Unfortunately, though, Winchell had become convinced that there had been men on earth earlier than the biblical Adam. Being a religious man, however, he tried to reconcile science and Scripture. He submitted a series of articles on the subject to a northern religious newspaper; whereupon the Methodist Episcopal bishop informed Dr. Winchell that "our people are of the opinion that such views are contrary to the plan of redemption," and asked him to resign his professorship. Winchell refused, replying, "If the board of trustees have the manliness to dismiss me for cause, and declare the cause, I prefer that they should do it. No power on earth could persuade me to resign." Thus, within twenty-four hours he was notified that his chair had been abolished, and its duties, with its salary, added to those of a colleague, while the public was given to understand that the reasons were purely financial. The Methodist Episcopal church (Tennessee Conference) complimented Vanderbilt University for having the courage to "lay its young and vigorous hand upon the mane of untamed speculation and say, 'We will have no more of this.'"

In the twentieth century—with the overwhelming and growing evidence on the great age of the earth, the universe, and man—the religionists have been backing away from extreme modes of resistance, ridicule, and attack, but they have not of course given up on Genesis. Now there are continuing efforts to reconcile Scripture and science. The words of the Bible are wrested from their natural meaning and forced to speak symbolically the language of science. There are efforts, for example, to twist the early chapters of the book of Genesis into apparent agreement by asserting that the days of creation were not really days, but eons of geological time—in other words, that "And the evening and the morning were the first day" does not refer to a day in our sense but to an immense flow of time in the course of eternity. The Deluge was not a single deluge, but a series of floods experienced by many peoples; and the story of the Ark was symbolic. Thus is the "revealed word" made permanently revealing!

THE CRUSADE AGAINST MEDICINE

The Christian churches' battles against astronomy and evolution have been equaled by their war against medicine or medical science. Universally, in all parts of the world, from the dim beginnings of man, there developed the idea that persons who were sick were afflicted or possessed by evil spirits or demons. Therefore, religious or mystic people came to believe that the healing of disease was effected by the casting out of these demons. This notion appears everywhere in the Old Testament. The leprosy of Miriam, the boils of Job, the dysentery of Jehoram, the withered hand of Jeroboam, the fatal illness of Asa—these are all attributed either to the wrath of God or to the malice of Satan. In the New Testament we see the casting out of the devil performed by Jesus himself.

The attitude of the early church toward the medical sciences can perhaps best be demonstrated by the views of some of the church fathers. Tertullian in the third century insisted that a malevolent angel is in constant attendance upon every person. St. Ambrose in the fourth century gave examples to show the sinfulness of resorting to medicine instead of trusting to the intercession of saints. St. Augustine in the early fifth century said, "All diseases . . . are to be ascribed to these demons; chiefly do they torment fresh-baptized Christians, yea, even the guiltless newborn infants." St. Bernard of Clairvaux in the twelfth century warned that to seek relief from disease in medicine was in harmony neither with religion nor with the honor and purity of his order, the Cistercians. Canon law declared that the precepts of medicine were contrary to divine knowledge. Thus a vast system of "pastoral medicine" was developed, which still survives today in such places as Lourdes.

Every cathedral, every abbey, every church claimed possession of healing relics, and the great cathedrals fought each other for the most powerful charms and relics, because they brought in huge revenues from the credulous faithful. For instance, in 1056 a French ruler pledged securities to the amount of 10,000 gold coins for the acquisition of the relics of St. Just and St. Pastor. The body of St. Sebastian brought enormous wealth to the Abbey of Soissons. The cathedral of Cologne acquired human skulls alleged to be those of the three wise men of the East, who, guided by the star of Bethlehem, brought royal gifts to the infant Jesus. And churches in Rome, Canterbury, Treves, Salzburg, Marburg, and elsewhere ventured considerable sums in the purchase of relics. It would have been expecting too much of human nature to imagine that pontiffs and churchmen, who derived great wealth and honor from shrines under their care, would have favored the development of any science that undermined their interests. When they could sell for high fees small blobs of wax on each of which was stamped the figure of a lamb—on the grounds that kissing the wax protected one from falling sickness, apoplexy, and sudden death for seven days—why should they be eager to see the source of their income discredited?

Superstition as well as greed and vanity checked the progress of medical science. For example, there was the idea of the resurrection of the human body. Because the body was the temple of the Holy Spirit and was to be resurrected on the final Judgment Day, it could not be mutilated. (The entire modern business of embalming corpses, beautifying them cosmetically, and sealing them in caskets and vaults derives ultimately from the idea of preserving the body for the Great Day.) In 1248 the Council of Le Mans forbade surgery for an added reason, on the incredible premise that the "Church abhors the shedding of blood"—this from an institution that had caused some of the greatest spilling of innocent blood in human history. The ban had the effect of stopping the development of surgery for centuries.

In the twelfth century the Council of Rheims forbade the study of "physic," meaning medicine, and a multitude of other councils enforced the decree. In the same century, Pope Alexander III forbade monks to study or practice medicine. In 1215 the fourth Lateran Council forbade surgical operations. A few years later Pope Honorius III reiterated and extended this ban. By 1243 the Dominican order was forbidding all practice of science and the art of medicine. Behind all this was the idea that, since supernatural means of healing were everywhere so abundant, it was irreligious to seek a cure by natural means.

Pope Innocent III decreed that no physician, under pain of exclusion from the church, would undertake medical treatment without calling in ecclesiastical advice. Three hundred and fifty years later Pope Pius V was renewing and enforcing this with penalties. Not only did Pius order that all physicians, before administering treatment, should call in a "physician of the soul" on the assumption that "bodily infirmity frequently arises from sin," but he also ordered that if at the end of three days the patient had not made confession to a priest, the medical man should cease his treatment, under pain of being deprived of his right to practice and being expelled from his university faculty should he be a professor.

(There was a faint, but disturbing, echo of this liaison in our own time. In 1963 the American Medical Association, meeting in Atlantic City, decided that religion could help at least psychologically in the cure of disease and that the AMA should start exploring the possibility of an association between physicians and churchmen. On January 6, 1964, the *AMA News* reported that forty-two state medical associations had approved formation of committees on medicine and religion. By 1965, in many cities, doctors were having ministers accompany them on their daily rounds in hospitals. If this trend continues, we would be right back to the situation in which the doctor hesitated to be present at the bed of a patient without "a physician of the soul" accompanying him.)

Even by the time of the Reformation and Counter-Reformation in the sixteenth and seventeenth centuries, things had scarcely improved. The Protestants took just as hard a line against medical science as did the Roman Catholics. Again and again, Martin Luther described his own ailments and diseases as "devil's spells" and declared that "Satan produces all the maladies which afflict mankind for he is the prince of death." The devil "poisons the air," but "no malady comes from God." The use of biblical and theological superstition to try to control the practice of medicine was by no means confined to the Middle Ages.

In the eighteenth and nineteenth centuries the battles continued and affected every aspect of medicine. When, for example, inoculation for smallpox was introduced in France, then in England, churchmen vigorously condemned it in the pulpit and in writing. When, in 1721 in America, Dr. Zabdiel Boylston made an experiment in inoculation with his own son the churches urged the authorities to try him for murder. They insisted that smallpox is "a judgment of God on the sins of the people" and that "to avert it is but to provoke him more." They said that such inoculation against disease was "an encroachment on the prerogatives of Jehovah, whose right it is to wound and to smite." The Boston authorities forbade him to repeat the experiment. By 1798 an Anti-Vaccination Society had been formed in Boston, composed of physicians and clergymen who were determined to suppress vaccination as being "unfaithful to the revealed law of God."

In Canada in 1885 a smallpox epidemic broke out among new immigrants to Montreal. There the Protestant population had finally accepted vaccination, and they escaped the disease almost entirely. The Roman Catholics, however, refused vaccination and suffered terribly. The plague became so serious that travel and trade were restricted. Spurred on by their priests, the Roman Catholic working classes resisted the demands of town officials for compulsory vaccination, declaring, "If we are afflicted with smallpox, it is because we had a carnival last winter, feasting the flesh, which has offended the Lord; . . . it is to punish our pride that God has sent us smallpox." The local board of health then addressed a circular to the Roman Catholic clergy imploring them to recommend vaccination. Only two or three responded. The Oblate Fathers, whose church was situated in the very heart of the infected district, continued to denounce vaccination. Instead, a great procession was ordered, with a solemn appeal to the Virgin Mary. Meanwhile the disease died out among the few Protestants that it touched, whereas it continued to flare among Roman Catholics, until ultimately the board of health was able to enforce the proper measures, and the epidemic was contained.

The use of anesthetics was another medical innovation that was widely attacked by the churches. One example may suffice. In 1847, James Young Simpson, a Scot physician, advocated the use of anesthetics to assist women in childbirth. This met with a storm of opposition from the clergy. Women *must* bring forth their children in pain. The Bible said so. From pulpit after pulpit Dr. Simpson's use of chloroform in childbirth was denounced. The vile aim of anesthesia, it was said, was "to avoid one part of the primeval curse upon woman." Feeling the need to change his tactics, Simpson retaliated with the following argument:

> *My opponents forget the 21st verse of the 2nd chapter of Genesis; it is the record of the first surgical operation ever performed, and that text proves that the maker of the universe before he took the rib from Adam's side for the creation of Eve, caused a deep sleep to fall upon Adam.*

The response was typical. The deep sleep was all right for a man having a rib operation, but not for a woman being assisted in giving birth, for the Bible commended women to suffer. Indeed, God himself had condemned women so (Genesis 3:16):

> *I will greatly multiply thy sorrow and thy conception; in sorrow thou shalt bring forth children.*

God had spoken.

EXORCISM AND MENTAL ILLNESS

The tragedy of the churches' superstition and restraint of knowledge is no more clearly revealed than in the history of psychiatry. When Christianity first gained ascendancy in the Western world, there was already established among scientists and thinkers a serious and sympathetic approach to the phenomenon of insanity. In the fifth century Hippocrates of Cos had asserted that all madness is simply disease of the brain. In the first century after Christ, the Greek physician Aretaeus living in Rome reaffirmed this idea. In the next century another Greek physician living in Rome, Soranus, continued the same line of inquiry. The famous Galen, resident in Rome toward the end of the second century, and Celius Aurelianus in the third century, also taught that insanity was a brain disease. This whole tradition stressed that madness was a disease requiring careful treatment and understanding. This tradition was interrupted and then overturned by Christian theology.

Early in Christianity there arose a current of belief which for centuries supported the infliction of torture, physical and mental, upon hundreds of thousands of innocent men, women, and children. The basic belief was that madness was mainly or largely possession by the devil. This was unquestioningly accepted by all the early church fathers and by theologians for many centuries thereafter. Indeed, it was considered proof of the divine origin of the Christian religion that the power of casting out devils had been given to Jesus Christ.

So strong was this belief that it took hold of even the most enlightened men in the church. The case of St. Gregory the Great in the sixth century is typical. He was a pope of exceedingly broad mind for his time, yet he solemnly related that a nun, having eaten some lettuce without making the sign of the cross, swallowed a devil and that, when commanded by a holy man to come forth, the devil replied, "How am I to blame? I was sitting on the lettuce, and this woman, not having made the sign of the cross, ate me along with it."

Thus did Christianity abandon the sensible, humane approach of the Greek and Roman scientists, substituting for it an elaborate dogmatic system for exorcising devils from persons possessed.

Sometimes the exorcisms were a form of magic tricks, employing strange mixtures of fetishes, herbs and balms, and incantations, as do the following characteristic pre- scriptions:

> A drink for a fiend-sick man, to be drunk out of a church bell: Githrife, cynoglossum, yarrow lupin, flow- er-de-luce, fennel, lichen, lovage. Work up to a drink with clear ale, sing seven masses over it, add garlic and holy water, and let the possessed sing the Beati Immac- ulati; then let him drink the dose out of a church bell, and let the priest sing over him the Domine Sancte Pater Omnipotens.

> For a fiend-sick man: When a devil possesses a man, or controls him from within with disease, a spew-drink of lupin, bishopswort, henbane, garlic. Pound these together, add ale and holy water.

Sometimes the exorcisms consisted of doing battle with the devil more directly. According to sacred Scripture, a main characteristic of Satan was pride. It was pride that led him to rebel. Therefore the first thing to do in driving him out of a lunatic was to strike a fatal blow to his pride. The theory was carried out logically, and to the letter. The treatises on the subject astound one by their wealth of blasphemous and obscene epithets. The *Treasury of Exorcisms,* published in Cologne in 1626, contains hundreds of pages packed with the vilest abuse imaginable for the purpose of overwhelming the in-dwelling Satan. A few excerpts:

> *Thou lustful and stupid one, . . . thou lean sow, . . . thou wrinkled and mangy beast, . . . thou beast, of all beasts the most beastly, . . . thou drunkard, most greedy wolf, . . . thou boor, . . . filthy sow, perfidious boar, . . . envious crocodile, . . . lousy swineherd, lowest of the low, . . . cudgelled ass. . . .*

In addition to wounding Satan's pride with this invective, there was also an attempt to scare him with tremendous words. For this purpose, thunderous names from Hebrew and Greek were imported. If those failed, efforts were made to drive out Satan with filthy and rank-smelling drugs. Urine and fecal matter loomed large in this, as did sulphur, all of which were smeared upon the persons in whom Satan had taken refuge. Still further to annoy Satan, pictures of the devil were spat upon and trampled underfoot, as well as sprinkled with foul compounds.

These were only the preliminaries. There were long litanies of cursing and threatening to follow, and occasionally the demon was even reasoned with. The results, according to the church, were nothing less than spectacular. One bishop of Beauvais, for example, was said to have proved so effective in one of his exorcisms that five devils gave up possession of a sufferer and then signed their names to an agreement that the possessed should nevermore be molested. On another occasion, in 1583, the Jesuit fathers in Vienna gloried in having cast out no less than 12,652 living devils in just one contest.

Another type of cure that was undertaken was the promotion of great religious processions. Troops of men and women, crying, howling, imploring saints, beating themselves with whips, visiting various sacred shrines, hoped to drive off the powers of evil. It is not uncommon to read of convents, entire villages, even large districts, ravaged by epidemics of diabolical possession.

With the Reformation there developed a rivalry between Protestants and Roman Catholics over the cure of madness. Whereas the Catholics used holy water and consecrated wax in their elaborate rituals, the Protestants used texts of Scripture and importunate prayer. Each side denied the efficacy of the other's efforts, and each insisted that the other's apparent success in running the devil out of a victim was actually only collusion between the devil and the other church. More than one poor victim had to run the gauntlet of exorcism by the Lutherans, the Roman Catholics, and then the Calvinists.

In the nineteenth and twentieth centuries, the theological conservatism of the Christian churches caused old abuses to be continued for years even after the theological bases for them had been discredited. Even in our own times there is a lingering fear of the insane, as if we subconsciously believe that they are possessed by unknown forces. Even in our times, a highly promoted motion picture, *The Exorcist,* could draw crowds to the theaters to be both shocked and instructed by the vilest of scenes involving possession and exorcism; in the course of things the movie squarely ridiculed scientific psychiatry and even inspired public discussions of the validity and efficacy of priestly exorcisms.

THE LONG WAR ON SCIENCE

For over twelve centuries the sciences were discouraged or perverted by religious orthodoxy. The orthodox held that the end of the world was at hand, that all existing physical nature was soon to be destroyed. Therefore, the greatest thinkers in the church poured contempt on all investigators into a science of nature, insisting that everything except the saving of souls was folly. This attitude—and its enforcement—arrested the development of the physical sciences for hundreds of years, because an atmosphere was created in which all seeking after truth in nature was regarded as futile.

For those hundreds of years the churchmen dominating European thought, who regarded all science as futile, diverted the mainstream of study into theology. As science came to be regarded as dangerous, persecutions became systematic and cruel. Laws were enacted and enforced with rigor. The most simple efforts in physics, chemistry, even mathematics, were frowned upon. The great cathedrals captured in stone the ideas that obsessed the theologians and the faithful alike: demons, saints, and gargoyles.

Every great theologian and church leader participated in the war on science. In the twelfth century Pope Alexander III issued a ban on the study of "physics or the laws of the world." In 1317 Pope John XXII issued his bull *Spondent Pariter,* which was leveled at the alchemists but in reality dealt a blow to the beginning of all chemical science. He called on all rulers, secular and ecclesiastical, to hunt down the miscreants who attempted the practice, and to this end he increased the powers of the inquisitors in all parts of Europe. Chemistry became known as the "devilish art." Pope Eugenius IV in 1437 and 1445 issued other bulls exhorting inquisitors to even more diligent searches for offenders. In the sixteenth century other popes similarly ruled.

The Protestants followed the same line. They simply vied with the Catholics to improve their orthodoxy by suppressing and punishing every independent mind that they could find. In Germany alone, from the mid-fifteenth to the mid-sixteenth century, more than 100,000 persons were victims of the search-and-destroy operation. Every independent thinker, in any field, was charged, harassed, imprisoned, or done away with. His works were destroyed and he was forced to recant.

It is truly one of the miracles of human history that despite the centuries-long effort by the churches to stamp out any vestige of scientific inquiry, there were enough courageous and dedicated men in every age to guarantee the survival, and eventual triumph, of the sciences. And it is no less a miracle of human ingenuity that when the sciences finally gained academic acceptance, the churches embraced their findings and announced to the world that they revealed the divine plan of God.

4 Suffer the Little Children
*The Churches' Attempts to
Control Childhood Education*

From the beginning of the Christian era onward, the churches have recognized the importance of gaining the child early and keeping the child late, in order to instill into the young mind those patterns of thought that will preserve the authority of the churches.

The churches recognize that this need is more urgent today than ever before, because the general intellectual atmosphere is rapidly changing as new technological and scientific ideas shatter old myths everywhere in the expanding world of knowledge. The ways in which the churches respond to the changes, however, can be quite various. Either they can resist the changes and try to maintain a rigid ideological environment in their teaching of the young, or they can try to modify a few areas of teaching to meet a changing world. Thus some institutions, such as the Roman Catholic church, are basically unyielding. The more "liberal" sects, on the other hand, at least attempt to rationalize or modify their body of ideas to make them more palatable to the earnest and inquiring mind.

As a matter of policy and principle, organized religion would prefer to maintain an unchanged ideological environment, chiefly by boycotting "irreligious" literature, art, and ideas and creating a protected "religious" atmosphere around the child. Such is the basis for the parochial or religious school. It represents an attempt to create an ideological environment in which the child's mind will respond in a manner favorable to the claims and teachings of a particular sect. Although the Jesuits are credited with the concept of "Give me a child until he is six and I have him for life," every religious group in America subscribes to the idea. This is evidenced in the words of a superintendent of Baptist day schools in California, in a report to his coreligionists:

> This all-essential Christian education must begin at the earliest possible moment—in childhood. College is too late. Children should be introduced to the Savior while their ears are susceptible and plastic. Delay is fatal. The cardinal principle in dealing with children about the things of God is to reach them early and reach them often.

Unhappily for the churches, traditional religious teaching conflicts with many scientific ideas and theories. Therefore, religious belief cannot be taught like other subjects. It must be *implanted*—"early and often." With other subjects one can wait until the child has the mental maturity to grasp them. One does not start a child on analytical chemistry or solid geometry. One begins with small numbers and lesser skills in every subject—except religion. Apart from the desire of religion to capture the mind early and indoctrinate it constantly, there is no reason at all why religion could not wait, as other subjects wait, until the child is old enough to understand and appreciate it. But with organized religion it is literally the child or nothing, for if it fails to get the child, it will almost certainly never get the adult.

The desire for the control of education is indicative of the churches' need to dominate the mind of the rising generation. The struggle for the child is a part of the fight for the future of civilization. This being true, the history of the United States naturally reflects the strenuous efforts of the churches to achieve a monopoly on the education of as many children as possible.

RELIGIOUS EDUCATION IN THE COLONIES

In each of the colonies of nascent America the churches practiced a rigid intolerance, fearful lest any of its brood be tainted by rival theologies. The dominant sect in any area used education as an instrument for keeping minds focused squarely on its own brand of orthodoxy. Organized religion was an educational as well as a political power in every colony.

The systems of education varied widely, however, from section to section. In New England the main pattern of human settlement was the town. Any group of New Englanders therefore had a convenient center for establishing a school. In the plantation South, on the other hand, towns scarcely existed, and homesteads lay great distances from one another. The scattered nature of settlement thus made community schools virtually impossible. By the time a child reached school by horseback or riverboat, he would have had to return right away to get home by nightfall. In rare instances, where a few plantations might be relatively close together, so-called Old Field Schools were established in which children were taught by a local clergyman, an indentured servant, or a planter's wife; the rich gentry of course could employ tutors or send their children to Europe for schooling. But usually education was left in the hands of individual families or groups of families to do what they could to instruct the young in piety and orthodoxy. In the middle colonies—Pennsylvania, New Jersey, and New York —patterns of settlement were mixed. Compared with the South, the middle colonies had more towns for the development of community schools; but, compared with New England, there was also a larger degree of individual settlement. Moreover, this section contained a host of rival sects —Moravians, Quakers, Baptists, Dutch Reformed, Congregationalists, and others—all at each other's throats, so that efforts toward community schools tended to fail. Almost all schools were parish or parochial schools.

New England thus could set the dominant pattern for colonial education. It had not only convenient settlement patterns for the development of community schools; it also had a sternly uniform Calvinistic—or Puritan—ethic that demanded of everyone that he be able to read the Scriptures and learn God's rules for existence (the region achieved 95 percent literacy for males in the period 1640–1700). It was thus the first region committed to compulsory elementary education, albeit doctrinaire religious education. In 1642, for instance, Massachusetts imposed fines for the neglect of reading and religious instruction. In 1647 it passed an act requiring every town of 50 or more families to set up an "elementary school" for reading and writing and requiring every town of 100 or more families to provide a Latin "grammar school" to prepare students for college (Boston Latin School had already been established, in 1635); the method of funding was optional but usually consisted of taxation. The Puritan ethic also demanded a ministry rigidly trained in theology and the classics. In 1636 Harvard College was established for the purpose in the town of Cambridge, across the river from Boston. It may be noted that among the early New Englanders (up to 1646) there were 130 alumni of the universities of Oxford, Cambridge, and Dublin. Virtually all these men of privilege and education were clergy, and they were the social and political theocrats of New England.

The clergy supervised the New England town schools. After the legislature had passed an authorization for a school, indicating how it would be funded, the smaller political unit, the township, was given the responsibility of organizing the school. It was at this point that the local minister exerted influence over the type of courses, the course content, and the choice of the teacher. Often the ministers were, in fact, the true supervisors even though administration was legally invested in the township trustees.

The pedagogy was doctrinaire. The Puritan ideal, derived from Calvin, included the belief that the state was the arm of the church and the church represented the word of God. Education stressed obedience. The educational life of the first communities was thus much given to rote-learning and catechizing. The catechism was an elementary book containing a summary, in the form of questions and answers, of the principles of the Christian religion, especially those of the sect. Because (in this theory of education) man existed for the glory of God, the only goal of education was "true piety." The first concern of life was to do God's will, and the point of death was to receive future happiness. The catechism taught that this was attainable through a succession of personal understandings:

> First, one's conviction of sin;
> then, one's call to grace;
> followed by one's evidence of saving faith;
> through one's growing of holiness in life;
> and one's glorification, in heaven.

So strong was the emphasis on catechizing that it continues to exist today in most American churches under the guise of "responsive reading."

EDUCATION IN THE YOUNG REPUBLIC

The American Revolution tended to disrupt what systems of education had existed. In many areas of British occupation, schooling ceased. And, as we saw in Chapter 2, the churches were thrown into disorder. Even before the war ended, however, the Founding Fathers, most of them Deists, were looking forward to the new nation that they believed should be guided by an enlightened people, rather than by a people obedient to religious dictates. Thus in 1779, for example, Thomas Jefferson offered a plan in the Virginia Legislature to provide secular education for children at public cost. The proposal, however, aroused the violent opposition not only of the rich gentry, who disdained putting out money for education of the poor, but also of the clergy, who, for obvious reasons, wanted the education of youth in their sole hands. Jefferson's plan was rejected.

A few years later, in 1784, the Virginia sectarians retaliated by advancing their own plan, asking the Legislature to levy a tax for the support of all Christian denominations, including facilities for parochial schooling. This bill especially aroused Thomas Jefferson and James Madison, causing the former to draft his famous Act for Establishing Religious Freedom (see Chapter 2) and causing the latter to write his celebrated essay, "A Memorial and Remonstrance." Madison later explained what prompted him to write the essay (letter to George Mason, July 14, 1826): "During the session of the General Assembly, 1784-5, a bill was introduced into the House of Delegates providing for the legal support of the teachers of the Christian religion, and being patronized by the most popular talents in the House, seemed likely to obtain a majority of votes. . . . [Some opponents of the bill] thought it advisable that a remonstrance against the bill should be prepared for general circulation and signature, and imposed me the task of drawing up such a paper." In that paper, we may note, Madison bluntly asked, "What influence in fact have ecclesiastical establishments had on civil society?" His reply: "In no instance have they been the guardians of the liberties of the people." The churches' bill was rejected by the Legislature.

Not until the second and third decades of the nineteenth century did there begin a real educational awakening in America. People like Josiah Warren began to push for proper schools, founded on the idea of practical education. He wanted students to be involved in observation as a means of instruction, and he wanted to link the school to the workshop. He regarded the development of the personality of the child as the true foundation of all education. To prepare the child for his future tasks in life (rather than for some hereafter) seemed to him the essential thing.

This line of reasoning was soon adopted everywhere in the new nation. Robert Coram, a seaman in the Revolution and later an intellectual leader in Delaware, called for the training of all children in the practical arts as a means of assuring personal independence and overcoming poverty. Thomas Jefferson pushed for the education of American youth on American soil and emphasized our potentials here for higher education with no need to send young persons abroad. Benjamin Rush proposed that not only state universities but also free schools be established in every township consisting of 100 families. Noah Webster advocated that schools be open for at least four months in a year. Samuel

Harrison Smith suggested that a fund be raised from the citizens in proportion to their property holdings in order to provide the money for schools. Philip Lindsley argued that schooling should be made available to all citizens, poor as well as rich, in order to safeguard the Republic.

More widespread education of children meant, of course, that public funds were needed to support the new common schools. The clergy wanted to secure the funds for themselves or, barring that, at least keep the funds away from secular schools. The rich did not want to be taxed to support common schools, for their children were not there. Also, the political orientation of the upper classes was not favorable to education that would make equality real.

Persuasive voices for free public schools were being heard, however. Thomas Jefferson proposed that American education should have as its object the "natural philosophy" of an education in chemistry, agriculture, natural history, botany, and the like. For this type of education South Carolina passed its "free school" law in 1811. In Pennsylvania a school tax was first required by law in 1827, and with this went a prohibition on sectarian teaching. In 1829 Ohio passed a law giving the city of Cincinnati the right to organize city schools and the authority to levy special taxes to support them. By 1834 New York recognized the need to have teacher training and to prepare secular teachers through public funding. Maryland, Ohio, and New Hampshire followed this example. Connecticut first financed its schools through taxation in 1838. In 1837 Massachusetts established the nation's first state board of education and, under the brilliant leadership of its first administrator, Horace Mann, set patterns of school appropriations, nonsectarian education, policy making, teacher training, and the like that would influence education everywhere in the United States.

During this first part of the nineteenth century, three general features made for the schools' progress, especially in the North. Most important, there was no dominant religious system. Second, there was a constant stream of immigrants who needed to be assimilated into the culture. Third, the control of schools remained with local boards. By 1840 roughly half of the children in New England were receiving free secular education, as were one-seventh of the children in the middle states and one-sixth of those in the West. By 1850, generally, educational opportunity was available everywhere to children of ordinary people in state-supported, state-supervised schools. Taxable property made possible government support, and grants of land were made for endowments. DeWitt Clinton of New York, Thaddeus Stevens of Pennsylvania, and Henry Barnard of Connecticut and Rhode Island, as well as Horace Mann of Massachusetts, saw the fight through. No Christian sects of organized religion helped anywhere along the way. Indeed, they feared how secular education might undermine the faith and obedience of youth in their charge, and thus they constituted the chief opponents of liberal innovators like Mann.

THE MOVEMENT FOR NONSECTARIAN SCHOOLS

The struggle for strong secular public schools went forward, slowly but steadily, against the protests of wealthy taxpayers and religious sectarians. Meanwhile, the religious community, finding itself unable to dominate the public school system, opted for private schools. The sects demanded and got free land grants and tax exemptions, and sometimes initially they even garnered part of the tax funds originally designated for the free school system. Fortunately for us, however, they eventually lost this largess. A few examples of what happened during this early period are quite illuminating.

In New York, for instance, beginning in 1805 and before true public schools developed, all schools, sectarian or nonsectarian, received public subsidies. Then in 1824 the state Legislature set up a special body to administer and distribute these funds and to choose those schools which merited aid. This Public School Society, as it was called, was supposed to be evenhanded in its policies, but actually its membership chanced to be dominated by Quakers, and the Quakers had odd ideas about education. They opposed what they arbitrarily defined as "formal" teaching of religion but favored what they arbitrarily defined as "general and scriptural" instruction. Only the latter, they held, could be subsidized by funds from the Public School Society. Roman Catholic schools, to the Quaker mind, did not qualify; theirs offered only "formal" sectarian instruction. Roman Catholics in New York, heretofore given school aid, were now cut off.

Denied the largess furnished to the Protestants, the Roman Catholic church began a barrage of complaints that culminated in a petition to the board of aldermen of New York City demanding that their eight New York schools be designated "as among the schools entitled to participate in the common school fund." The petition was rejected, whereupon the Roman Catholics, under the leadership of Bishop John Hughes, organized the Church and State party in New York and nominated a slate of two senators and thirteen assemblymen to represent New York City in the state Legislature. After a bitter campaign all their candidates were elected. With this new balance of power in the Legislature, a bill was introduced to give control of the schools to local school boards, which could then decide which religion would dominate in each geographical school district. The proposal passed the House of Representatives 65 to 16 on March 31, 1842. However, the New York Senate, receiving the bill, amended it by banning the teaching of any specifically denominational tenet in a state-funded school. After heated battle, the amended form was approved 13 to 12. A board of education was set up in every community, sectarian instruction was outlawed in the public schools, and a universal system of secular education was established. When word of this reached New York City, mobs of Roman Catholics and Protestants fought in the streets, rioting and looting for several days. Yet, out of this very sectarian fight came the nonsectarian public school system of New York; the Public School Society ceased to function.

A more diffused struggle developed in Massachusetts. There a law of 1827 decreed that no book purchased or used in any school could favor "any religious sect or tenet." When Horace Mann became secretary of the first board of education in 1837 he found widespread disregard of the law. He began a program of strict enforcement—and immediately reaped a harvest of religious abuse. The

American Sunday School Union attacked Mann with such vigor that the controversy was known across the nation. Mann, it should be noted, was not asking for the elimination of Christian instruction; as a Protestant, he approved silent, uninterpreted Bible reading in school, and he encouraged teachers to show by precept and example what he conceived to be the essentials of Christianity. Nevertheless, such zealous organizations as the Presbyterian Synod of New Jersey regarded such limited religious teaching as calculated to develop "infidel youth who will not be fit to maintain our free institutions." The religious community opted to attack the whole concept of universal free education rather than to give up their full-ranging influences.

Henry Barnard in Connecticut was equally involved in the fight, which included elementary public schools, training schools for teachers, and free libraries in towns.

While organized religion lost its grasp on the elementary schools, it increased its hold on the colleges. Each denomination strove to outdo the other in the number of colleges each could sponsor. From 1820 to 1850, eighty-seven such private colleges were founded, and from 1850 to 1860 there were ninety-one more. What these colleges were, and represented, is best illustrated by remarks of William S. Tyler of Amherst College as he summarized the arguments for church-affiliated colleges in 1855:

> *Princeton College was founded by the Synod of New York for the purpose of supplying the church with learned and able preachers of the Word. And its paramount religious design and spirit are well expressed in the language of President Witherspoon: "Cursed be all that learning that is contrary to the cross of Christ; cursed be all that learning that is not subservient to the cross of Christ."*

THE CATHOLIC REACTION TO "PROTESTANT" PUBLIC SCHOOLS

Although the Protestant establishment in the mid-nineteenth century might not be pleased with how men like

Mann tried to limit religious teaching, the public school system nevertheless was predicated generally on Protestant beliefs. Protestants were able to influence legislators and school boards, and Protestants were increasing the number of their colleges. Roman Catholics, on the other hand, were being treated like aliens and were unhappy about it. In 1829, and again in 1849, for example, the Roman Catholic bishops convened councils in Baltimore to emphasize the danger to Roman Catholic children of attending public schools that had a Protestant atmosphere.

Because the Roman Catholic church had brought along from Europe its hierarchical structure, it could face the problem with united strength and vigorous resolve. The church thus decided to rear the children of its faith in the closed protection of its own school system. While it might continue to attack the public school system, it more realistically began a gigantic effort to establish its own educational system. Every parish was urged to establish a school to protect the Roman Catholic children from contamination. Parents were admonished to be certain to have children attend and to financially support such schools. The following is one such appeal that was used:

> How would your hearts be torn with grief did your minds foresee, that throughout eternity your children will be cast into outer darkness, where there is weeping and gnashing of teeth! Believe us, it is only by the religious education of your children that you can train them up, as to ensure that, by their filial piety and steady virtue, they may be to you the staff of your old age, the source of your consolation, and reward in a better world.

For the teachers and the administrators of parochial schools the church had set a decidedly Christianizing mission. This mission would later be spelled out by Pope Pius XI in his encyclical On the Christian Education of Youth, which stated that the

> . . . only school approved by the Church is one where . . . the Catholic religion permeates the entire atmosphere and where all teaching and the whole organization of the school and its teachers, syllabus, and

textbooks in every branch is regulated by the Christian spirit.

In short, the child was to be wholly enveloped.

TRENDS TOWARD SECULARIZATION OF PUBLIC SCHOOLS

When the Roman Catholics themselves would not provide enough schools, the Catholic church turned to fight the public schools where the Catholic children were in attendance. Some people today even credit our now totally secular schools to the fact that the Roman Catholic church fought so vigorously for the removal of all the religious matter in the curriculum which might be interpreted as adverse reflection on Catholicism. Conversely, rather than have an intrusion of Roman Catholic doctrines, the Protestants agreed to secularize the schools. During the nineteenth century, then, both the Protestants and the Roman Catholics feared the influence of secular education on the faith and morals of the young people, but they each, equally, feared the theological supremacy of the other more.

The road to secularization, however, was not free of difficulties or even of violence. In 1844, for instance, at the urging of a local bishop, the Philadelphia school board permitted Roman Catholic children in the public schools to read from their own version of the Bible, the Douay Version. The American Protestant Association was outraged. Mass meetings were held, two Roman Catholic churches were burned, and the rioting was stopped only when the bishop ordered all his churches closed. At the Church of St. Philip Neri several people were killed. The church was broken open and only the presence of the militia, the mayor, and the governor prevented its being burned to the ground.

When this measure of self-determination proved so provocative of violence, the Roman Catholic church felt the need to go to the courts. One of the earliest cases attempting to stop Bible reading and prayer recitations in the public schools was brought by the Roman Catholic church in the case of *John D. Minor et al.* v. *The Board of*

Education of the City of Cincinnati et al. on November 26, 1869. The litigants complained that the Protestant Bible was used in classes and that, in the view of the Roman Catholic church,

> . . . *the version of the Scriptures taught [was] incorrect as a translation and incomplete by reason of its omission of a part of the books held by [the Catholic] church to be an integral portion of the inspired canon.*

The church also charged

> . . . *that the Scriptures ought not to be read indiscriminately, inasmuch as [the Catholic] church has divine authority as the only infallible teacher and interpreter of the same, and that reading of the same without note or comment and without being properly expounded by the only authorized teachers and interpreters thereof is not only not beneficial to the children in said schools but likely to lead to the adoption of dangerous errors, irreligious faith, practice and worship.*

In a legal system dominated by Protestant ideals, the Catholics, in this instance, lost their fight. Nevertheless, Bible reading within the confines of the school was now fully a public question for debate, whereas before it had been taken for granted.

Beginning in 1855 in Massachusetts, various states began to adopt state constitutional provisions forbidding the granting of public funds to denominational or sectarian institutions, especially schools. President Grant entered the fray in 1876 with a speech in Des Moines, Iowa, to the Army of the Tennessee:

> *Now, the centennial year of our national existence, I believe, is a good time to begin the work of strengthening the foundations of the structure commenced by our patriotic fathers a hundred years ago at Lexington. Let us labor to add all needful guarantees for the greater security of free thought, free speech, a free press, pure morals, unfettered religious sentiments, and equal rights and privileges to all men, irrespective of nationality,*

color, or religion. *Encourage free schools and resolve that not one dollar of the money appropriated to their support shall be appropriated to the support of any sectarian school; that neither the state or nation, nor both combined, shall support institutions of learning other than those sufficient to afford to every child in the land the opportunity of a good common-school education, unmixed with sectarian, pagan, or atheistical dogma.*

Leave the matter of religion to the family altar, the church, and private schools entirely supported by private contributions. Keep the church and state forever separate. With these safeguards I believe the battles which created the Army of the Tennessee will not have been fought in vain.

In a message to Congress later in the year he reiterated his stand. A debate ensued in Congress, arousing large public interest. Finally James G. Blaine, later a Republican candidate for the Presidency, introduced a resolution to amend the Constitution thus:

No State shall make any laws respecting an establishment of religion or prohibiting the free exercise thereof; and no money raised by taxation in any State for the support of the public schools, or derived from any public fund be under the control of any religious sect, nor shall any money so raised or lands so devoted be divided between religious sects or denominations.

The proposed amendment passed the House by a vote of 180 to 7 (98 not voting) and was referred to the Senate judiciary committee. The final vote by the Senate on the resolution, slightly modified, was 28 to 16 (27 not voting). Forty-eight votes were needed for passage, and Blaine's proposed constitutional amendment failed.

A strong current of opinion held that the matter was best left to the states. Still, the Congress utilized at least one safeguard. It required territories seeking admission as states in the Union to adopt ordinances guaranteeing that public schools would be established "free from sectarian control." Montana, North Dakota, South Dakota, and Washington, admitted in 1889, and Idaho and Wyoming, admitted in 1890, were the first to comply.

'PLANS" FOR RELIGIOUS EDUCATION

From this time on, a series of "plans" and legislative ploys were continually put forward in an effort to evade the new restrictions on sectarian teaching in the public schools or somehow even to reimpose religious observance in the schools.

One of the first of these plans developed as the National Education Association met in St. Paul, Minnesota, in 1890. In a speech to that body, Archbishop John Ireland proposed that states subsidize general nonsectarian instruction in parochial schools, leaving to the churches the expense of providing religious education. Out of this proposal came the "Faribault Plan," involving the Roman Catholic schools in Faribault and Stillwater, Minnesota. Under the plan, each local school board leased the Roman Catholic school buildings in the area and put the teaching staff, most often consisting of nuns, on the public payroll. The children went to mass, usually on the school premises, each morning before school officially opened, and they were taught the catechism at the end of the school day; in between they received so-called general education. The appearance of the school remained about the same. This plan was accepted in many small, principally Roman Catholic, communities for many decades. It was finally to come to national attention in the 1940s when it was attempted in a major American city. That city was Cincinnati, Ohio, or, rather, one of its major suburbs. The National Education Association investigated and reported:

> This school enrolled only Catholic pupils and was taught largely by Catholic Sisters, wearing the garb of their religious order. It was conducted as a sectarian school, but paid for out of public funds. Sectarian religious instruction was given each day as a regular part of the school program. The symbolic decorations of the building were of a sectarian nature. The Sisters were paid

from public funds under contract with the local board of education.

This particular situation aroused heated controversy in the Cincinnati community from 1940 to 1947 before the plan was finally discontinued there. One of the main arguments against this plan, designed allegedly to separate general education from religious education, was that it was a ruse. Roman Catholic teachers were under express papal orders not to try to separate the two. Leo XIII, in his encyclical *Militantes Ecclesiae* of August 1, 1897, had stated:

> It is necessary not only that religious instruction be given to the young at certain fixed times, but also that every other subject taught be permeated with Christian piety.

Meanwhile, the so-called North Dakota plan was evolving. Under this plan, biblical studies were to be pursued outside the schools, but public school authorities were to award credit for the studies. The state school board of North Dakota actually prepared and published the syllabus for such studies. Vestiges of this system still exist in the public schools of other states.

Another proposal was the so-called released-time plan. It developed because Protestant religious or parochial schools had never been able to attract any appreciable number of students, and Protestant educators were thus casting around for a plan to establish a weekday church school. This plan had already been adopted by Jewish communities with some success. Finally, in 1913, a superintendent of schools in Gary, Indiana, suggested that the public schools "release" to the churches some of the time that the child spent in the public schools. The Protestants had faith in the idea and were eager to utilize it. By the end of 1915 a program had been worked out whereby approximately 600 Gary schoolchildren were being excused one period a week to attend church school.

When this plan was tried in New York City, the resultant controversy actually developed into brawls at public hearings. Nonetheless, legislation was passed requiring schools to provide released-time if a duly constituted religious body in the community requested it. Seeing benefits to its own in the midst of the battle, the Roman Catholic church suddenly reversed its prior disapproval of the plan and enthusiastically embraced the idea.

Both the U.S. Office of Education (in 1932 and 1940) and the National Education Association (in 1945) reviewed the program. By 1950 about forty-five states were participating in this exercise, involving about 500 school systems and about 165,000 children. By the most liberal calculations, however, not more than 5 percent of the school population participated in this program, and of the 5 percent about 75 to 80 percent were Roman Catholic children. Begun by the Protestants, this experiment became a boon to the Roman Catholics, and as such was then attacked by the Protestants.

The original idea behind the released-time plan was to bolster declining Protestant schools and to enforce attendance at religious classes by resorting to the authority of the public schools. Public school property and employees were used to assemble groups, with all the pressures to conform which come in such a situation; public school administration processes were used to keep records and distribute literature. This enforced attendance at church schools could not have been obtained if classes had been held during the free time of the pupils.

The program unmistakably interrupted regular classroom work and required the reorganization of scheduled school programs for all students. Those children remaining in school could not be given tests, work, or instructions which the released pupils would be missing. The children who left and the children who remained were identified for all to see, and children were made very conscious of their religious differences. The lesson was driven home: the 5 percent of the children who were religious and who were included in this program could and did disrupt the schooling process of the other 95 percent.

So what happened? A substitute plan was proposed. Instead of the children going off to the church school, the church school would in effect come to the children. A local clergyman would come into the public school to give his religious lessons. This plan was started in Champaign,

Illinois, in 1940. It was tested in the courts by an Atheist, Vashti McCollum, who finally brought it to a Supreme Court review. The Court found that the plan constituted use of tax-supported property for religious instruction, and thus was forbidden.

Naturally, the next test was to see if the released-time plan itself was unconstitutional. The test case arose in New York City, where the majority of released-time children resided. In this instance the Supreme Court went along with the churches and declared:

> When the state encourages religious instruction or cooperates with religious authorities by adjusting the schedule of public events to sectarian needs, it follows the best of our traditions.

Encouraged by this decision, the churches continued with the plan until lack of interest on the part of both children and parents brought failure. Out of it came the idea of "shared time." In this practice, which continues currently, the religious schools teach the "value" subjects of sociology, history, religion, and the like. The parochial children then go to the public schools for the other courses, such as chemistry, math, and physics.

These long battles over religious teaching concerned not only what was taught in the public schools but also what the children read there. Back in the nineteenth century, in the alarm over growing Roman Catholic influences, the Protestant community stood firm in its insistence that the King James Version of the Bible should remain in the public classrooms. In 1855 Massachusetts became the first state actually to enact a law requiring public school Bible reading. Before, it had been simply customary. The Roman Catholics meanwhile fought valiantly to have that Bible removed from the public schools. The most stubborn resistance came in Maine in 1854, in Massachusetts in 1859, and in Indiana in 1880. But by the beginning of the twentieth century more and more states began to require Bible reading—King James Bible reading—in the public schools *by statute,* as advocated by the Protestants. Naturally such enactments came easily in the South— Alabama in 1910, followed shortly by Florida, Tennessee,

Delaware, and the District of Columbia. By 1913 Bible reading was mandatory in twelve states. By the mid-1940s twenty-four states "permitted" the practice.

PRAYER IN THE SCHOOLS

A further wish of Protestants was that prayer be regularly observed in the public schools. Opposition to this forced prayer arose as early as 1866, when a little girl who refused to bow her head was expelled from school. Her expulsion was approved by the Supreme Court of the State of Massachusetts. The issue was again tested in Iowa in 1884, with similar results. In Kansas in 1904, again those who did not desire to pray were coerced by the state courts to do so. In 1929 in South Dakota and in 1950 in New Jersey dissatisfied Roman Catholic parents fought against the forced prayers, which they deemed Protestant, but our legal and court system was so overwhelmingly Protestant that the Roman Catholic litigants had little chance of success. In the New Jersey case the state court declared that

> . . . the Old Testament and the Lord's Prayer, pronounced without comment, are not sectarian, and that the short exercise provided by the statute [of the state of New Jersey] does not constitute sectarian instruction or sectarian worship but is a simple recognition of the Supreme Ruler of the Universe and a deference to His majesty . . . and that, in any event, the presence of a scholar at, and his participation in, that exercise is, under the directive of the Board of Education, voluntary.

Always the prayers were attacked, as had been the Bible, as being sectarian. The King James Version of prayers was used, and the Roman Catholics wanted the Douay Version. The Jews did not care for the prayer of Jesus Christ from the New Testament at all. Certain fundamentalist religionists who do not believe in public prayer also balked. They interpreted that Jesus Christ, in the Sermon on the Mount, had forbidden such a display.

Because prayers in the public schools were being challenged not for being unconstitutional but for being sectarian, the state of New York in 1951 attempted to devise a "nondenominational" prayer. This only created more difficulties. The reasons underlying the intrusion of religion into the schools in this "nondenominational" form were apparent in the policy statement issued by the New York State Board of Regents. It asserted that the American people had always been religious and that a program of religious inspiration in the schools would assure that schoolchildren would acquire "respect for lawful authority and obedience to law." The so-called Regents' prayer, however, was nondenominational only with respect to the sects of Judaism and Christianity. It took into consideration none of the other religions of the world. This practice of using a prayer composed by a governmental body—in this case the New York State Board of Regents—was challenged all the way up to the U.S. Supreme Court, where in 1962 the practice was found to be unconstitutional.

By 1960 I had personally, in Maryland, challenged *all* prayer or Bible reading, not on the basis that it was sectarian but on the bases that it violated the principle of separation of church and state and that it was an intrusion of the Christian religion into the public schools. In Baltimore the habit in schools had been to recite "The Lord's Prayer" or the prayer given by Jesus Christ to the masses in his Sermon on the Mount. This was accompanied by "reverential" reading of Bible script. In June 1963 the U.S. Supreme Court agreed with my contentions that this was indeed "a religious exercise" and did not properly belong in the public schools.

We have already surveyed (in Chapter 2) the reactions to this decision in the halls of Congress, where scores of amendments to the Constitution were offered in efforts to overturn the Supreme Court's ruling. The most famous of the proposed amendments was offered by the late Senator Everett Dirksen, but the proposed amendments are still coming. In June 1973, to "commemorate" the tenth anniversary of the removal of prayers from public schools,

Senator Richard S. Schweiker, Republican of Pennsylvania, was proposing yet another amendment:

> Nothing contained in this Constitution shall prohibit the several states and the District constituting the seat of government of the United States from providing for voluntary prayer in the public schools of that jurisdiction, nor shall it abridge the right of persons lawfully assembled in any public building to participate in voluntary prayer.

Indeed, as of the time of the writing of this book, the Senate had six prayer amendments being proposed and the House of Representatives thirty-six. Many of the measures had several sponsors. Schweiker's proposal, for example, had twenty-eight cosponsors.

MORE PLANS

After the Supreme Court ruled out prayer and Bible reading, the religious community immediately changed course with a massive push to get an allegedly "objective" study of religion introduced into the public schools. The most favored plan currently is the Pennsylvania Plan, so called because it was significantly promoted by Pennsylvania State University. It does not involve educators bringing religion to the classroom overtly. The idea is to publish and introduce into the public schools textbooks containing religious material—such as science textbooks "impartially" adding the biblical account of creation, or literature anthologies that include some Bible stories. Other examples are history books describing the impact of religion on American culture (always couched in favorable terms, of course) and sociological books containing comparative studies of various religions (with an obvious bias in favor of Christianity). All this is known as "producing materials for the academic study of religion."

To train teachers "objectively" for this kind of religious instruction has proved rather difficult. The organizers of training programs have professed that their intent is to equip teachers to handle religious topics without any subjective sectarian bias. At this writing, however, no nonreligious persons have been admitted into the seminars developed at Pennsylvania State University, the University of Alabama, and California State University at Northridge. So, once again, the desires and wishes of those Americans who are not religious have not been taken into account.

PUBLIC AID TO PAROCHIAL EDUCATION

Some decades ago, the various states of the union became aware that, in order to enlarge and improve their public educational systems, they needed better financing than that derived from property taxes. Thus, as early as the 1920s and 1930s they began soliciting grants from the federal government. The Roman Catholic church initially, however, waged intense and effective campaigns against such aid. Because Roman Catholics were bearing their share of the federal tax burden, the church did not desire federal funding to an old enemy—secular public schools of a Protestant persuasion. The church's initial opposition to all federal aid to education was modified, nevertheless, in 1937, when the church agreed to relax its stand should parochial schools be included in the benefits.

One of the Roman Catholic church's initial strategies was to try to get federal funding decisions put on the state level, where it exercised more political power. Thus it began demanding that the states be permitted to decide for themselves whether or not federal money given to the states could be passed on to parochial schools. By 1941 this strategy had been changed to include a demand that parochial schools in every state receive some specified part of any funds voted by Congress. By 1945 Roman Catholics were advocating a complicated trustee device whereby funds could be channeled indirectly into their schools. Concurrently with these strategies, the Roman Catholics repeatedly and successfully blocked all federal funding legislation that excluded aid to the parochial schools. Moreover, whenever the federal government devised a proposal that did include the parochial schools, Protestant church groups and the National Education Association did their bit to successfully kill such legislation. It was a standoff for more than thirty years, and the only victims of this game of theological politics were the kids in school.

The Roman Catholic efforts were more successful on the state level. We may consider the example of textbooks. The average person seeing children going to parochial or public schools, arms loaded with books, seldom gives thought to who pays for the books, but it is a considerable sum. Parochial schools knew this from the beginning. If they could persuade local taxpayers to purchase the schoolbooks used by Catholic children, there would be much more money free to invest in the religious thrust of the schools. And the campaigns began—with religious schools asking for free books, notably in Kentucky, Louisiana, Maryland, Mississippi, and California. In those states the religious community won, both in the legislatures and in the courts, with the court case in Louisiana constituting a landmark. There in. 1930, in *Cochran* v. *Louisiana State Board of Education,* a principle was established that came to serve the parochial schools well. The Louisiana State Board of Education had purchased textbooks and supplied them free of cost to all schoolchildren, including those in parochial schools. The state court upheld the practice, noting:

> *The schools, however, are not the beneficiaries of these appropriations. . . . The school children . . . are the beneficiaries.*

This so-called child-benefit theory, however, was not accepted by many other states, including New York, Delaware, Oklahoma, Washington, Wisconsin, and South Dakota, where the state courts held that such aid was aid to the *schools,* not *children,* and therefore unconstitutional.

The matter finally came to the U.S. Supreme Court in 1947 in a case up from New Jersey, called *Everson* v. *Board of Education of Ewing Township.* In this instance, the issue involved busing. The state had been reimbursing parents for fees charged their children on ordinary bus transport; the reimbursements covered children attending public and Roman Catholic schools, but not children attending any other parochial or private schools. A taxpayer complained, and in a bitterly divided decision (5 to 4) the U.S. Supreme

Court applied the child-benefit theory and ruled against the taxpayer. In this famous decision, the dissenting justices pointed out:

Two great drives are constantly in motion to abridge, in the name of education, the complete division of religion and civil authority which our forefathers made. One is to introduce religious education and observances into the public schools. The other, to obtain public funds for the aid and support of various private religious schools.

Both avenues are closed by the Constitution. Neither should be opened by this Court. The matter is not one of quantity, to be measured by the amount of money expended. Now as in Madison's day it is one of principle, to keep separate the separate spheres as the First Amendment drew them; to prevent the first experiment upon our liberties; and to keep the question from becoming entangled in erosive precedents.

The precedents, however, were already there—in the Cochran decision and in countless unheralded administrative decisions of government. After World War II, for instance, the church schools began sharing in funds provided by the School Lunch Act; how and when they did so is obscure, since the sources of some administrative decisions are almost impossible to uncover. They just seem to happen sub rosa.

It is worthy of mention that in 1950 a young Roman Catholic Congressman, John F. Kennedy of Massachusetts, introduced a bill in Congress which would have set aside a percentage of any proposed federal school funds for the transportation of pupils to all schools, including parochial schools. The bill failed, but the issue of federal subsidy for the transportation of parochial students remained, and still remains.

ROMAN CATHOLIC SUCCESSES IN ACQUIRING PUBLIC AID

Meanwhile, in the years from the 1930s to the 1960s, many hallowed traditions of the separation of church and state were being slowly demolished, and many precedents

were being set in the funding of religious schools. During
the Great Depression, the National Youth Administration
and the Works Progress Administration had made funds
available to parochial schools. By the 1940s, twenty states
were providing funds for the free transportation of children
to parochial schools. Under the G.I. Bill of 1944, war
veterans could attend denominational colleges, universities,
and special schools, to which the government made direct
payments. In this last instance, a distinction came to be
made between aid to colleges and universities and aid to
elementary and secondary schools; and, because it was aid
for an ex-G.I., aid to religious higher education was
deemed satisfactory. By the end of 1963 a law had been
enacted granting direct financial aid to religious colleges for
the construction of buildings (although the funded buildings had to be used ostensibly for secular or nonsectarian
activities). This crucial breakthrough came during Lyndon
Johnson's administration, and it was followed by the even
more radical Elementary and Secondary Education Act of
1965, which gave religious elementary and secondary
schools both loans and money for building, for acquisition
of equipment, for payment of teachers, for educational
radio and television equipment, for mobile educational
services and equipment, for books, and for teacher in-
service training.

Still, it was not enough! The Roman Catholic church
turned to its old friends, the state and local governments. In
a staggering array of demands made in different cities and
states, the church asked that Roman Catholic parents who
paid tuition for their children in religious schools be given
either tax credits, direct tuition grants, or money reimbursements. It asked the states to provide their schools with
teachers or, alternatively, to lend some teachers. It asked
the states to pay the salaries of teachers handling allegedly
secular subjects in Roman Catholic schools, or at least to
supplement the salaries paid by the churches. It asked for
money for the repair and maintenance of the buildings,
under the guise of money for "health and safety." It asked
for state-paid scholarships for Roman Catholic children at
every level of education up through college. It asked for
money to assist low-income families to send their children

to religious schools. It asked for help to build and maintain and to staff and administer poverty area schools for children of the Roman Catholic faith. It asked for money for the private busing of Roman Catholic children to schools or, alternatively, for state-operated transportation. It asked the states to purchase books for the Roman Catholic schools or at least to "loan" books, as well as all kinds of teaching equipment, materials, and supplies. It asked for auxiliary services and for enlarged school lunch programs. It asked the states to "purchase services" from Roman Catholic schools or to rent its buildings. It asked for shared-time or dual-enrollment, meaning that Roman Catholic children could go to public schools for all secular subjects and to religious schools for "sacred" subjects. In all such demands, the church frequently appealed to the child-benefit theory: the aid, so it was said, was "aid for the child," not the church.

This massive campaign over the five years from 1964 to 1969 resulted in legislation in thirteen states, thus giving aid to religious schools. Let us look at one state, New York, for the school year 1971–72. The New York religious and private schools received more than $10 million that year from federal aid under the 1965 Elementary and Secondary Education Act. In addition, they received $28 million under the state's 1970 Mandated Services Law; $32 million under the state's 1971 Secular Educational Services Act; $23 million for busing; and $5 million for textbook "loans" for grades 7 to 12. Altogether, the aid added up to more than $100 million in a year in this one state alone. New York's total population is about 18 million persons. This means that every man, woman, and child in the state was forced to donate $5.50 a year to the "nonpublic" schools.

How many of these nonpublic schools are in fact sectarian religious institutions? According to a government report commissioned by the New York State Commission on Quality, Cost, and Financing of Elementary and Secondary Education, 19.6 percent of the children in New York attend nonpublic schools. Of these, 84.5 percent go to Roman Catholic schools, 6.3 percent to Jewish schools, 2.7 percent to Protestant and Eastern Orthodox schools, and 6.5 percent to nonsectarian private schools. Thus, 93.5 percent of the children in nonpublic schools are actually in religious schools.

Moreover, if New York taxpayers believe that they are burdened only with $100 million a year for nonpublic schools, they are deceived. This sum does not include the increased tax that each New Yorker pays on his real estate because church school property is tax-free, or the increased postage that he pays because the church schools can mail for about one-tenth of what he pays. It does not include the increased taxes on his estate or for the probate of his will because the church schools are free from all inheritance taxes. It does not include the increased income tax that he pays because federal income tax law permits gifts to church schools to be deducted from income taxes. Every New York family is heavily involved in the church school business, as is every family in every other state in the United States.

THE CENTRAL ISSUES

Ever since the battle over government support for religious education began, organized religion, especially the Roman Catholic church, has been using the same arguments to insist that the taxpayer finance church schools. The arguments, however, do not address themselves to the real issue. There is only one real issue. It is this: Should all of the citizens of the United States be coerced into subsidizing, by whatever scheme, the religious indoctrination of the children of any faith?

At the time of the birth of our nation this question was firmly settled. It was decreed that there would be complete and absolute separation of church and state which would preclude the possibility of any tax-supported religious institutions. But now we are being asked by organized religion to reevaluate that principle and to either circumvent, override, or undermine it. Therefore we should examine closely the arguments advanced in behalf of the various schemes to divert tax revenues into church schools.

ARGUMENT: *Without aid to church schools, the parents of parochial schoolchildren become victims of "double* taxation"—paying a state tax for public schools and a private tuition tax for their parochial school.

I believe that the best answer to this argument is provided in a brochure published by the American Civil Liberties Union in 1967. Here is an excerpt:

> A tax is something one is forced to pay. No one is forced to send his children to a parochial school and therefore, is not being "taxed" for parochial schools. An important part of the American tradition of separation of church and state is that churches may not levy or receive taxes.
>
> Taxes are the required share of all who pay for governmental services. We all pay taxes for libraries, hospitals, roads, and other public facilities which we may never use. But even if we make no direct use of a particular public institution, every citizen has the right to direct its policies through normal participation in the political processes (school board elections or bond issues, etc.). Furthermore, tax supported institutions are not permitted to discriminate on grounds of race, religion, or national origin in their services or employment policies, and it would violate our religious liberty if we were forced to support an institution which would discriminate religiously.
>
> Parochial schools in this sense are not public institutions, and contributions to them are entirely voluntary. In return for this private status, parochial schools have the right to discriminate in admission and employment, to teach a particular religion, and to set their own academic standards and financial policies.
>
> If parochial schools received tax funds we would have a true case of double taxation. All citizens would be taxed for public schools and in addition for parochial schools which in many cases would exclude them on religious grounds from admission, employment, or a voice in the school policies.

Fundamentally, the church's argument is more an appeal to sympathy than an appeal to logical thinking. Most Americans recognize the need for an educated citizenry

108 O'Hair: Freedom Under Siege

and are generally willing to assume the burden of financing general public educational facilities. Over and above this, however, there is no reason why Americans should finance special-interest groups or individuals seeking their own peculiar brand of private education—be it instruction in religion, yoga, horseback riding, bartending, or karate. such additional education is beyond the scope of government to provide. Each group or individual has the perfect right to get the special schooling that one desires, within one's ability to pay. No obligation exists for the taxpayer to finance this self-interest, and the government is specifically precluded from assistance to religious education because of the First Amendment to the Constitution.

ARGUMENT: *Aid to church schools gives parents true freedom of choice in education by allowing them to send their children to public or private schools.*

Given the Roman Catholic hierarchy's own views on education, this amounts to a rather specious or even dishonest argument. Roman Catholic Canon Law number 1374 scarcely allows Roman Catholic parents any freedom of choice. It states specifically:

> *Roman Catholic children shall not attend non-Catholic, neutral, or mixed schools, that is, those which are open also to non-Catholics. It pertains exclusively to the local bishop to decide, in accordance with instructions of the Holy See, under what circumstances and with what precautions against the danger of perversion, attendance at such schools may be tolerated.*

To ask the American taxpayer to support this command of the church would be to ask him to support a religious tenet that seeks to segregate or isolate the children of one religion from those of all other religions. It also asks him to support schools to which his own children may not freely gain admission unless they profess the Catholic faith. None of this is freedom of choice at all. True freedom is that described by Thomas Jefferson when he said:

> *To compel a man to furnish contributions of money for the propagation of opinions which he disbelieves is*

sinful and tyrannical. . . . Even forcing him to support this or that teacher of his own religious persuasion . . . is depriving him of liberty.

ARGUMENT: *Aid to church schools is not necessarily aid to religious studies; the public funds given to church schools can be specifically reserved for general or secular studies.*

The fallacy of this argument has already been suggested. Earlier I quoted two papal encyclicals that expressly deny the separation of religious and secular studies. The one encyclical stated that the only kind of "school approved by the church" is one in which "the Catholic religion permeates the entire atmosphere" and in which "teachers, syllabus, and textbooks" are all "regulated by the Christian spirit." The other encyclical insisted, "It is necessary not only that religious instruction be given to the young at certain times, but also that every other subject taught be permeated with Christian piety." Similar prescriptions can be found in countless Roman Catholic documents and essays.

There is even evidence more specific than these general pronouncements. Dr. George R. LaNoune, for instance, surveyed the textbooks used in 100 Roman Catholic and other parochial schools and published his conclusions in the *Phi Delta Kappan* of June 1962:

1. *Religious symbols and subjects are commonly used in mathematics and language arts texts.*
2. *Specific sectarian doctrines are presented where controversial matter appears in science, geography, and language texts.*
3. *All subjects are presented with a general Christian theistic approach.*
4. *Texts in some subjects request that pupils concern themselves with specific church goals, such as working and praying that non-Western cultures will adopt Christianity or playing one's part in spreading the gospel message.*
5. *Appeals are made to church authority to prove points in many subject areas.*

6. Selective emphasis is placed on denominational institutions and contributions to culture and on facts favorable to the particular church, while contributions to culture by other churches and facts unfavorable to the particular church are omitted.
7. Texts in a number of subjects defend denominational social ideas and regulations.

Justice William O. Douglas, in my appeal case concerning Bible reading and prayer recitation (*Murray* v. *Curlett*), very fundamentally spoke to this issue in another way when he said:

> *The most effective way to establish any institution is to finance it; and this truth is reflected in the appeals by church groups for public funds to finance their religious schools. Financing a church either in its strictly religious activities or in its other activities is equally unconstitutional, as I understand the Establishment Clause. Budgets for one activity may be technically separable from budgets for others. But the institution is an inseparable whole, a living organism, which is strengthened in proselytizing when it is strengthened in any department by contributions from other than its own members.*
>
> *Such contributions may not be made by the State even in a minor degree without violating the Establishment Clause. It is not the amount of public funds expended; as this case illustrates, it is use to which public funds are put that is controlling. For the First Amendment does not say that some forms of establishment are allowed; it says that "no law respecting the establishment of religion" shall be made. What may not be done directly may not be done indirectly lest the Establishment Clause become a mockery.*

ARGUMENT: *Aid to church schools is really aid to the students, not aid to the church.*

This of course is the child-benefit theory, and Justice Douglas, in the passage just quoted, addressed himself to one of the basic elements of the issue. What is most annoying about this argument of the church, however, is its deceitfulness. In point of fact, the church is concerned more about perpetuating its authority than about nurturing the aspirations of individual children. Justice Robert H. Jackson, in *Everson* v. *Board of Education*, stated the issue squarely:

> *I should be surprised if any Catholic would deny that the parochial school is a vital, if not the most vital, part of the Roman Catholic Church. If put to the choice, that venerable institution, I should expect, would forego its whole service for mature persons before it would give up education of the young, and it would be a wise choice. Its growth and cohesion, discipline and loyalty, spring from its schools. Catholic education is the rock on which the whole structure rests, and to render tax aid to its Church school is indistinguishable to me from rendering the same aid to the Church itself.*

Frequently, in defense of this argument for child benefit, the church appeals to the precedent allegedly set by the G.I. bill. If veterans, says the church, can receive funds to go to religious schools, why should not students generally be funded to allow them to do so? In an excellent article in *Church and State*, Dr. Hugh Wamble, professor of church history at Midwestern Baptist Theological Seminary, answered this question by pointing out six basic differences between the G.I. bill and aid to parochial schools:

1. *The G.I. Bill comes under "Veterans' Benefits" and not under the "Education" section of the U.S. Code.*
2. *The G.I. Bill is compensation to the veteran—not really just aid to students. It is actually compensation for the interruption in the education careers which military service has caused.*
3. *The G.I. Bill requires military service as a prerequisite and is compensation for services already rendered— parochiaid [aid to parochial schools] is simply a gratuity.*
4. *Parochiaid imposes no conditions of eligibility—a veteran's eligibility is directly related to his length of service.*

5. Parochiaid is aimed at private schools only. Under the G.I. Bill, a veteran does not have to attend a private school.
6. Parochiaid is a euphemism for getting public funds directed into church channels. The G.I. Bill has no such ulterior purpose.

ARGUMENT: *Church schools save the taxpayers money by educating children who otherwise would have to be enrolled in public schools.*

No one in his right mind would contend that money could be saved by having duplicate police forces or highway departments or fire departments or any other agencies of public service. Yet the claim is made that money can be saved by having duplicate educational systems. Certainly, on a long-term basis, any saving for society would be illusory, for the operation of duplicate or multiple school systems is always much more costly than the operation of a single public school system. In fact, aid to church schools would eventually diminish the economic efficiency of running public schools because unquestionably many new systems would spring up as public funds became freely available. Supporting a number of competing, smaller school systems will always cost the taxpayer more than supporting one public school system available free to all children.

The tax burden of all citizens would be increased should they be required to support both a public school system and a number of religious school systems. One should recognize, however, that taxpayers are already forced indirectly to support the churches and their parochial schools. Whenever churches—or contributors to churches—are excused from paying taxes, the average citizen's tax burden must be increased correspondingly. And these religious exemptions are unending (as we shall see more fully in later chapters). For example, the entire operation of every parochial school is tax-exempt. The school buildings and the land on which they stand are not taxed. Donations given to the church schools are tax-deductible. Funds bequeathed to the schools are exempt from estate taxes. Gifts from corporations or foundations are tax deductible. No sales taxes are paid on any materials purchased for the schools. And thus on and on. In short, even now the churches are not really saving taxpayers on the cost of supporting children in parochial schools. Taxpayers already have the burden in great degree—wrongfully, in my view.

Before we leave this particular issue, it should be pointed out that tax exemptions for religious schools give preferential treatment to one church over all others—in a nation that is supposed to be committed to "religious pluralism." Certain national enrollment statistics are available:

Distribution of Enrollments in Church-Related
Elementary and Secondary Schools,
by Religious Affiliation, 1965-1966

Roman Catholic	91.8%
Lutheran	3.2
Seventh-Day Adventist	1.0
Jewish	0.9
Protestant Episcopalian	0.8
Christian Reformed	0.7
Society of Friends (Quaker)	0.2
Methodist	0.1
Presbyterian	0.1
All others	0.8

In viewing these figures, one can readily see that the Roman Catholic church is being rather devious when it bountifully declares that parochial schools are of many, many religious denominations. True, there are some Jewish schools, and they support the concept of tax aid; and there are some Lutheran schools, which also support the idea. All the various types of religious schools, indeed, whether they ask for tax breaks or not, certainly do take the breaks afforded to all churches. However, the percentages above indicate that the Roman Catholic claim, that all kinds of religions are involved in schooling, is simply weak and specious. The Roman Catholic schools account for 91.8 percent of the total, and all the other percentages are ridiculously small.

NEW SCHEMES FOR AID TO CHURCH SCHOOLS

And so the battle goes on. Each year a new argument or a new scheme is devised whereby it is hoped that the American taxpayer can be forced to support religious education in the United States. During the year 1971, for example, the "voucher" plan had priority. Under this plan, vouchers were certificates that a government agency would issue to parents for one year's tuition for their children. The parents could then shop around for their children's education, "cashing" the certificates at any public or private school of their choice. The national average cost of educating a pupil in a public elementary school in 1970 was about $650. There were about 27.5 million students in elementary schools in that year. So the plan could involve spending $18 billion a year just to satisfy the parents of less than 5 percent of the pupils. The United States government agency most involved in this plan has been the Office of Economic Opportunity, the federal antipoverty agency, which has issued grants to four cities where the voucher system is being tried: Seattle; San Francisco; Rockland, Maine; and Alum Rock, a suburb of San Jose, California.

The President's Commission on School Finance, heavily loaded with proponents of federal aid to religious schools, recommended in April 1972 that parents be permitted to deduct half the tuition costs for private schooling from their final income tax liability. It also urged the creation of federal loan programs for the construction of private schools and a system of extra payments to families on welfare to be used for private school tuition. It recommended nothing for public schools.

In addition, several bills were introduced into both houses of the Congress to give aid to religious schools. The most significant was that of Representative Wilbur A. Mills, chairman of the powerful House Ways and Means Committee. This was a tax credit bill, beginning with grants of about $2.5 billion a year. At hearings on the bills, the Secretary of the Treasury, the Secretary of Health, Education, and Welfare, and the Director of the Office of Management and Budget all testified enthusiastically for such aid to religious schools. By the time the fuss was over, H.R. bill 17072 had been approved by the committee. This bill would allow the parents of children in religious and private schools to subtract from their total federal income tax liability either 50 percent of the tuition paid for each child or $200 per student, whichever is less. It would also exempt the religious schools from any public examination of their accounts or activities, thus giving churches the unrestricted use of public funds for their religious schools. The bill is still pending in Congress.

Meanwhile, at last count, thirty-two states had become involved in litigation over aid to religious schools, as the advocates of tax aid keep testing one theory after another in their efforts to discover some formula that may be legally permissible.

Currently, more than one-half of the states provide some form of transportation, at taxpayer expense, for children to attend parochial schools. Textbooks are furnished, under various theories and in diverse ways, in eleven states, including some of the biggest and the most populous: California, Pennsylvania, New York, New Jersey, Indiana, Louisiana, Mississippi, New Mexico, Rhode Island, Missouri, and Nebraska.

Rulings by the U.S. Supreme Court in 1971 and again in 1973, together with several lower court decisions, outlawed a number of state plans for providing tax aid for parochial schools. Some of the plans that were found to be violative of the First Amendment consisted of

1. Purchase of secular education services
2. Salary supplements for parochial teachers
3. Grants for parochial school maintenance and repair
4. Tax credits for parochial school tuition
5. Reimbursements for parochial school tuition
6. Payments for testing and record keeping by parochial schools
7. The lending of public school teachers to parochial schools
8. The lending of public school equipment to parochial schools
9. The locating of public school "annexes" in parochial

schools for the purpose of aiding the parochial schools

Other devices that continue to exist consist of

1. State contracts with nonpublic (a euphemism for parochial) schools to provide "educational opportunities" for certain rural students (example: Alaska)
2. Driver education grants (examples: Connecticut, Delaware, Ohio, Pennsylvania, North Carolina)
3. Grants for remedial programs and special tutoring for the educationally disadvantaged (Connecticut)
4. Grants for auxiliary services, instructional materials, and services for educationally disadvantaged students (Iowa)
5. Dual enrollment (Kentucky)
6. Tax credits (California, Louisiana, Minnesota)
7. Tuition reimbursement (Louisiana, Minnesota)
8. Shared time (Michigan, Minnesota, South Dakota, Washington)
9. Grants for pupils with learning disabilities (Mississippi)
10. Grants for auxiliary services (Ohio, Washington)
11. Grants for health and welfare services (Rhode Island, Pennsylvania)
12. Joint public and parochial purchasing (Washington)
13. Leasing of office space in parochial schools to administer federal programs

It must be borne in mind that these are state or local programs. Under the 1965 Elementary and Secondary Education Act, federal aid also is given to parochial schools in every state of the Union.

There were, as of January 1, 1974, only seventeen states that provided no state aid to parochial schools on the primary and secondary levels. They are:

Alabama	Hawaii	Tennessee
Arizona	Idaho	Texas
Arkansas	Montana	Utah
Colorado	Nevada	Virginia
Florida	Oklahoma	Wyoming
Georgia	South Carolina	

THE BATTLE AHEAD

In America now, we are back where we were a hundred years ago, in a bitter battle over government aid to religious schools. Today scores of cases go forward in various states. Legislation is disrupted, hundreds of thousands of dollars are spent on litigation, lobbying, and propaganda. With all this going on, however, the national media pretend that nothing is happening. Beleaguered voters in Ohio may feel that the parochial school problem is peculiar to them, for they are most likely unaware that neighboring Pennsylvania is deeply in the throes of a politico-legal convulsion over the same issue. In almost every state of the union, the struggle goes on.

In the years ahead, we will probably find that the battle has become even fiercer. Organized religion in our nation fully recognizes the difficulties in which it finds itself, and therefore it will increase its efforts in the struggle for the child. For it knows that if it does not, the child may step into a totally secular twenty-first century.

5   Speak No Evil,
See No Evil, Hear No Evil
The Censorship of Books, Films, and Broadcasting

The Virginia Bill of Rights, enacted in 1776, declared "that the freedom of the press is one of the great bulwarks of liberty, and can never be restrained but by despotic government." After the American Revolution, the First Amendment to the United States Constitution guaranteed that "Congress shall make no law . . . abridging the freedom of speech, or of the press." This First Amendment was later applied to the states by judicial interpretation of the Fourteenth Amendment. Through all these scores of years down to the present, perhaps no freedom in America has been so jealously guarded and steadily enlarged as that of freedom of speech. As the Virginia delegates well knew, the loss of freedom of speech is allied with despotism. It is the first freedom to go under when an authoritarian order seizes power.

In recent years in America, freedom of expression in print, picture, and spoken word has become greater than ever before. The profusion of media—in all kinds of books, films, and broadcasts—has become astonishingly great and indescribably wide-ranging in content. This freedom of expression, nonetheless, has never in the past escaped attack, and does not now. It is a favorite target for attack by doctrinaires who stress obedience to authority and intolerance of beliefs or life styles unlike their own. On the leading edge of the attack have always been the churches.

Clearly, any church or subgroup within a church is eager to exert its right to advise its members on what to read, what to listen to, and what to see. It wants to shield its members from ideas that are alien to its creed and from ideas that may undermine its authority or reputation for revealed truth. The problem facing any church, however, is that generally under the guaranties of the First Amendment it can usually rely only on threat and persuasion to restrain its members from reading or seeing works that are generally available in the public marketplace. At times, this limit on its powers can rankle any church, knowing that its parishioners may easily be exposed to products and promotions that are pervasive in the mass media. In its zealousness, therefore, one church after another has frequently—and often successfully—sought to subvert the First Amendment and compel all people, adherents and nonbelievers alike, to bow to its judgments by denying them a free choice in the marketplace. It has sought a total ban on what it dislikes, and it achieves this ban either by enlisting civil government in official censorship or by intimidating publishers and distributors. Both means have been employed by American churches and continue to be used to this very day. This we shall see in the following pages devoted to discussions of censorship of books, films, and broadcasting.

HISTORICAL BACKGROUND OF CHURCH CENSORSHIP

Church censorship of the written or spoken word goes back almost to the birth of Christianity. St. Luke recorded with satisfaction that the Ephesian converts had set a bonfire of thousands of books alleged to be poisoned by pagan superstition (Acts 19:19). This was long before official recognition of Christianity. After 313, when the Roman Emperor Constantine decreed toleration of Christianity, the organized persecution of unorthodox opinion began. In 325 the Council of Nicaea condemned a book by Arius, who had denied the godhood of Jesus, and eight years later Constantine ordered the burning of all books by Arius upon pain of death. In 391 the Emperor Theodosius I had all the great classical libraries of Alexandria razed and burned. This pattern of condemnation and burning continued for centuries, until 1233, when Pope Gregory IX founded the Inquisition, which enthusiastically set about burning authors as well as their books. Torture and the fiery stake were considered fitting ends for foul heretics like Savonarola, whose chief crime was to expose the political and sexual scandals of the papal court.

With the invention of printing in the fifteenth century and with the awareness of its fearsome potential of getting more and more knowledge into the minds of the faithful, the church decided that it had better do something. In 1487 a papal bull ordered that all manuscripts be subjected to prior examination by ecclesiastical authority, which would officially authorize or prohibit their publication. The secular governments—whether Roman Catholic or, later Protestant—supported this prior ecclesiastical censorship by imposing punishments under civil law.

The Reformation that divided Christendom not only divided the agents of censorship but also tended to make preventive censorship difficult. A book that was banned in one place was apt to get published somewhere else, and often all that the churches could do was to get it banned locally after publication. Under Pope Paul IV, in 1557, the first Index of Forbidden Books (*Index librorum prohibitorum*) was issued, listing books that Roman Catholics were forbidden to read because of their theological error or immorality. Thereafter, through four hundred years, numerous editions of the Index of Forbidden Books were issued, the last in 1948, which had a list of more than 4,000 banned titles, including all the works of Emile Zola, Anatole France, and André Gide; many of the works of Voltaire, Descartes, Balzac, and the Dumas, father and son; Gibbon's *Decline and Fall of the Roman Empire;* Rousseau's *Social Contract;* Kant's *Critique of Pure Reason;* Hugo's *Les Misérables;* Flaubert's *Madame Bovary;* and many others of the world's classics. The Vatican did not abolish the post of censor until 1965 or discontinue use of the Index of Forbidden Books until 1966. Even then, the discontinuance was not the result of any liberalizing of Catholic attitudes. As Cardinal Ottaviani observed in the Vatican's weekly *L'Osservatore della Domenica* in May 1966, the Curia was ceasing publication of the Index only because the sheer volume of published materials in today's world had made impossible the task of reviewing and compiling a central list of forbidden books. The responsibility for censoring literature would pass from the Vatican to the several national conferences of bishops.

The Protestants were no better than the Catholics. The great "reformers" like Martin Luther and John Calvin might seek freedom of conscience for themselves but were not about to give that liberty to others. Protestant authorities eagerly sought out and persecuted papists and nonconformists. In lands under Calvinist domination especially, regulation of private conduct and individual opinion was harsh, and censorship was rigorous. This spirit was transported to the theocratic communities of New England, and much of the puritanical censorship of ideas and morals in the United States can be traced to these New England sources. The reason is that New England was the center of much of American literary and intellectual life for 250 years or more. The first American press, for example, was established in Massachusetts Bay colony in 1639, and in subsequent years its productivity was amazing. Its output exceeded that of the presses of both Oxford and Cambridge in England. Its publications were strictly Calvinistic, mostly sermons or theological treatises; even the occasional poetry or nonfiction conformed to religious orthodoxy. A bestseller was Michael Wigglesworth's *Day of Doom*, a long, ponderous epic in verse, describing the terrifying Day of Judgment. It was said to have been read by half the population of New England. Another book, however, met an unhappier fate. Somehow slipping past the censors, William Pynchon's *The Meritorious Price of Our Redemption,* a religious treatise at odds with Puritan orthodoxy, was published, only to be met with a storm of denunciation. In 1650, it became the first book to be publicly burned in what is now the United States. At the order of the legislature, it was put to fire in the marketplace by the common executioner, and the author, after public censure, soon left for England.

In the seventeenth and eighteenth centuries all the thirteen colonies made blasphemy, profanity, and obscenity statutory crimes. Massachusetts specifically made it criminal to publish "any filthy, obscene, or profane song, pamphlet, libel or mock sermon" in imitation or mimicking of religious services. Over and above this, the puritan climate continued to exercise pervasive limits on what publishers might be willing to publish or writers might be willing to write. Self-censorship to avoid harsh criticism from the public or especially from powerful pressure groups never ceased. All kinds of extralegal pressures can enforce the observance of "morality."

After the founding of the Republic, the first known obscenity case in the United States happened to center on the erotic novel *Fanny Hill,* which was banned in 1821 in (naturally) Massachusetts. Before the Civil War, however, there were few prosecutions for obscenity because of the prevalence of puritan mores and the effectiveness of self-censorship. The U.S. Congress in 1842 did pass a law forbidding the "importation of all indecent and obscene prints, paintings, lithographs, engravings, and transparencies," and in 1865 it passed its first law making the mailing of obscene matter a criminal offense; but means of enforcing these laws were perfunctory.

COMSTOCKERY

Then there appeared Anthony Comstock, a YMCA crusader from New York who became one of the most famous names in the history of censorship, giving his name to the word "Comstockery," the puritanical hunting down of vice and immorality in printed materials. As head of a YMCA vigilante committee, he authored New York State's first obscenity law, and the YMCA forced its passage in 1868. In 1873 the YMCA transformed his informal committee into the New York Society for the Suppression of Vice, which in that year aggressively pressured Congress into passing an antivice law drafted by Comstock; the law banned from the mails any "obscene, lewd, lascivious, or filthy book, pamphlet, picture, paper, letter, writing, print, or other publication of any indecent character" and any advertising for such materials and set up a penalty of a $5,000 fine and/or five years' imprisonment. This so-called Comstock Law passed Congress virtually without debate. "Little Comstock laws" were subsequently enacted by a number of state legislatures.

In New York, Comstock's YMCA antivice society was actually given legal power in the form of warrants to search for and seize materials suspected of obscenity. It swept down on all suspected malefactors and virtually dictated New York arrests and convictions, even though it was a private religious organization unanswerable to the electorate. In its first seventy-three years the New York Society for the Suppression of Vice confiscated 397,000 books and secured the arrest of 5,567 defendants. Comstock and the YMCA also inspired the formation, in Boston, of the New England Watch and Ward Society, which eventually came under the crusading leadership of the Reverend J. Franklin Chase. Its success in fiercely guarding proper Bostonian morality and suppressing the obscene is reflected in the nationwide notoriety of the phrase "Banned in Boston." Working under the favoring eye of public officials, the Watch and Ward Society seldom had to resort to securing arrests or prosecutions; it effectively intimidated and put private pressure on New England booksellers to withhold from circulation any books condemned by the society. Most of the books, it should be noted, were not deemed obscene by the U.S. Post Office Department under the Comstock Law, and they included such works as Whitman's *Leaves of Grass,* Upton Sinclair's *Oil!,* Sinclair Lewis' *Elmer Gantry* (condemned as much for its antireligious theme as for its supposed obscenity), Theodore Dreiser's *An American Tragedy,* Ernest Hemingway's *The Sun Also Rises,* Aldous Huxley's *Antic Hay,* John Dos Passos' *Manhattan Transfer,* and Sherwood Anderson's *Dark Laughter.* Erich Maria Remarque's *All Quiet on the Western Front* was banned in Boston, even though the American edition had been expurgated, missing two "obscene" passages included in the European version.

Although the New York Society for the Suppression of Vice, the New England Watch and Ward Society, and similar Protestant societies in other cities were to play a role in antivice campaigns for several more years, their power began to weaken in the 1920s and 1930s. America after World War I began to experience a revolution in standards regarding sex, the human body, and other matters of morality—a revolution that continues to this day. Protestant fanatics who carried on in the traditions of Anthony Comstock and the Reverend Chase were discredited through ridicule and public indifference. The nation's courts were also putting the puritans on the defensive. In 1922 the New York State Court of Appeals, in *Halsey* v. *New York Society for the Suppression of Vice,* held that a book could not be ruled obscene because of selected words or passages; the work must be considered as a whole. In 1934 a U.S. Circuit Court of Appeals applied this "dominant effect" standard in ruling that James Joyce's *Ulysses* was not obscene and could be imported into the United States. In 1946, in *Hannegan* v. *Esquire,* the U.S. Supreme Court curbed the Postmaster General's power to punish a magazine by refusing it second-class mailing privileges; the law, declared Justice William O. Douglas, does not "clothe the Postmaster General with the power to supervise the tastes of the reading public of the country."

NODL

By the early 1950s our major Protestant antivice societies had ceased to count. The New York Society for the Suppression of Vice evaporated forever, and the New England Watch and Ward Society abandoned censorship issues and turned to the cause of crime prevention. Similar societies in other cities tended to weaken. In place of these organizations, however, there arose a Roman Catholic organization, the National Organization of Decent Literature—or NODL, as it was popularly known. Established by the Catholic Bishops of the United States in 1938 and subsequently sponsored and run by the Archdiocesan Council of Catholic Women in Chicago, NODL declared its purpose to be "to organize and set in motion the moral forces of the entire country . . . against the lascivious type of literature which threatens the moral, social and national life of our country." It determined to rid America's stores of such literature—by any means possible. It was going to make the population as a whole bow to its literary and moral opinions, and during the Great Fear of the 1950s, it was especially successful. It proceeded to compile weekly blacklists of paperbound books and magazines (as well as lists of approved publications) and print the lists in the national Catholic weekly *Our Visitor* or, beginning in 1956, in its own *N.O.D.L. Newsletter*. Eventually it worked out a system of boycotts and pressures against noncomplying book vendors and distributors; and prosecutors and police chiefs, especially in many heavily Catholic cities and counties, regularly used the blacklists in their raids, arrests, and book bannings. By the 1950s NODL had become by far the most important antiobscenity pressure group in the United States, the sole one of national scope. Only some Baptist, evangelical, and other fundamentalist groups, chiefly in the South, could match its effectiveness locally.

NODL's operational methods were something out of the early Nazi era. In any given area, for example, action groups, armed with NODL lists, would visit local merchants and ask them to clear their shelves of NODL-listed books and return them to the distributors. If the merchant refused, further visits were scheduled, often with not-too-subtle demonstrations. If the merchant yielded, he received a certificate, renewable monthly. Parish newsletters or sermons from the pulpit then urged Catholics to buy books and magazines only from merchants displaying the certificates in their windows. In April 1957 the Executive Secretary of NODL, Monsignor Thomas J. Fitzgerald, boasted that NODL lists were also "implemented by other organizations such as PTA's, American Legion posts, women's clubs, Junior Chambers of Commerce" and that "some organizations applying NODL procedures have been organized by public officials." NODL also put its lists in the hands of wholesalers.

In many localities, municipal authorities gave official recognition to the NODL lists. In Port Huron, Michigan, for instance, the county prosecutor delivered to retailers in his jurisdiction a letter declaring that "the pocket-books and digest-type novels listed below are those which have been found to be in violation of the Michigan state statutes." This was a lie, for the list was wholly a NODL list, and many of the books had never been outlawed in Michigan or banned from the U.S. mails, and included such honored works as John Dos Passos' *1919*, Ernest Hemingway's *To Have and Have Not*, James T. Farrell's *A World I Never Made*, James Jones's *From Here to Eternity*, and J. D. Salinger's *Catcher in the Rye*. Larger cities than Port Huron, however, were also affected. An attorney for the American Civil Liberties Union in Pittsburgh gave this report:

(a) In July 1956 we learned that a six-page list of titles of paper-bound books and magazines was being distributed to retailers and distributors of books by policemen. (b) Our inquiry in the city police department revealed that the list of titles came from Father Lackner, the head of the Holy Name Society. Our source in the police department said the list was the NODL list. We were informed that 500 mimeographed copies were prepared (without any identification to show that the list was an NODL list) and that the city policemen were distributing the list to retailers and distributors of books with information that this was the NODL list of objectionable titles, and the dealers were asked "Will you cooperate?" (c) An official of the Triangle News Company, wholesale distributor, informed me that the NODL list was distributed to practically all the dealers in the Pittsburgh area. He said that some dealers reported threats from policemen if the dealers would not cooperate.

The dangers of police censorship are obvious. The dangers of private exactions like those of NODL are maybe even more frightening, for they place the freedom to read in the hands of a religious group that lacks even the accountability to the public that a prosecutor or police chief has.

CONFUSIONS AND BATTLES IN THE COURTS

Beginning in 1957 the U.S. Supreme Court began handing down new decisions in efforts to legally define obscenity. The decisions were always split, with vigorous dissents from some justices; and the results have sometimes produced as much confusion as clarification. In 1957, in the famous *Roth* case, the Court said, "Obscene material is material which deals with sex in a manner appealing to prurient interest, and the test of obscenity is whether to the average person, applying contemporary community standards, the dominant theme of the material appeals to prurient interest." In 1964, in a clarification of the *Roth* ruling, it said that the "contemporary community standards" were to be defined as national standards rather than individual local standards. In 1966, in a ruling in favor of the publishers of the book *Fanny Hill,* it declared a work to be pornographic only if it was "utterly without redeeming social value," thus allowing the publication of virtually anything. In June 1973, in *Miller* v. *California,* however, the Court, now heavily weighted with four Nixon appointees, apparently reversed course. It declared that states and localities might ban the printing or sale of works "which appeal to prurient interests in sex, which portray sexual conduct in a patently offensive way, and which, taken as a whole, do not have serious literary, artistic, political or scientific value." It held that the definition of "prurient" should be that of "the average person, applying contemporary community standards," and that it would be no defense for a work to have some "redeeming social value." The ruling seemed to imply that local communities could apply their local standards, rather than national standards. Just one year later, in June 1974, in the *Carnal Knowledge* case, the court reinforced this criterion of local standards by asserting that juries were free "to rely on the understanding of the community from which they came as to contemporary community standards" and that state legislatures had considerable freedom in defining "community." A state "may choose to define an obscenity offense in terms of 'contemporary community standards' . . . without further specification . . . or it may choose to define the standards in more precise geographic terms." In a companion case, the federal courts and juries were similarly instructed to apply local community standards in obscenity cases.

These latest decisions of course would work right in the churches' favor. The churches have always been eager to get public decision making brought down to the community level, where they are more powerful and have more access to the governing machine.

For the time being, nevertheless, the general climate of public opinion had a liberalizing effect, as witness the immensely greater freedom of sexual expression in books, magazines, and newspapers across the land. Still, rock-ribbed religionists, especially in the Roman Catholic church, were fighting on. In a speech on August 6, 1964, for example, Cardinal Spellman of New York decried the early Supreme Court decisions as an "acceptance of degeneracy and the beatnik mentality as the standard way of American life." The judges had standards "substantially below the standards of the communities over which they sit in judgment. . . . I would ask you to join with me in a plea to those judges who have weakened America's efforts to protect its youth, to reconsider their responsibilities to Almighty God and to our country." The cardinal urged a boycott of "dealers who traffic in pornography" (pornography, in his mind, of course, included such works as D. H. Lawrence's *Lady Chatterley's Lover,* Henry Miller's *Tropic of Cancer,* and the magazine *Playboy*). Boycotts, he said, may not be a "welcome method these days, but this approach may be the only weapon the interpreters of the law have left to us. Once it becomes clear to the neighborhood shopkeeper, the corner newsdealer, and the local drugstore owner that we intend to use it, then the purveyors of filth will be dealt a stunning and maybe even fatal blow."

The cardinal, in other words, was championing the NODL strategy—at a time when NODL itself was on the skids. After a steady decline in subscriptions, the *N.O.D.L. Newsletter* at last ceased publication in December 1969, and the organization disappeared thereafter.

Into the breach had already stepped another predominantly Roman Catholic organization, founded and headed by the Reverend Morton A. Hill, priest of New York's St. Ignatius Loyola Church; also among its leaders, however, were a Lutheran minister and a Jewish rabbi. Originally called Operation Yorkville when founded in 1962 (so called for the section of Manhattan where the parish is located), the organization changed its name to Morality in Media in the late 1960s. Local chapters were established in many American cities. The organization's aim, according to Father Hill, was to destroy not only so-called hard-core pornography—"adult" books and movies and the like—but also what he called "soft core smut"—X-rated commercial films, teen-age sex and romance magazines, homosexual magazines, and even general-release films "with an anti-hero image." Even critically acclaimed works depicting illicit or immoral sex should in his opinion be banned; for the greater the literary quality of such material, he said, the greater its attraction, and thus the more dangerous it is. As one of the eighteen members of the President's Commission on Obscenity and Pornography from 1968 to 1970, he rejected the majority report approved by fifteen members, who had found that exposure to erotica did not "play a significant role in the causation of social or individual harms," that "a majority [almost 60 percent] of American adults believe that adults should be allowed to read or see any sexual materials they wish," and that laws against pornography for consenting adults should be repealed.

The main thrust of Morality in Media has been to assist in court battles and in legislative enactment of new antiobscenity laws on the state and municipal levels. Father Hill and his colleagues were apparently the driving force behind a successful effort to draw the U.S. Department of Justice on their side in this antismut drive. In 1973 the Justice Department's Law Enforcement Assistance Administration set up a so-called National Legal Data Center on the Law of Obscenity on the campus of California Lutheran College in Thousand Oaks, California. Father Hill was named a member of the center's advisory board, and Philip Cohen, a law professor, became its project director. The center received an initial grant of $137,625 in federal funds and a prospect of $200,000 more and has received assistance from Morality in Media—all for the purpose of abetting prosecutors and legislators across the country in a crackdown on allegedly obscene literature and films. Liberal groups have been looking into the legality of these grants, both on the issue of church-state separation and on the issue of the constitutionality of the center's activities and links with the government.

In a quarterly report issued by the Law Enforcement Assistance Administration, the center's mission was described as follows:

1. To write antiobscenity laws for local municipalities.
2. To provide "model pleadings and court orders" to be used by prosecutors and judges in obscenity actions and, in general, to fashion "trial tactics"
3. To provide lists of expert witnesses who can testify for the prosecution in obscenity trials
4. To maintain a "brief bank" or indexed collection of briefs and pleadings used in past obscenity trials
5. To issue a prosecutor's manual to guide local district attorneys in obscenity issues
6. To conduct antiobscenity conferences or workshops everywhere in the nation, at which prosecutors may be instructed in trial preparation
7. To issue "training films" for local prosecutors.
8. To make presentations about censorship and antiobscenity laws to groups of librarians and to library associations
9. To seek out information on what the Justice Department calls "the shady legal tactics frequently employed by one of the nation's most prominent pornography defense attorneys" (Watergate again!)

The Supreme Court's decisions of 1973 and 1974, which specified that local community standards could apply in determining what is obscene, truly paved the way for this massive legal conspiracy by church and state.

Actually, Morality in Media's New York office had long been engaged in some of the activities now funded by the federal government at California Lutheran College. (In fact, it provided the California center with copies of its own collection of trial transcripts—but not for free; it sought $2,000 in payment from the college.) Morality in Media has, for instance, loose-leaf-bound collections of obscenity statutes, both domestic and foreign, with commentaries on their appropriateness and effectiveness. It maintains a similar collection of pending legislation. It maintains a "brief bank." In addition, Morality in Media publishes two "obscenity law" journals. In a report on its activities, it declared:

> *We intend to announce the availability of our service and our clearinghouse to the following:*
> 1. *Every County Prosecutor*
> 2. *Every City Attorney*
> 3. *Every Attorney General*
> 4. *Every Judge*
> 5. *Every Federal Prosecutor*
> 6. *Every Police Department Legal Advisor*
> 7. *Every Law Library*
> 8. *Every Law School Law Library*
> 9. *Every Bar Association*
> 10. *Every State Library*
> 11. *Library of Congress*

The signs are so ominous that the American Booksellers Association has dubbed the 1970s as the era of "The New Censorship." Now that the Supreme Court has turned over the power of censorship to local government, the sectarian moralists are having a field day. By late spring 1974 new obscenity bills had been passed in ten states (Connecticut, Delaware, Kentucky, Nebraska, North Carolina, Oregon, South Dakota, Tennessee, Vermont, and West Virginia), and eighteen states had bills pending. According to the Media Coalition, a liberal watchdog organization, many of the passed and pending bills contained restrictive and dangerous provisions: (1) Most did not provide for mandatory civil proceedings prior to arrest or seizure; only two states (North Carolina and Vermont) had included this provision, despite a Supreme Court recommendation. (2) All bills defined community standards of judgment in rather clear geographical terms—either state, county, or area from which the jury is drawn. (3) Most bills contained extensive detailed descriptions of prohibited conduct, written or visual; and the prohibitions on minors often applied to adults as well. (4) Many bills had strict provisions on public display of prohibited materials; several bills went so far as to prohibit minors from even entering a library or bookstore containing prohibited materials—thus possibly eliminating works of literary or educational merit from general libraries and bookstores. Two states (Nebraska and Tennessee) provided for out-of-state extradition. In Delaware, individual citizens could bring action. In general, the new value test of "local community standards" puts all kinds of materials—educational and literary as well as pornographic —under the threatened stamp of suppression.

THE MOVIES AND THE LEGION OF DECENCY

In his survey, *Censorship of the Movies* (1968), Professor Richard S. Randall of the University of Nebraska affirmed:

The Roman Catholic Church probably ranks as the most important single group in the control of movies in this country at any level: production, distribution, or exhibition. As censorial pressure, Catholic strength rests on numbers, a potential for militancy, and a programmatic development which includes a moral evaluation and a systematic rating of all leading commercial films shown in the country.

Although we have already touched on the issue of films in our survey of religious censorship, we might do well to give added attention to the special pressure put on movie producers and moviegoers by the churches, especially by the Roman Catholic church.

In the post–World War I era, movies increasingly tended to reflect the new upper-class morality of the Jazz Age and even no doubt overstated the uninhibited freedoms of flappers and sheiks. As one film historian has noted:

Sophisticated sex had suddenly become big box office, whether in comedies or played straight. Drinking scenes abounded in pictures, despite the recent adoption of prohibition. Divorce, seduction, the use of drugs were presented in film after film as symbols of the fashionable life.

Movies like *Flaming Youth* (1923) or *Fascinating Youth* (1926), with their deliriums of partying, scarcely resembled average American life. Yet the 1920s experienced a kind of lull in movie censorship, and not until talkies arrived late in the decade, with their potential for adding free talk to free display, did the religious moralists really begin crying out their disapproval. Initially, the leading publication to undertake the fight was the weekly journal of the Protestant Episcopal Church, *The Churchman*. In the issue of June 29, 1929, it began a campaign for "better movies" and for "honesty and sincerity" from the motion picture industry in its dealings with the public. It was supported and encouraged by other church publications. By October 1933 the Vatican's Apostolic Delegate to the United States announced in New York that an important crusade was necessary:

> *Catholics are called by God, the Pope, the Bishops, and the priests to a united and vigorous campaign for the purification of the cinema, which has become a deadly menace to morals.*

Then at the annual Roman Catholic bishops' conference that year the bishop of Los Angeles proposed that an organization be set up to oversee motion pictures and to try to make producers more responsive to "Christian" morality.

In 1933 the Legion of Decency was planned, and in 1934 it was formally established, with priests and monsignors on its executive staff, administratively answerable to an Episcopal Committee for Motion Pictures, composed of five bishops. The Legion's official functions were declared to be:

1. To maintain membership in the Legion through the annual pledge of the faithful;
2. To publish classification of the Legion ratings of films in the diocesan newspapers;
3. To organize protests against showings of condemned films.

To attain the first goal, the Legion of Decency's hierarchy began and sustained a membership drive. With all Roman Catholic churches' congregations participating, as

many as 9 to 11 million Catholics would annually sign
pledge cards, which stated:

> *I wish to join the Legion of Decency, which con-
> demns vile and unwholesome moving pictures. I unite
> with all those who protest against them as a grave
> menace to youth, to home life, to country and to
> religion.*

> *I condemn absolutely those salacious motion pic-
> tures which, with other degrading agencies, are corrupt-
> ing public morals and promoting a sex mania in our
> land.*

> *I shall do all that I can to arouse public opinion
> against the portrayal of vice as a normal condition of
> affairs, and against depicting criminals of any class as
> heroes and heroines, presenting their filthy philosophy
> of life as something acceptable to decent men and
> women.*

> *I unite with all who condemn the display of sugges-
> tive advertisements on billboards, at theater entrances
> and the favorable notices given to immoral motion
> pictures.*

> *Considering these evils, I hereby promise to remain
> away from all motion pictures except those which do
> not offend decency and Christian morality. I promise
> further to secure as many members as possible for the
> Legion of Decency.*

> *I make this protest in a spirit of self-respect and with
> the conviction that the American public does not
> demand filthy pictures, but clean entertainment and
> educational features.*

To effect its second goal, the Legion appointed the
International Federation of Catholic Alumnae, composed of
women graduates of Roman Catholic universities and colleges, to review and rate films. (Reviewing and rating would
later be performed also by other Roman Catholic organizations, but the Catholic Alumnae would always remain the
chief agency.) The principal guide to reviewing was Pope
Pius XI's encyclical *Vigilanti cura,* which asserted that films
were to be judged on the basis of whether or not the theme

was moral, the treatment was moral, a clear voice articulated moral principles, and sin was treated as a shameful transgression. Until 1958 four rating categories were used:

A-I   "morally unobjectionable for general patronage" (i.e. the film is acceptable for all age groups)

A-II   "morally unobjectionable for adults and adolescents" (i.e., the film is not acceptable for children)

B   "morally objectionable in part for all" (i.e., the film barely passes)

C   "condemned" (i.e., the film may not be viewed by Catholics, on pain of mortal sin)

In 1958 two more categories were added:

A-III   "morally unobjectionable for adults" (i.e., the film is not acceptable for minors)

A-IV   "morally unobjectionable for adults, with reservations" (i.e., the film is deemed so devious or specious in moral reasoning that "the uninformed" should be cautioned "against wrong interpretations and false conclusions")

In 1934, with at least 9 million Roman Catholics signed to pledges and with a Catholic rating system established, the way was paved for fulfilling the Legion's third goal, that of effectively protesting against, as well as putting a stop to, films to which it objected. The very threat put the Hollywood motion picture industry into a state of alarm. After all, when a cardinal in Philadelphia ordered local Catholics to stay away from all movie houses in 1934 as an act of protest, business dropped by 40 percent. The motion picture industry came to heel.

The Motion Picture Association of America (then called the Motion Picture Producers and Distributors of America) had drafted in 1930 a "Production Code" of dos and don'ts regarding film content. However, it remained merely advisory — and thus was largely ignored. In 1934, to pacify the Legion of Decency, which was threatening a national boycott, the Motion Picture Association set up the Production Code Administration (PCA) as a semi-independent body charged with enforcing and interpreting the code. Indeed, the industry panicked and stiffened the code with new restrictions and prohibitions that even clergymen had not contemplated: "vulgarisms" became taboo, as did the approved use of liquor or drugs, any reference to venereal disease or sexual deviations, and unfavorable references to the clergy, or any scenes explicitly indicating that man and wife might enter the same bed. The self-regulation of the industry turned into self-abnegation. When all this was found "acceptable to the Bishops," the PCA was given authority to impose a fine of $25,000 on any member company that produced, distributed, or exhibited any film not bearing the PCA's seal of approval. Even smaller independent producers that were not members of the Motion Picture Association had to obey the code, since, in order to make money, they had to make films that could be shown in theaters controlled by members of the association.

As it turned out, this was still not enough. The Legion of Decency stayed in operation and actually insinuated itself into the filmmaking process itself. Many of the major film producers began routinely to let Legion officials sit in on screenings of films before release so that the Legion could rate the films or suggest cuts and revisions to save the films from condemned or "B" ratings. As one writer has noted, the power of the Legion came from "the cowardice of most picture producers" who would "grovel before" the Legion's ratings.

The Legion's sanctions for noncompliance were formidable. The Roman Catholic bishops could forbid the faithful of their dioceses to see a film, under pain of sin. They could order a boycott, or place a theatre off-limits for six months, or simply forbid the laity to see a film at all. Indeed, in 1936 Pope XI issued an encyclical on the motion picture industry's portrayal of sin, in which he lamented the "havoc wrought in the souls of youth and childhood, of the loss of innocence so often suffered in motion picture theaters." He also noted, rather menacingly, that Jesus Christ had condemned the corruption of the little ones:

Whosoever shall scandalize one of these little ones who believe in Me it were better that a millstone be hanged

around his neck and he be drowned in the depths of the
sea.

In this encyclical the Pope specifically complimented the
Legion of Decency and its work and exhorted Catholics of
other countries to follow its lead. He praised government
censorship and hoped all Catholics would unite to "place a
ban on bad motion pictures."

The Legion lost very few battles with Hollywood during
the first decade that it was in operation. Incredibly, from
1936 to 1943, not one major studio film condemned by the
Legion was ever issued. When films contained scenes found
offensive by the Legion, the industry was quick to cut. It
hacked words, phrases, sequences, even basic themes. These
included anything that showed public officials in an indeco-
rous light, suggestive sex sequences, suicide, murder, traffic
in drugs, implied antireligious attitudes, "sordid atmos-
pheres," abortion, any scene of debauchery and anything
with homosexual overtones. The overall criterion was not
the general level of sophistication of the nation but rather
what the Roman Catholic hierarchy felt was safe for its
least-educated faithful to see.

Over the years, what were the Legion of Decency's
reactions to various kinds of motion picture themes? We
might look at a few examples.

When, in 1938, Walter Wanger produced *Blockade*—an
adventure film starring Henry Fonda and Madeleine Carroll,
concerned with the Loyalist side of the Spanish Civil War
(the Vatican supported Franco)—the picture was condemned by the Legion as "foreign political propaganda." In
1937 *Damaged Goods,* a film by an independent maker, was
condemned because it dealt with venereal disease; another
film on the same subject, *No Greater Sin,* was condemned
in 1941. In 1939, the film *Yes, My Darling Daughter* was
attacked because it ridiculed certain premarital conven-
tions. The film had to do with an unchaperoned weekend
spent together by an engaged couple. The weekend was
totally without sex, as explicitly agreed to by both parties.
Yet the Legion objected to the woman putting herself into
"an occasion of sin," so the producers cut out 1,300 feet of

film, eliminated much dialogue, and reduced any emphasis
on the unconventional theme of the film. It still got only a
"B" rating.

In 1943, when Russia was our wartime ally and the
pro-Soviet film *Mission to Moscow* was released, the Legion
noted that the "sympathetic portrayal of the government
regime in Russia makes no reference to the antireligious
philosophy and policy of said regime." In 1953, when the
Lutherans issued the film *Martin Luther,* the Legion found it
to "contain theological and historical references and interpretations which are unacceptable to Catholics."

In 1956 Bette Davis starred in *Storm Center,* which won
the Prix Chevalier de la Barre at Cannes for being "the film
which contributes most to international tolerance and
understanding." The same film, under the title *The Library,*
had not even got beyond the planning stage four years
earlier because the Legion of Decency had attacked it thus:

> The highly propagandistic nature of this controversial
> film offers a warped, over-simplified and strongly emo-
> tional solution to a complex problem of American life.
> Its specious arguments tend seriously to be misleading
> and misrepresentative by reason of an inept and dis-
> torted presentation.

The film, incidentally, was the story of a strong-willed
librarian who would not knuckle under to local bigots. But
because the Roman Catholic church had itself been too
often in the struggle to remove books from library shelves,
it could not permit a heroic presentation of the struggle
against censorship. In 1962 a film on a similar theme,
Fahrenheit 451, still received only an A-II rating.

Battles raged around two plays by Tennessee Williams
when they were transferred to film. *A Streetcar Named
Desire* was condemned by the Legion of Decency in 1951
before the film's release. The director, Elia Kazan, described
what followed:

> The studio's reaction was one of panic. They had a
> sizable investment in the picture, and they at once
> assumed that no Catholic would buy a ticket. They
> feared further that theaters showing the picture would

be picketed, might be threatened with boycotts of as long as a year's duration if they dared to show it, that priests would be stationed in the lobbies to take down the names of parishioners who attended.

As a result, twelve different cuts were made without the director's approval. A climactic scene was altered for being "too carnal." Yet even with these changes, the film—which won the acclaim of critics and public alike—received a mere "B" rating from the Legion.

In 1956, concerning Tennessee Williams's film *Baby Doll,* which involved marital infidelity among decadent Southerners, the Legion said:

The subject matter of this film is morally repellent both in theme and treatment. It dwells almost without variation or relief upon carnal suggestiveness in action, dialogue and costuming. Its unmitigating emphasis on lust and cruelty are degrading and corruptive. As such it is grievously offensive to Christian and traditional standards of morality and decency.

For the first time in eight years Cardinal Spellman came to the pulpit to warn all those in his New York jurisdiction to avoid the film "under pain of sin." The bishop of Albany, New York, forbade Catholics in his diocese to patronize for six months any theatre that showed the film. In Providence, Rhode Island, the bishop banned the film to all Catholics there. The bishops of Hartford, Bridgeport, and Norwich in Connecticut prohibited Catholics from seeing the film.

We will never know how many potential film projects were abandoned in these years because of fear of the Legion, since the very existence and demonstrable power of the Legion kept many projects from even being considered, much less produced or released. If the distributors believed that the Legion's judgment might ruin a potential film financially, they abandoned it. The Legion's ideas about "compensating moral value" determined what films got approval. As a result, the "Hollywood ending" is still with us. Basically, the "Hollywood ending" can be summed up thus: "Wrongdoing, whether intentional or unintentional, must be shown to bring suffering to the wrongdoer." This prescription resulted in a "C" rating for motion pictures as diverse as *Forever Amber, The Moon Is Blue,* and *Blow-Up.*

With regard to foreign films the Legion of Decency had difficulty. After the Second World War, more and more came to be introduced into the United States and could not be stopped at the source. The Legion reacted harshly. *Shoe Shine* was deemed to have "suggestive dialogue and gesture." *The Bicycle Thief* had "unsuitable material." *La Strada* tended to "arouse sympathy for immoral characters." And *I Vitelloni* was guilty of "suggestive costuming and situations."

In 1948 Roberto Rossellini made *The Miracle,* starring Anna Magnani in a story written by Federico Fellini. Hardly any credentials could be more prestigious. The film is about a simpleminded peasant girl who is plied with wine and seduced by a bearded stranger whom, in her mental confusion, she believes to be St. Joseph. She believes, despite the mockery of the villagers, that the son resulting from the liaison is the Messiah. The film was shown throughout Europe. Although the Vatican, under the Lateran Agreement, can bid the Italian government to suppress any story, play, or film that offends the Catholic religion, the Vatican did not exercise its prerogative when the film was shown in Italy. However, when the film was shown in New York City in December 1950, Roman Catholics here took a different, dimmer view. The Legion of Decency condemned the film and strongly emphasized that it "presents a sacrilegious and blasphemous mockery of Christian and religious truth." Twelve days later the city commissioner of licenses, an ardent Roman Catholic, ordered showings stopped, thereby exceeding his legal right since the distributors had already obtained all necessary licensing. It took five days to get a restraining order to overrule him. When the film finally opened again, the chancellor of the archdiocese of New York characterized the reopening as "an open insult to the faith of millions of people in this city and hundreds of millions throughout the world." Cardinal Spellman called upon all Catholics everywhere to boycott the film. He then went on to attack the laws of our nation:

If the present law is so weak and inadequate to cope with this desperate situation then all right-thinking citizens should unite to change and strengthen the federal and state statutes to curb those who would profit financially by blasphemy, immorality and sacrilege.

A Roman Catholic fire commissioner in the city issued a summons to the theater, picket lines were formed, a bomb threat was received. The New York Film Critics, who wanted to give an award to the film, were forced to a change of venue for their award giving in order to avoid a confrontation with the Legion's legions. Finally, the license to exhibit *The Miracle* was withdrawn by the state Board of Regents, and in the resultant legal actions the case went all the way to the U.S. Supreme Court. In May 1952 the Court unanimously reversed the New York ruling and held that

. . . the state has no legitimate interest in protecting any or all religions from views distasteful to them which is sufficient to justify prior restraints upon the expressions of those views. It is not the business of government in our nation to suppress real or imagined attacks upon a particular religious doctrine, whether they appear in publications, speeches, or motion pictures.

In *The Miracle* case the Supreme Court for the first time brought motion pictures under the guaranties of the First Amendment, thus weakening the Legion of Decency's claims of rights to censorship. Moreover, gradually the studios themselves were maturing and becoming more courageous. By way of evidence, in 1955, 36 percent of the films produced were found to be objectionable by the Legion but were released anyway. Critics, backed by the Supreme Court decision in *The Miracle* case and by a number of Protestant ministers, began to stand up to the Legion.

Finally, the Legion was supplanted in 1966 by the National Catholic Office for Motion Pictures, which was to concentrate as much on the rising tide of nudity in movies as on matters of morality and theology. Nevertheless, the

International Federation of Catholic Alumnae continued to review films and make ratings, along with two other Roman Catholic offices—the New York Board of Consultors and the National Center for Film Study in Chicago—and Roman Catholic newspapers still carefully carried the reviews and ratings.

ORGANIZED RELIGION AND THE AIRWAYS

Perhaps in no other area is collusion between the churches and the government more obvious, and the results so suppressive of independent thought, than in the broadcast media. Here one sees in its most blatant form the effect of religious influence when applied to the means of social communication.

The Federal Communications Commission has been concerned with religious broadcasting since its beginning. The FCC is the successor to the Federal Radio Commission, established by the Radio Act of 1927, which empowered the Commission to assign broadcasting frequencies and to prescribe the nature of the services rendered by broadcasting stations. The act prescribed that licenses should be granted to applicants who could best serve public convenience, interest, and necessity; and one of the first things that the new Commission attempted to do was to define what "public convenience, interest, and necessity" might be. After conferring with various broadcasters, it came up with a formula whereby broadcasters were obliged to devote a certain amount of air time to each of seven different subject areas. Religion was one of those subject areas (the others included such areas as entertainment, education, and news). When the FCC succeeded the Federal Radio Commission in 1934, it continued these seven categories, which persisted until 1960, when they were further refined to fourteen.

Although the FCC has officially denied that the program categories are "intended as a rigid mold or fixed formula for station operation," they have in fact operated and been applied as prima facie minimum requirements of acceptable programming. Over the years individual commissioners and staff members have stated explicitly that the Commission favors and requires religion as one element of broadcast programming. The decisions of the Commission have also demonstrated that inclusion of a significant percentage of religious programming is a practical necessity for applicants and licensees. The Commission has given preference to some applicants in comparative proceedings because of the content of their proposed religious programs; conversely, the Commission has given demerits to some applicants in such proceedings because of a lack or "weakness" in religious programming. In Evansville, Indiana, for example, the Commission held that the proposed religious programming of one applicant for a television station license was superior to that of another because it afforded a "more positive proposal for providing time to diverse religious faiths" (whatever that meant). In another case it gave a comparative demerit to one of two competing applicants because one had failed, in its proposed program schedule, to include "any strictly religious programs" and thus had left a "void in overall program structure." In Oswego, New York, two applicants for a license submitted programs in which one had three hours of free religious programming and the other had two hours of commercially sponsored (paid) religious programming; the FCC held that "while the Commission does not regard commercial religious programs as inherently objectionable, nevertheless it is concluded that the provision of more religious programming and all on a sustaining [free] basis is better calculated to serve the varied religious needs of the community."

The basic idea that free time for religious programs is somehow superior to paid time has often surfaced with the FCC. For instance, in 1947 the FCC refused a Chicago applicant a license for a radio station, charging that the station devoted practically all its Sunday time "to commercial religious programs and that no time has been set aside for the carrying of religious services on a sustaining [free] basis from the churches of established faiths in the Chicago area."

Perhaps the single most instructive example of the FCC's favoritism for religion came in 1959 and concerned a Puerto

Rican law that prevents any government department in Puerto Rico from engaging in sectarian activity. In that year, two applications were received for a license, one from a private applicant and one from Puerto Rico's Department of Education. The latter, as a government department, included no scheduled religious broadcasts because of the existing statute forbidding it to do so. The FCC then held:

> In conformance with existing Puerto Rican law, the Department [of Education] does not propose to broadcast any strictly religious programs, whereas Sucesion [the private applicant] plans to devote 6.6 percent of its broadcast time to religious programming, more than half of which would be live. While the Department's failure to propose any strictly religious programming was required by law and therefore does not indicate an inattentiveness on the Department's part to demonstrated public needs, it nevertheless leaves a void in the overall program structure for which it must suffer comparatively.

The station was awarded to the private applicant.

The FCC has even awarded licenses to religious organizations. In 1965 I received from the National Religious Broadcasters their list of stations owned and operated by churches and other religious institutions. There were ninety-four of them, in every state of the Union. This raises a vital constitutional question: If the FCC is an instrument for regulating the public airways and one that was set up by an act of Congress, can it assign radio wavelengths or television channels—which are in the public domain—to religious organizations? The First Amendment to the Constitution states specifically that "Congress shall make no law respecting an establishment of religion." Yet a radio or television station owned by a religious organization and using the public airwaves surely represents an "establishment of religion."

The Federal Communications Commission has obviously gone far beyond the limits that have been marked by the Supreme Court as permissible governmental action in the field of religion. Likewise, the FCC rushes in where other government agencies are forbidden to tread when it requires religious programming and determines that a certain amount of religious broadcasting is or is not adequate, or that the public interest is or is not served by the broadcasting of particular views on religion or the views of particular churches, or when it awards a preference or demerit on the basis of an official judgment as to the quantity or quality of religious broadcasting—all of which it has done in reported cases. The time seems to be long past due for the FCC to reconsider its practices and doctrines in the light of the First Amendment and to extend the constitutional principle and the great spirit of religious liberty to American broadcasting.

The problem currently is that the National Association of Broadcasters itself abets this infringement of religious freedom—which includes the freedom to forgo religion as well as to practice it. The NAB Television Code, Part IV, Section 5, states:

> *Attacks on religion and religious faiths are not allowed. Reverence is to mark any mention of the name of God, His attributes and powers. When religious rites are included in other than religious programs the rites shall be accurately presented. The office of the minister, priest or rabbi shall not be presented in such a manner as to ridicule or impair his dignity.*

The NAB Radio Code, Section F (similar to the Television Code, Part VIII), prescribes:

1. *Religious programs shall be presented by responsible individuals, groups or organizations.*
2. *Radio broadcasting, which reaches men of all creeds simultaneously, shall avoid attacks upon religious faiths.*
3. *Religious programs shall be presented respectfully and without prejudice or ridicule.*
4. *Religious programs shall place emphasis on religious doctrines of faith and worship.*

The Federal Communications Commission, the National Association of Broadcasters, and individual broadcasting stations, by the way, have all held that stations are in no way obligated to give Atheists or other nonreligionists any air time, either free or paid. In 1948, in writing to the Religious Radio Association, the chairman of the FCC declared that the FCC "has never stated or indicated that atheists or persons with similar views are entitled to radio time upon request to answer or reply to the various religious broadcasts which may be carried by a radio station." Religionists, in other words, can attack Atheism on the air, but Atheists cannot reply. In 1964, I myself attempted to obtain air time and was refused by the fifteen stations located in Honolulu, where I was then living. The refusal was referred to the FCC, which, however, characteristically and deviously declared, "there is no single party or group entitled as a matter of right to present its viewpoint" on the airways.

Most broadcasters tend to lean over backward not to offend organized religion, and it is not just a question of denying Atheists their rights to defend themselves. It is also a question of churches imposing their views on broadcasters generally. In November 1972, for example, the popular CBS television show, *Maude,* courageously and quietly, without fanfare, offered a two-part episode on the issue of abortion; the frank talk about abortion, in which the heroine Maude ponders whether or not to end her supposed pregnancy, took the churches by surprise and threw some of them, particularly the Roman Catholic church, into an uproar. When the two episodes were scheduled for a summer rerun in August 1973, the outcry from the Catholic community was so great that thirty-nine CBS affiliates refused to show the reruns. Vengefully, the United States Catholic Conference waged an extensive campaign to persuade national advertisers not to purchase commercial spots on the two episodes; as a result, CBS reported that only one of the twelve half-minute spots got sold. The Catholic Conference sent out statements to 160 dioceses and 20,000 priests calling upon them to urge local CBS affiliates not to carry the abortion episodes. From Milwaukee the Catholic League for Religious and Civil Rights urged a boycott of the show by the country's 48 million Roman Catholics. Members of the Knights of Columbus met with Frank Stanton, CBS vice-chairman, to demand two half-hour slots in prime time to present the Roman Catholic stand against abortion (the request was denied). Not only stations in cities dominated by Catholics were affected; the two stations owned by the Mormons in Salt Lake City also refused to rerun the two episodes. When CBS did finally show the episodes, it ran a spoken and printed warning at the beginning of the programs:

> *Tonight's episode of* Maude *was originally broadcast in November of 1972. Since it deals with "Maude's Dilemma" as she contemplates the possibility of abortion, you may wish to refrain from watching it, if you believe the broadcast may disturb you or others in your family.*

THE CHURCH AND MODERN COMMUNICATIONS

As a final note on organized religion's views on the uses of modern media of communication, we might well take a look at "The Communications Decree" promulgated by Vatican II, the great conference of all Roman Catholic bishops and other Roman Catholic dignitaries held in Rome from 1962 to 1965.

In this decree the church recognizes that the communications media now have such power that they are capable of exerting a serious influence on society as a whole. Whereas man's character as a social being was formerly described in terms of such groups as family, nation, or church, it is now evident that modern technology has produced a "communications group" consisting of people affected and joined together by certain "communicators." In fact, the Roman Catholic church calls all mass media "social communication."

The church also acknowledges how these instruments can "spread and strengthen God's own kingdom." In fact, "the Roman Catholic Church has been commissioned by the Lord Christ to bring salvation to every man" and "claims as a birthright the use and possession of all instruments"—cinema, radio, television, theater, and the press—"to satisfy . . . the will of God himself."

The church further notes that the mass media can be so compelling that people "can be taken unawares and thus rendered scarcely able to reject its influence, should they want to do so." The media can employ "indirect persuasion by means of casual comment, secondary characters, or the settings," especially when such "indirect" persuasion is carried on for an "extensive period." The church approves of such tactics and even approves of "subliminal or subaudial projection of messages to audiences in television, radio, and cinema"—that is, the projection of messages so fleetingly or evanescently that an audience, while affected, may remain consciously unaware of being affected. (Subliminal advertising has been generally banned in the United States for its deceit and deviousness.)

The Roman Catholic church recognizes that "certain issues . . . are rather sharply debated in our times" and that these merit special handling. In this context, "the search for news and the publication of it" becomes extremely important because "the information process has clearly grown very useful and generally necessary." The church therefore recommends that the "matter communicated always be true"—except when "the norms of [Roman Catholic] morality" must be held "sacred." In this event, "knowledge is sometimes unprofitable" to man and "not all knowledge is worth having." Likewise, the church takes a dim view of "what is called art" in the mass media if it is based on ethical and artistic theories that are "false" in the eyes of the church; the church demands of the social communications "absolute allegiance to the moral order of the church."

The church also warns that "readers, viewers, and listeners" who "freely choose to receive what these media have to communicate" have a burden to honor "the moral law" of the church and to "inform themselves" of "the judgments made in these affairs by competent authorities." This in essence is an admonition to mind the authorities of the church and to accept their decision as to what is good, moral, and decent. Pointing out that the "chief moral duties respecting the proper use of instruments of social communication fall on newsmen, writers, actors, designers, pro-

ducers, exhibitors, distributors, operators, sellers, and critics as well as advertisers, marketers, public relations men,
propaganda engineers, and psychological researchers," the
church directs the faithful to assume "the task of regulating
the commercial, political, and artistic aspects of these
media."

With respect to government regulation, the church
states boldly and without equivocation that "civil authority
is bound by special duties," one of which is that "this
authority should foster religion" and should make sure in a
"just and vigilant manner that serious danger to public
morals . . . does not result from a perverted use of these
instruments." It emphasizes that "the freedom of individuals and groups is not at all infringed upon by such
watchful care."

6 The Crosier and the Distaff

The Churches' Oppression of Women and the Battle Against Birth Control and Abortion

Judeo-Christian tradition is "the oldest and most entrenched enemy" of women striving for "full human dignity and personhood," a Roman Catholic theologian told a convocation of Lutheran pastors in early 1973 in St. Paul, Minnesota.

Dr. Rosemary Ruether, one of the first two women to become lecturers at Harvard Divinity School, said that, since the time of the earliest Christian fathers, women have been viewed as "flesh, a sort of headless body," even the "symbol of sin" for the spiritually superior male to control and use, "either as the means of procreation or the remedy of concupiscence." Both the early fathers and the medieval theologians agreed "that for any spiritual companionship another male is always more suitable." "Not too surprisingly,' she went on, "the most concerted foes of the women's movement in the 19th Century and down to our own times have been the Christian clergy, and it has been the Biblical, especially the Pauline, texts which have been used continually as the bludgeon to beat women back into their traditional place."

During the same week, Dr. Mary Daly, professor of theology at Boston College, spoke before the 1973 Nobel Conference. Here are her words:

Compare the high status of women under the Celts with that of women under Christianity, . . . a patriarchal religion which functions to maintain patriarchy. Male Deity, the incarnation of God in a male Christ, feminization of evil, sexist scriptures, disregard of women's experience are means by which this is achieved. A sexist society spawns a sexist religion, which, in turn, produces a sexist society.

Organized religions have always bent their efforts to suppressing and oppressing. Whether the suppressed were communities within their own ranks, primitive tribes on whom they inflicted their rituals of worship, or other countries whose different god they tried to destroy, each of the large branches of Christianity has struggled to suppress the spirit of human and cultural individuality. Perhaps organized religions' grandest and most tyrannical effort in this regard has been their attempt to subjugate half the human race—women.

WOMEN IN THE BIBLE

Is it really all that bad? Has that really been the history of organized Judaism and Christianity? To find out, we really must consult the Bible.

In its story of how the human species began, the Bible tells us that the first in order of creation was the male, who is created in the image of the Lord: "And God said, Let us make man in our image" (Genesis 1:26). The creation of the female emphasizes her subordinate position: "And the Lord God caused a deep sleep to fall upon Adam, and he slept: and He took one of his ribs, and closed up the flesh instead thereof; and the rib, which the Lord God had taken from man made He a woman, and brought her unto the man. And Adam said, 'This is now bone of my bones and flesh of my flesh: she shall be called Woman, because she was taken out of Man' " (Genesis 2:21–23).

The story of the origin of the female played a decisive part in old Jewish society. It solidified the master position of the male. According to the *Jewish Encyclopedia*, "The wife was regarded as property." Indeed the morning prayer of the Hebrew male, from time immemorial, has included the thankful line, "Blessed be Thou, our God and Lord of Host, who has not created me a woman." Conversely, the Hebrew female must pray daily to the God "who has created me after thy way."

After this ignominious start, the female immediately committed the supreme transgression. She enticed the man to fall from grace. She disobeyed God. She succumbed to temptation. She corrupted the male. For her crime of eating of the fruit of the tree of knowledge she caused man to be expelled from the Garden of Eden. So God said to woman, "thy desire shall be to thy husband, and he shall rule over thee" (Genesis 3:16); "I will greatly multiply thy sorrow and thy conception; in sorrow thou shalt bring forth children." Two concepts derived from the story of Eve in the garden. First, through her disobedience she had caused the fall of man and brought death to the human community and its expulsion from the Garden of Eden. She had sought after knowledge that only God could have: the knowledge of good and evil. Second, the myth developed that her disobedience had been bound up with sexual activity, with sexual intercourse, and so woman became the living symbol of the "demands of the flesh" as opposed to the true "spiritual" life of man. Woman became Evil personified.

The sexual ownership of women became the warp and woof of Judeo-Christianity. Man owned woman, and his first command was that she abstain from intercourse with other men. At the same time the man reserved to himself the right to have sexual relations with other women. Besides his own wife, or wives, he could have as many concubines as his condition allowed. In Genesis, Abraham's wife, Sarah, bearing no children, gave her handmaid Hagar to her husband so that children could issue to Abraham. Also in Genesis, Rachel was unable to bear children to Jacob and so gave him her handmaid Bilhah for the purpose. The Hebrews were also given to raping the women of peoples they had conquered, provided the women were virgin. If the women "had known men," they were slaughtered. Captured women became slaves and concubines. Moses's reaction (Numbers 31:14–18) to the capture of the Midian women is typical:

> *And Moses, and Eleazar the priest, and all the princes of the congregation, went forth to meet them without the camp. And Moses was wroth with the officers of the host, with the captains over thousands, and captains over hundreds, which came from the battle. And Moses said unto them, Have ye saved all the women alive? Behold, these caused the children of Israel, through the counsel of Balaam, to commit trespass against the Lord in the matter of Peor, and there was a plague among the congregation of the Lord. Now therefore kill every male among the little ones, and kill every woman that hath known man by lying with him. But all the women children, that have not known a man by lying with him, keep alive for yourselves.*

Significantly, the Ten Commandments delivered by Moses were addressed only to the men. In the tenth commandment (Exodus 20:17) woman is bracketed with servants and domestic animals when man is warned not to covet anything that belongs to his male neighbor, such as, first, his property and then his wife, or a manservant, or ox, or an ass.

Biblical women were so little thought of that they were excluded from inheritance. This was changed only at a later date, when the father left no sons. Nor had a woman any right, generally speaking, to choose her own husband. Her father selected the man she was to wed.

The importance a man attached to his daughter is clearly indicated in two Old Testament stories. In Judges 19:23–29, some sodomists beat at the door of a home at which "a certain Levite" was visiting. The sodomists demanded: "Bring forth the man that came into thy house, that we may know him" ("know him," meaning to bugger him). The head of the house replied:

> *Nay, brethren, nay I pray you, do not so wickedly; seeing this man is come into mine house. Do not this*

folly. Behold, here is my daughter, a maiden, and his concubine; them I will bring out now, and humble ye them, and do with them what seemeth good to you: but unto this man do not so vile a thing.

The sodomists took one woman and "abused her all the night until the morning" and left her dead upon the doorstep.

The Old Testament is everywhere full of contempt for women. According to Mosaic Law, for example, there was to be a period of cleansing after childbirth (Leviticus 12:1):

If a woman have conceived seed, and born a man child; then she shall be unclean seven days; according to the days of separation for her infirmity shall she be unclean.

However, if she produced a girl, things were different:

If she bear a maid child, then she shall be unclean two weeks, as in her separation, and she shall continue in the blood of her purifying threescore and six days.

In other words, it was twice as dishonorable to bear a child who was female.

Warnings against woman's perfidy also occur throughout the Old Testament. The story of Jezebel (I Kings 16–21) concerns a woman who tried to influence her husband and who, because of this, lost her life when the Lord passed judgment on her. "In the portion of Jezreel shall dogs eat the flesh of Jezebel: And the carcase of Jezebel shall be as dung upon the face of the field" (II Kings 9:36-37). Indeed, Delilah's betrayal of Samson was a warning not to trust in women.

The New Testament increased the hostility toward women. Paul, in his First Epistle to the Corinthians, laid down the rules:

But I would have you know, that the head of every man is Christ; and the head of woman is the man; and the head of Christ is God. (I Corinthians 11:3)

Then he explained why woman must cover her head to engage in prayer:

For a man indeed ought not to cover his head, foras-much as he is the image and glory of God; but the woman is the glory of the man. For the man is not of the woman; but the woman of the man. Neither was the man created for the woman; but the woman for the man. (I Corinthians 11:7–9)

Later in the same epistle Paul leaves no doubt as to the true Christian's attitude toward women:

Let your women keep silence in the churches: for it is not permitted unto them to speak; but they are com-manded to be under obedience, as also saith the law. And if they will learn anything, let them ask their husbands at home: for it is a shame for women to speak in the church. (I Corinthians 14:34–35)

When viewed as the incarnation of sexual desire, woman takes on a more sinister aspect in the New Testament. Jesus Christ, when approached directly with the question of women and whether it is or is not good to marry, said:

All men cannot receive this saying, save they to whom it is given. For there are some eunuchs, which were so born from their mother's womb: and there are some eunuchs, which were made eunuchs of men: and there be eunuchs, which have made themselves eunuchs for the kingdom of Heaven's sake. He that is able to receive it, let him receive it. (Matthew 19:10–12)

Clearly, Jesus felt that self-castration was preferable to sexual entanglement with a woman. Paul understood the implications and set them forth in his First Epistle to the Corinthians:

Now concerning the things whereof ye wrote unto me: It is good for a man not to touch a woman. Nevertheless, to avoid fornication, let every man have his own wife, and let every woman have her own husband. Let the husband render unto the wife due benevolence: and likewise also the wife unto the husband. The wife hath not power of her own body, but the husband. (I Corinthians 7:1-4)

For I would that all men were even as I myself. But every man hath his proper gift of God, one after this manner, and another after that. I say therefore to the unmarried and widows, it is good for them if they abide even as I. But if they cannot contain, let them marry: for it is better to marry than to burn. (I Corinthians 7:7-9)

There was an absolute aversion to both sex and woman in Paul's interpretation of Christianity.

THE CHURCH CONTINUES THE TRADITION

Paul goes on and on in this vein in his other epistles, and his attitude was enthusiastically embraced by the church fathers who came after him. Tertulian exclaimed; "Woman, thou should ever walk in mourning and rags, thy eyes full of tears, present the aspect of repentance to induce forgetfulness of your having ruined the human race. Woman, thou art the Gate of Hell!" And "Celibacy is preferable, even if the human race goes to ground." And "Woman, you are the devil's doorway. You have led astray one whom the devil would not dare attack directly. It is your fault the Son of God had to die; you should always go in mourning and rags." Finally, "The judgment of God upon your sex endures even today; and with it inevitably endures your position of criminal at the bar of justice."

St. Jerome said, "Marriage is always a vice; all that we can do is to excuse and cleanse it." Hence it was made a sacrament of the church. Origen declared, "Marriage is something unholy and unclean, a means of sensuality" (in order to resist the temptation Origen emasculated himself). St. Ambrose affirmed, "Adam was led to sin by Eve and not Eve by Adam. It is just and right that woman accept as lord and master him whom she led to sin." John Chrysostom added, "Among all savage beasts none is found so harmful as woman." Anthony, the first Christian monk, instructed the Christian brothers, "When you see a woman, consider that you face not a human being, but the devil himself. The woman's voice is a snake's hiss." A little more humanely, St. Thomas Aquinas declared that woman was only an "occasional" and incomplete being, a kind of imperfect man.

By decree of the Council of Auxerre in A.D. 578, women were forbidden to receive the sacraments with their naked hands. They were too impure. Women were also forbidden by canon law to receive the Eucharist when menstruating. They were forbidden to sing in church because of their inherent wickedness, and male eunuchs were created to furnish the high-pitched voices. Women were totally excluded from the priesthood.

Abuse was lavished on the woman. She was called filthy, indecent, shameless, immoral. For hundreds of years it was debated whether she even had a soul; the sixth-century Council of Macon finally granted, by a majority of one vote, that woman had a soul.

For millennia women in Christendom were trained to suppress all their thoughts, personality traits, and desires and to be in complete subservience to men. Free action, free speech, and free thought all were denied to women. All gainful occupations remained closed to them. They were forbidden to make depositions in court or to give testimony. Divorce was not available to them. A woman was married without her consent, and disposed of at her husband's whim.

Wherever Christianity went, it took along its ferocious antifeminism, forcing civil governments to adopt the harsh and woman-hating laws of the church. Civil law finally placed women in the absolute power of men. This was predicated on the doctrine that woman had brought sin into the world, rendering the sacrifice of the Son of God necessary, for which she never could be forgiven.

By feudal times in Western Europe it was natural that the *droit du seigneur* would come into being with full sanction of the church. The landlord possessed the absolute right to give any female under his care to whatever man he had designated for her husband. In addition, he had the privilege of taking her maidenhead on the night of her marriage. The prospective husband was required to stand by until the deflowering act was accomplished. This *jus primae* noctis, or "right to the first night," was even exercised by churchmen when the church was the landlord.

Everywhere the right to subdue women by force was upheld by the church. Organized religion preached from the pulpit the right of men to beat their wives, and the wives' obligation to kiss the rod that beat them. Christianity deliberately sanctioned violence against women. In a burst of pity for women, Bernardino of Siena in 1427 finally suggested that for "not every cause" should the wife be beaten.

We remember that women were burned as witches, but we forget that women were burned for many other reasons during the Middle Ages: for talking back to a priest, for stealing, for prostitution, for adultery, for masturbating, for scolding and nagging, for bearing a child out of wedlock. All this occurred when the only real laws were the laws of the church and when civil courts were little other than agents of the Christian hierarchy.

The full extent of organized Christianity's animosity toward women came out in the witch-hunts. Under the banner cry, "Thou shalt not suffer a witch to live," women were blamed for everything. The use of torture was rapidly adopted throughout Europe. In 1437 and 1445 Pope Eugene IV issued bulls commanding punishment of witches who caused bad weather. In 1484 the bull *Summis Desiderantes,* by Pope Innocent VIII, started a wave of torturing and execution in which many thousands were killed. Similar bulls were issued by Julius II and Adrian VI. The estimates of the number of persons slaughtered as witches vary with every author, but the number is staggering by any method of count. Moreover, calculations based on court and other records indicate that it was in the most advanced and civilized countries of Europe—Spain, England, Germany, and France—where executions for witchcraft were most frequent. Under the Spanish Inquisition, as many as 100 witches might be burned in a day. This auto-da-fé, as it was called, took on the character of a carnival, with the selling of food, souvenirs, rosaries, and holy relics. The Protestants also participated fully in the carnage. Martin Luther once said, "I would have no compassion for a witch, I would burn them all." In America, the witch trials were products of American Protestantism. Massachusetts, Maryland, New Jersey, and Virginia passed laws designating witchcraft as a crime; Pennsylvania, New York, Virginia, and Delaware made it a capital offense.

One of the greatest injustices to come out of organized religion was the convent. Thousands of women's lives, liberty, and happiness were sacrificed for hundreds of years as forced religious vows came to prevail throughout Europe. When a family could not or did not desire to pay a dowry to obtain a husband for a daughter, it was not uncommon to assign her to a nunnery, whether or not she desired to go. This abuse has never been fully explored, although the case of Marguerite Delamarre is particularly interesting. Marguerite Delamarre was a young nun in a convent of Longchamps, near Paris, who in 1752 instituted court proceedings to be released from her religious vows. She pleaded that she had been forced to make them under duress. In 1758, however, the Paris court ruled against her, and Marguerite was forced to remain in the convent. A fictionalized version of the case was written by Diderot, the great French encyclopedist, which in 1966 was made into a film entitled *The Nun*. There was an outcry, and then the French censorship board, at the insistence of the Roman Catholic church, placed a total ban on the film both for France and for exportation. In addition, President Charles de Gaulle ordered that no mention of the film be made on radio or television.

The Protestant flowering brought with it even more misery for women. It was simply a reversion to the older, biblical antifeminism, but now even more carefully enforced. The logical outcome of the Protestants' increased devotion to the Holy Bible was the phenomenon of Puritanism, directed specifically against human sexuality and women. Martin Luther believed that women were naturally secondary to men and that sexual relations perpetuated original sin. Philip Melanchthon, the great associate of Luther in the Reformation, proclaimed, "If a woman weary of bearing children, that matters not. Let her only die from bearing, she is there to do it." John Calvin also was completely contemptuous of women, and held that their only useful function was childbearing. He spoke against political equality for women as a "deviation from the original and proper order of nature." John Knox went so far as to write "The First Blast of the Trumpet Against the Monstrous Regiment of Women." In Protestant England in 1661, it was decreed that every woman coming to church must be veiled, and as late as 1867 in New York the sacraments were refused to women patients at a sanatorium because their heads were uncovered.

Education was almost universally denied to women. During the sixteenth and seventeenth centuries, for example, a woman could learn only needlework, singing, drawing, or playing a harpsichord—if she was of the upper class. The lower-class woman knew only the work of drudgery in home and farm. Her children belonged to the father and bore his name, as did she herself. She could not maintain a bank account or hold property in her name. She was not permitted to make contracts or wills. She had no control over money she earned or inherited. She had no civil rights; she could not vote, make a will, testify in court, serve on juries, or obtain a divorce. Her condition was equal to that of an infant.

CHRISTIANITY AND AMERICAN WOMEN

The Puritans, Anglicans, and other sects carried their prejudices to the American colonies. There were no women at the Constitutional Convention, no women in the First Continental Congress, no women who could vote. Later, the woman's only admission to any institution outside her home was to the mills and factories of the new capitalism where her wages and working conditions did not even approximate those of the lowest class of laboring man. As late as 1879, in a famous case tried in Ohio, the "Lucy Walker Case" (involving a suit over alienation of affection), it was held that a man has a property interest in his wife and his daughter which they do not possess in him. At no time did organized religion lift its voice against such abuses. Historians Charles and Mary Beard, in *The Rise of American*

Civilization (1927), sadly noted: "Teachings of the Church fathers on the wickedness of human nature, consecrated by centuries of Catholic propaganda and taken literally by Puritan and Anglican, were made, like due process, the law of the land in their new home. Fines, public confessions, brands, and lashings were usually prescribed, . . . and the records seem to indicate that, as a rule, it was the woman, not the man, who got the heavier punishment."

Not until the mid-1800s in the United States did the first concerted efforts to liberate women begin. The situation before then had been desperate. The Christian ethic of female depravity had so penetrated every aspect of Western culture for 1,500 years that it was totally accepted. Then in 1848 in Seneca Falls, New York, Elizabeth Cady Stanton, Lucretia Mott, and a few others organized the first woman's rights convention in the United States and drew up a public protest against the political, economic, and social inferiority that had been clamped on women by the civil government with the approval of the churches. Three years later, in 1851, Mrs. Stanton met Susan B. Anthony, and the two became the acknowledged leaders of the woman's movement in the United States.

THE WOMEN FIGHT BACK: THE FEMINIST MOVEMENT

In 1893 Matilda Joslyn Gage wrote a book entitled *Woman, Church and State,* the preface of which noted:

This work explains itself and is given to the world because it is needed. Tired of the obtuseness of Church and State; indignant at the injustice of both towards woman; at the wrongs inflicted upon one-half of humanity by the other half in the name of religion; finding appeals and arguments alike met by the assertion that God designed the subjection of woman, and yet that her position had been higher under Christianity than ever before: Continually hearing these statements, and knowing them to be false, I refuted them. . . . Read it; examine for yourselves; accept or reject from the proof offered, but do not allow the Church or the State to govern your thought or dictate your judgment.

With compelling logic, Mrs. Gage then went on to show that "the most grievous wrongs" inflicted on woman have been through the cooperation of state with church. She argued that civilization as known in her time was so permeated with Christian thought that the existing laws of the states were blind to a consideration of justice for women. She summed up her arguments by saying that "freedom for woman underlies all the great questions of the age."

During the late nineteenth century Elizabeth Cady Stanton also came to believe that not disfranchisement but the Bible and the churches were the main obstacles to the equality of the sexes. She felt that, if she could demonstrate that the subjection of women was *not* divinely ordained, men would be more willing to admit women to an equal place in society, and women would feel less hesitant about asserting their rights. She wrote:

> *Every form of religion which has breathed upon this earth has degraded woman. Man himself could not do this; but when he declares, "Thus saith the Lord," of course he can do it.*

She decided that, if the authority of the Bible were to continue to be admitted, it would have to be rewritten in order to defend the cause of women. She and some chosen feminists thus took upon themselves the task of such a rewriting, and in 1895 she issued her *Woman's Bible*. She denied divine authority and saw the Bible as a collection of writings that were "wholly human in their origin." Women's subjugation by men had grown out of the Bible: their social and political degradation was simply an outgrowth of their status in the Bible and in the codes of the churches.

Regrettably, many members of the feminist movement tried to dissociate the movement from the *Woman's Bible*. Thereupon, Susan B. Anthony came to Mrs. Stanton's defense: "I was born a heretic . . . I always distrust people who know so much about what God wants them to do to their fellows." But the religionists won out, and a religious department was founded within the National American Woman Suffrage Association, severely weakening that organization.

This did not stop great women from recognizing the pernicious influence of organized religion. Jane Addams, in founding Chicago's Hull House, America's first settlement house providing community services to the poor, completely excluded religion from it. Attacked again and again by religious groups and by newspaper editorials, she continued on her resolute way. And Margaret Sanger, in her single-minded fight for birth control, was impelled by what she characterized as "the memory of my own suffering . . . with religion."

THE BIRTH CONTROL MOVEMENT

In the course of the movement for "emancipation," which focused primarily on women's right to vote, it became apparent that a more specific right of woman had to do with knowledge about her body functions. This manifested itself in the first fights for sex education, which included information on how to prevent pregnancy or alternatively, how to terminate an unwanted pregnancy.

The churches and men of puritanical persuasion were in concert to prevent birth control material from coming into female hands, basing their arguments on the fear that the ability to avoid pregnancy would foster promiscuous sexual conduct on the part of the female and lead to adulterous premarital or other uncontrolled sexual activity. Another aspect, however, was that information was also to be withheld from the young male, since the Protestant work ethic heavily emphasized fidelity to the employer and the home, long hours, and rigid self-control.

From the nineteenth century well into the twentieth century, the advocates of birth control were few and were systematically persecuted. Probably the most detailed essay on contraceptive techniques to be written since ancient times was *The Fruits of Philosophy: or, The Private Companion of Young Married People,* written by an American, Charles Knowlton, and published in nine editions from 1832 to 1839. Knowlton was eventually prosecuted, and the dissemination of such information was quashed. In 1873 the U.S. Congress enacted the "Comstock law," named after Anthony Comstock of New York, the fanatical YMCA crusader against vice whom we met in Chapter 5. The law specifically classed birth control literature with obscene matter and forbade its distribution in the mails. The Tariff Act of 1890 banned the importation of such literature, and "little Comstock laws" with provisions against birth control literature were adopted in many states.

Concurrently, prosecutions continued. In 1877 Dr. Sarah B. Chase advertised and sold the first hygienic syringe, only to be prosecuted for doing so. In 1878, a contraceptive manual, *Cupid's Yokes,* brought a jail sentence not only for the author, E. H. Heywood, but also for the editor of a militant Atheist journal, D. M. Bennett, who had championed Heywood. Later, Dr. E. B. Foote, who had issued a booklet with "hints for the prevention of conception," entitled *Words of Pearl,* was also arrested and fined.

However, it was the great American lawyer and orator Robert Ingersoll, author of such books as *Why I Am an Agnostic* and *Superstition,* who most offended the religious community. In an address to the Free Religious Society of Boston in June 1899 he said:

> *Science must make woman the owner, the mistress of herself. Science, the only possible savior of mankind, must put it in the power of woman to decide for herself whether she will or will not become a mother.*

Not until the second decade of the twentieth century, however, when Margaret Sanger and her followers appeared on the scene, did there develop really organized efforts to overturn the Comstock laws and to establish birth control clinics and regular publication of contraceptive information. In 1912 a New York socialist newspaper, *The Call,* published Mrs. Sanger's articles "What Every Woman Should Know" and "What Every Girl Should Know"; both urged the use of contraception to emancipate women from the burdens of unlimited childbearing. Upon return from a trip to Europe to learn more about contraceptive techniques, she began to publish articles in her new monthly magazine, *Woman Rebel,* on the masthead of which was the slogan "No Gods, No Masters." With the inauguration of the magazine she declared that she was bent on breaking the law banning contraceptive information, and she thus proceeded to publish a booklet entitled *Family Limitation* (in which, incidentally, she coined the phrase "birth control"). For this publication she was prosecuted, but the case was dismissed, establishing her first victory for free dissemination of contraceptive information. In 1916 in Brooklyn she opened the first American birth control clinic, was arrested for "maintaining a public nuisance," and in 1917 spent thirty days in jail. Gradually, however, she won approval from the public and the courts, and in January 1918 a New York judge ruled in her favor; and from that point on it began to be possible for physicians in more and more states to give contraceptive information for reasons of health. Yet when Margaret Sanger later scheduled a meeting on birth control at the New York City town hall, the Roman Catholic archbishop, using his influence with the police department, had the meeting closed.

In 1917 Mrs. Sanger helped organize the National Birth Control League (which in 1921 became the American Birth Control League and in 1942 the Planned Parenthood Federation of America), which fought long legal and political battles, always against rancorous religious opposition. The Clinical Research Bureau, which Margaret Sanger established in New York in 1923, was being raided as late as 1929 at the behest of the city's Roman Catholic hierarchy. In one raid, birth control information cards concerning individual women were seized, and when the court ordered the cards returned, those of the Roman Catholic women were missing.

By 1930 there were fifty-five birth control clinics in twenty-three cities, and in 1936 the U.S. Court of Appeals ruled that physicians could mail whatever was needed "for the purpose of saving life or promoting the well-being of their patients." Finally, in 1937, the American Medical Association also came out in support of birth control. By the 1970s the Planned Parenthood Federation had affiliates in almost 200 U.S. cities.

While the legal position was gradually becoming more flexible, the position of the Roman Catholic church was, if anything, hardening. In Massachusetts in 1942 the Roman Catholic hospitals, under orders from the Roman Catholic hierarchy, demanded that doctors on their staffs either resign or terminate any association with Planned Parenthood. In 1945 St. Elizabeth's Hospital in Newark, New Jersey, asked any doctor bringing patients to the hospital to sign an agreement not to give any patient advice on birth control or other activities at variance with Roman Catholic morality either in the hospital or in private practice. Under the same proscriptions, six Protestant physicians were dismissed in 1947 from three Connecticut hospitals—St. Mary's in Waterbury, St. Joseph's in Stamford, and St. Vincent's in Bridgeport.

In 1952, delegates from Roman Catholic countries to the World Health Organization warned that if birth control information were included in WHO programs it would endanger the very existence of the organization. The organization, consequently, dropped birth control information from its programs. One of the results of this was that WHO health teams in India limited instruction in birth control methods to the religiously approved "rhythm method." In the 1970s the Roman Catholic church was still trying to block all effective sex education and birth control programs in the Roman Catholic countries. WHO, however, as well as such other UN organizations as UNESCO and UNICEF, had finally evaded the obstructionism of organized religion and were now extensively engaged in family planning efforts around the world.

In December 1952, representatives of Planned Parenthood were excluded from membership in the Welfare and Health Council of New York City, due solely to the opposition of the Roman Catholic Charities of New York. When, in June 1953, Planned Parenthood was voted in, fifty-three Roman Catholic agencies resigned from the council, pleading that Planned Parenthood was "contrary to the law of Almighty God." In Princeton, New Jersey, in 1955, Planned Parenthood had to withdraw from participation in the Community Chest drive as a result of a Roman Catholic boycott of the fund-raising campaign. And in Austin, Texas, in 1957 a birth control clinic was removed from Brackenridge Hospital because of Roman Catholic pressure.

A confrontation in New York City in 1958 well illustrates the willingness of hospital administrators to bow to religious influence. On July 16, 1958, the New York hospital commissioner ordered a Protestant physician not to fit a Protestant patient for a contraceptive device at Kings County Hospital. On September 17, 1958, the full hospital commission reversed the order. Thereupon the Roman Catholic Archdiocese of New York attacked the commission's decision as introducing "an immoral practice in our hospitals that perverts the nature and dignity of man." Five days later the city's bureau of medical and hospital services issued a memorandum stating that henceforth such a fitting would require certification of medical necessity by two physicians and the written consent of both the patient and her husband. There was also a recommendation that the patient consult initially with her spiritual adviser as well as with members of her family. In addition, physicians, nurses, and other hospital personnel who had religious or moral objections were "excused from participation in this procedure."

What makes these instances of religious interference with the rights of women particularly reprehensible is that they also involve the misuse of public funds, since, in effect, public funds are being used in aid of religious doctrine, contrary to the constitutional principle of separation of church and state. The Roman Catholic hospitals of Massachusetts, for instance, which of course deny patients birth control aid, have taken $5 million in federal funds under the Hill-Burton Act alone. St. Elizabeth's Hospital in New Jersey has similarly received $877,247. The three Connecticut hospitals noted above have received $927,316. One may also point out that the Brackenridge Hospital in Austin and the Kings County Hospital in New York are both owned by the people in those cities, not by the church groups that brought pressure to bear on them.

Finally, we may consider the case of William R. Baird, who in 1964 decided to give lectures on sex education and birth control and in 1965 was arrested in New York for his efforts (the arrest, ironically though, served eventually to help change the archaic New York law). He was arrested also in New Jersey and in Massachusetts in 1967, in

Wisconsin in 1970, and again in New York City in 1971. In each case he was attempting to give information concerning birth control. The 1971 arrest in New York was particularly laughable—or sinister. A married woman had brought her fourteen-month-old daughter to a lecture, and so Baird was arrested for "contributing to the delinquency" of a minor!

THE ABORTION CONTROVERSY

One of the saddest things about all this is that if all the birth control advocates from Margaret Sanger to William R. Baird had been fully successful in their campaigns to get contraceptive information easily and widely disseminated, the other great women's issue of our time, induced abortion, would probably be of only marginal concern. Unfortunately, though, by systematically trying to block the free flow of information regarding contraception, the Roman Catholic church has ensured that abortion should become both tragically widespread and bitterly controversial.

Historically, in the United States, the first abortion statute was passed in Missouri in 1835. It prescribed that an abortion could be performed only when the life of the mother was at stake. For the better part of a century, as other states followed Missouri's example, this remained essentially the only circumstance under which pregnancy could be terminated through induced abortion. Even when the feminist movement began in 1848, the state legislatures could not be induced to broaden the law. We were a growing nation, and an increased population was thought necessary. The desires or well-being of women were little considered when the manifest destiny of the United States was involved. In 1865 the American Medical Association decided that the unborn child was a human being from the time of conception, an argument that would be used more than 100 years later by antiabortionists.

By the turn of the century, only twenty-four states had laws permitting induced abortion, and all of these prescribed that the life of the mother had to be endangered by a full-term pregnancy. In every instance the physician and the husband were legally empowered to make this determination. During the first half of the twentieth century, these restrictions on women continued without any serious challenge in the courts or the public forum, so well did women know their place.

When the women's liberation movement began to make an impact in the 1960s, however, states like Alaska, Hawaii, Washington, and New York began to liberalize their laws. Thirty other states began considering new abortion legislation, and the American Law Institute came up with a "liberal" prototype law. Then court rulings in Illinois and California expanded access to abortion in those states. Contrary to the stand of the Roman Catholic church, opinion polls indicated that 56 percent of Roman Catholics believed that abortion should be a matter for decision between a woman and her physician alone. Protestants, ignoring the increasingly violent fulminations of their fundamentalist brethren, agreed by a thumping 65 percent. When abortions were legalized in Washington, D.C., in 1971 the number of such operations increased by 56 percent over the year before. In New York the cost of abortions dropped from around $600 in 1970 to less than $200 in 1972. Women no longer were forced to submit themselves to exorbitant quacks for hazardous butchery in squalid back rooms. At last they could rely on competent medical care from licensed physicians.

Some churches even began cautiously supporting women's rights. The United Presbyterian Church in the U.S.A. felt that women should have "full freedom of personal choice" about completion or termination of pregnancy. The American Baptist churches held that, although the choice of abortion should be controlled by legislation, it should be sanctioned within the first three months of pregnancy. Other groups gave approval in varying degrees (although, admittedly, often with prominent individual members in sharp disapproval). The Episcopal church, the Lutheran church, the United Church of Christ, and the United Methodist church generally agreed that the women concerned should have some say in the matter.

The Roman Catholic church, on the other hand, was adamant in its stand against abortion. As early as 1869 the Vatican had enunciated its firm position, which held that, because the embryo is "ensouled" at conception and because this living soul must be protected for Christ, no mother may be allowed an induced abortion for any reason whatsoever. In the 1960s the church reaffirmed this stand and quickly began to muster its forces. By the early 1970s the church's political savvy began to pay off. From its thousand or more years of experience in dealing with every conceivable type of government, the church knew where and how to proceed. In 1972 a law professor at Notre Dame University fashioned an antiabortion amendment to the Constitution, which was introduced into Congress. It was described as a bill to ensure that due process and equal protection would be afforded an individual from the moment that he is conceived. Dubbed the "Right to Life" amendment, it contained this passage:

> *An individual, from the moment that he is conceived, shall not be deprived of life, liberty, or property, without due process of law. No State shall deprive any individual, from the moment that he is conceived, of life, liberty, or property, without due process of law; nor deny to any individual, from the moment that he is conceived, within its jurisdiction the equal protection of the law.*

Suddenly a full-fledged offensive developed, as antiabortion groups sprang up everywhere. The biggest of these—and the one that was ultimately to swallow up almost all the rest—was the "Right to Life" group, headquartered in the United States Roman Catholic Conference Building in Washington, D.C., and staffed 98 percent by Roman Catholics. It soon had about 300 smaller "grass roots" groups (of which more than half were tax-exempt even though their main purpose was clearly to effect legislation). With an initial annual budget of $50,000, the group had branches in virtually every state, conducting mail campaigns, lobbying, protesting, and "educating" for their points of view. A favorite means of politicizing was to lecture communicants at mass (a captive audience) and to hand them lists of senators and congressmen, together with a printed message containing these instructions:

> . . . *In effect, this [Right to Life] amendment, when ratified, will ABOLISH ALL liberalized abortion laws, in all the States without exception.*
>
> *In view of this important amendment, we strongly urge all who desire to repeal the liberalized abortion laws to:*
> 1. *WRITE TO YOUR CONGRESSMAN in your own congressional district, stating your approval of this amendment and urging him to vote for its passage.*
> 2. *GET OTHERS TO DO THE SAME. A few hundred letters will show a congressman that people want change. (This letter may be photocopied and passed on to others.)*
> 3. *Don't worry about the form or about any misspelling of any words, nor how long or short the letter is, do not copy from another letter, your own original words are preferable.*

In New York a showdown came early in 1972. A liberal abortion law had been put into effect there two years before. The Roman Catholic church wanted the law repealed, and legislators reported that they were under extreme pressure to vote for that repeal. They were telephoned at their homes; petitions were presented to their offices; demonstrators gathered in Senate chambers. Into the midst of this stepped President Nixon. On May 7, 1972, Terence Cardinal Cooke released a letter that he had received from the President on the eve of the vote and which was certainly calculated to influence it. The letter read:

> *Recently, I read in the* Daily News *that the Archdiocese of New York, under your leadership, had initiated a campaign to bring about repeal of the state's liberalized abortion laws. Though this is a matter for state jurisdiction, I would personally like to associate myself with the convictions you deeply feel and eloquently express.*

*The unrestricted [sic] abortion policies now recom-
mended by some Americans, and the liberalized abortion policies in effect in some sections of this country,
seem to me impossible to reconcile with either our
religious tradition or our Western heritage. One of the
foundation stones of our society and civilization is the
profound belief that human life, all human life, is a
precious commodity—not to be taken without the
gravest of causes.*

*Yet, in this great and good country of ours in recent
years, the right to life [sic] of literally hundreds of
thousands of unborn children has been destroyed—
legally—but in my judgment without anything approaching adequate justification. Surely, in the on-going
national debate about the particulars of the "quality of
life," the preservation of life should be moved to the top
of the agenda. Your decision, and that of tens of
thousands of Catholics, Protestants, Jews, and men and
women of no particular faith, to act in the public forum
as defenders of the right to life of the unborn, is truly a
noble endeavor. In this calling, you and they have my
admiration, sympathy, and support.*

By a bare majority of one vote, the New York Legislature
thereupon voted for repeal of the law permitting abortions.
Fortunately, however, the situation in New York was saved
by Governor Nelson Rockefeller's veto of the repeal bill. In
Pennsylvania the same thing happened when a liberal
abortion law repeal was also blocked by the governor's
veto. On the other hand, legislative efforts to liberalize
abortion laws were defeated in Georgia, Indiana, Rhode
Island, Colorado, Delaware, Maine, Kansas, Iowa, Illinois,
Michigan, Massachusetts, and Connecticut. In states already blessed with liberalized laws, the Right to Life groups
continued to shout for their repeal.

In Connecticut, when a federal court ruled unconstitutional the state's 112-year-old antiabortion law, the governor called a special session of the state Assembly to
overrule the court. A staunch Roman Catholic himself, in a
heavily Roman Catholic state, he called for an even stricter

antiabortion law, which was quickly passed. Massachusetts followed, with the Legislature giving initial approval to a state constitutional amendment that would grant the fetus "the rights of all citizens . . . from the moment of conception."

In Michigan the fight erupted into a court suit. There the president of a Roman Catholic association known as the Men of the Sacred Heart erected billboards featuring a picture of Jesus Christ and the command:

> *Stop Abortion Now! Thou Shalt Not Kill.*
> *Don't take away a life that I have given.*
> *Vote No in November.*

The Michigan Abortion Referendum Committee immediately filed suit alleging a violation of the Michigan election law, which states:

> *No priest, pastor, curate, or other officer of any religious society shall impose or threaten to impose any penalty of excommunication, dismissal, or expulsion, or command or advise, under pain of religious disapproval, for the purpose of influencing any voter at any election or primary election.*

Nevertheless, the Detroit area parochial schools still excused students from classes to permit them to canvass voters and to distribute antiabortion literature near the polls on election day. Indeed, a baby-sitting service was given free to mothers who wanted to go and vote, and volunteers drove persons to the polls. When the final vote was counted the antiabortionists won with 61 percent of the vote.

In the midst of all this, the U.S. Supreme Court on January 22, 1973, handed down a critical decision. By a vote of 7 to 2, it overturned a Georgia law and a Texas law and decreed that in the first three months of pregnancy the decision on an induced abortion should be left solely to the mother and the doctor. In the second three months of pregnancy the state could establish restrictions, through such maternal health legislation as the licensing of abortion clinics; in the final three months the state would be permitted (not required) to prohibit abortion to protect the "potential life" of the fetus after its viability had been demonstrated. At the time of the Supreme Court decision, there was abortion "on demand" (more or less) in New York, Washington, Hawaii, and Alaska. Thirteen other states required some justification, such as rape, incest, or German measles, and thirty-three states permitted abortions only if the mother's life was endangered.

The reaction by Catholic hospitals was predictable. The Sacred Heart Hospital of Eau Claire, Wisconsin, which had received $3,794,081 in federal funds, immediately declared that it would "refuse to allow abortions to be done here." St. Mary's Hospital in Ladysmith, Wisconsin, issued a statement that "We have not changed our policies" (of not performing abortions).

The Roman Catholic cardinals of the United States also spoke up. Cardinal Krol of Philadelphia said, "It is hard to think of any decision in the 200 years of our history which has had more "disastrous implications for our stability as a civilized society"; and Cardinal Cody of Chicago accused the Supreme Court of having "overstepped itself" and said that Roman Catholics must oppose abortion as an immoral act. This was immediately followed, on February 13, 1973, by a warning from the National Council of Catholic Bishops that Roman Catholic women who undergo or perform an abortion "place themselves in a state of excommunication." Then, announcing that it would seek ways to reverse the Court's decision, the council stated:

> We find that this majority opinion of the court is wrong and is entirely contrary to the fundamental principles of morality. Those who obtain an abortion, those who persuade others to have an abortion, and those who perform the abortion procedure are guilty of breaking God's law.

Concurrent with this announcement, the Family Life Division of the National Council of Catholic Bishops sent out a "pastoral letter" to every priest in the country declaring, "No one is obliged to obey any civil law that may require abortion." Their reasoning was that "our American law and way of life comprise an obvious and certain recognition of the law of God, and that our legal system is both based on it, and must conform to it."

The Roman Catholics were not entirely without other religious support. The leaders of the Church of Jesus Christ of Latter-Day Saints (the Mormons) agreed that "abortion must be considered one of the most revolting and sinful practices of this day." The Archbishop and Primate of the Greek Orthodox Archdiocese of North and South America said that the Supreme Court decision was "regrettable." A split developed in the Methodists with a Perkins School of Theology (Southern Methodist University) professor criticizing the Court and the dean of the Boston (Methodist) University School of Theology charging that the decision was a "cheapening of human life."

On the actual day of the Supreme Court decision, the bishops of the state of Illinois, in conjunction with the National Catholic Hospitals Association, declared that no Roman Catholic hospitals in Illinois would perform abortions. In Cook County (Chicago) alone there are fourteen Roman Catholic hospitals (which from 1957 to mid-1971 had taken $14.2 million of federal funds from the federal government under the Hill-Burton Act). Four days after the decision the 880,000 Roman Catholics in greater Cleveland were told that the hospitals there would remain a "safe haven" from abortion. The decision was made by the Cleveland Catholic diocese and announced by the bishop of Cleveland, who also ordered special prayers against abortion in future masses. (Four Roman Catholic hospitals in Cleveland had accepted $3 million in federal grants from 1957 to 1971 under the Hill-Burton Act.) In Massachusetts the Catholic Conference of Roman Catholic Hospitals issued a statement that the state's Catholic hospitals would close and that their doctors would go to jail rather than perform abortions. The statement indicated that eighteen hospitals were involved. Almost immediately a bill was introduced in the Massachusetts Legislature to allow public or private hospitals or medical personnel the right to refuse to perform abortions and sterilizations and the right to refuse to dispense birth control products or information. (The Massachusetts Roman Catholic hospitals had received more than

$4.5 million in federal funds.) It should be noted that in each of these states the hospitals not only were tax-exempt but had benefited from state, county, and city funding as well. They were frequently the recipients of gifts from corporations and from individuals, all of which could be taken as tax write-offs by the donors. The hospitals enjoyed massive financial support from the public to whom they were refusing to grant perfectly legal operations; they were denying a right guaranteed by the Supreme Court decision.

In March of 1973 New Jersey began a constitutional amendment fight to restrict abortion. In the same month Rhode Island passed a strict antiabortion bill. In April in Texas there were attempts to introduce legislative bills to curb abortions. By May Michigan had drafted a constitutional amendment that protected "a person" with full rights from the "moment of conception." Within ninety days of the Supreme Court decision New Hampshire had passed a resolution in its Legislature opposing the decision, and refused to pay for abortions out of welfare funds. Virginia voted down a bill to bring its abortion law into conformity with the decision. Pennsylvania was considering two resolutions calling for amendments to the Constitution. Massachusetts, North Dakota, and Utah had already passed such resolutions. The Georgia Legislature considered a petition to Congress. Rhode Island began writing a new bill. Even in the U.S. Congress there were proposals for eight different constitutional amendments, one of which was cosponsored by Representative Gerald Ford, future President of the United States. This one would have made abortion a matter of state's rights and ended the Supreme Court's right to rule on the issue. This is a classic political move of the Roman Catholic church on any issue. That body has much more political influence in states where heavy Roman Catholic population is concentrated.

As Representative Bella Abzug of New York said, "The opposition is very well-organized and very strong."

To give some idea of the success of the campaign against legalized abortion, we may note that in the first seven months after the Supreme Court decision, thirty-two state legislatures adopted "conscience clause" laws, which were designed to exempt both medical personnel and institutions from involvement in abortion operations if participation would violate religious scruples. By early 1974 there were pending 228 bills and 68 resolutions in state legislatures, designed to tighten or close abortion laws.

Every phase of the fight against induced abortion is based in theology and is being waged with the full political power of organized religion. But unfortunately the basic issue has become completely obscured. Abortion is a radical surgical procedure, which should be used only when birth control has failed. The real issue, therefore, is the distribution of birth control information. If every woman had the necessary educational material, the need for abortions could be so drastically reduced as to present scarcely any problem.

In any event, despite all the religious propaganda and lobbying and pressure, a 1972 Gallup Poll did reveal that 73 percent of those questioned thought that abortion during the first three months of pregnancy was a matter that should be left solely to the woman and her physician. Not that this will make any difference in the churches' attitude. We already know what they think of women.

THE CHURCH AND WOMEN TODAY

After all is said and done, organized religion remains one of the most powerful forces in the Western world. The teachings of Christianity still carry enormous weight, and the churches have fantastic power to implement their doctrines. Regrettably, these teachings and doctrines are out of the dark ages. As late as 1912 the *Roman Catholic Encyclopedia* announced that "The female sex is in some respect inferior to the male sex, both as regards body and soul." In 1931 Pope Pius XI restated the position of the husband in Christian marriage in an encyclical: "Married life presupposes the power of the husband over the wife and children, and subjection and obedience of the wife to the husband." As recently as 1968 Pope Paul VI again shattered the hopes of women throughout the world in his *Humanae Vitae,* in which he held fast in his determination to withhold birth control means from the Roman Catholic women of the world.

Today, looking at the books written by the proponents of women's liberation, one is struck by the fact that almost no reference is made to the human religious history that underlies the cultural abuse of women. So steeped are we in the fabric of this prejudice that we cannot see it. The standard published biographies of Margaret Sanger, Jane Addams, Elizabeth Cady Stanton, Susan B. Anthony, Lucretia Mott, and Frances Wright contain few hints of their antichurch, antireligious stand.

In her autobiography, *Eight Years and More* (1898), Elizabeth Cady Stanton wrote:

> *I found nothing grand in the history of the Jews nor in the morals inculcated in the Pentateuch. I know of no other books that so fully teach the subjection and degradation of women.*

In the *Free Thought Magazine* of September 1896 she said that "The Bible and Church have been the greatest stumbling blocks in the way of women's emancipation." And a statement signed by Mrs. Stanton, Susan B. Anthony, and Matilda Joslyn Gage was equally unequivocal:

> *To no form of religion is woman indebted for one impulse of freedom, as all alike have taught her inferiority and subjection. . . . Throughout this protracted and disgraceful assault on American womanhood the clergy baptized each new insult and act of unjustice in the name of the Christian religion, and uniformly asked God's blessing on proceedings that would have put to shame an assembly of Hottentots.*

This is a fight against 6,000 years of history and of sacred custom. Until and unless we recognize the source, and repudiate it, women will never be free.

It is ironic that today one of the leading minds in the ability to perceive what the basic problem is should be that of a Roman Catholic woman, Dr. Mary Daly, who perceives that the history of Christian ideology has been one of an "all pervasive misogynism and downgrading of women as persons." All the talk of the value and dignity of the human person, she asserts, is concerned with the male while the depredation and oppression of the feminine continues. Yet, characteristically, she believes that the solution lies within the church and with acceptance of women within its structure. Even she does not see that there cannot be a change in the theology without a destruction of it.

Mrs. Stanton did not perceive that her *Woman's Bible* was a contradiction in terms. Dr. Daly does not perceive that her "Christian theology of women" cannot exist. The essence of it is antisexual, anti-life-force, antifemale. To change it is to destroy it. It can only be abandoned. It is a part of the childhood of the human race. Women, more than the men of our era, must realize that humanity is grown now.

In the United States, the churches' bias against women has been so all-pervasive and so overpowering that neither man nor woman now sees from what source it derived. With 2,000 years of depredation in Western civilization and more than 400 years of the same in North America, the discrimination is so systemic in our culture that only a complete intellectual revolution can begin to perceive it and to counter it. "Women's liberation" cannot come near to understanding the issue until it attains the awareness that last century's women leaders had: there can be no civil rights for women until there is, first, absolute separation of government and religion in America.

7 **Render Not Unto Caesar**
The Churches' Tax-Free Wealth

In the introduction to this book I quoted an official statement of the Methodist church, which unmistakably boasted of the newly found economic power of the churches in America:

> *Churches have acquired a large amount of economic and social power. They employ labor, provide social services, and operate educational institutions; they sponsor recreation, entertainment, and cultural enterprises; they are landlords as well as tenants; and they collect, expend, and invest money, as well as administer retirement and pension systems. Clearly churches now have the power to make economic and social decisions that vitally affect the lives and welfare of millions of people. . . .*

The boast is awesome. The facts are perhaps even more frightening. In the twentieth century the churches' wealth and estates, especially in profit-making businesses, have expanded enormously, in a manner rivaling the growth of great industrial corporations, so that today the churches' holdings are measured not merely in millions, but rather in billions of dollars. Almost all of it is tax-free.

Item: The churches' total real estate wealth—estimated between $80 billion and $103 billion—exceeds the combined assets of the nation's ten largest industrial corporations.

Item: The visible assets of the churches—land and buildings—are double the combined assets of the nation's five largest industrial corporations.

Item: The churches' gross (nontaxable) revenue is greater than the combined income, after taxes, of General Motors, American Telephone and Telegraph, Standard Oil, Ford, Texaco, and Sears, Roebuck.

Item: Seven major Protestant denominations have combined assets estimated at $160 billion and combined disbursements estimated at $22 billion a year—second only to the assets and disbursements of the United States government.

Item: Roman Catholic assets and real estate holdings in the United States exceed the combined assets and holdings of Standard Oil, American Telephone and Telegraph, and U.S. Steel.

Item: Mormons control the greatest aggregation of capital to be found in the states of the Rocky Mountain region.

Item: Boys Town is richer than any Nebraska industrial farm.

Comparisons like these could go on endlessly. The wealth of American churches, tax-free, is awesome.

THE CHRONICLE OF TAXATION AND TAX EXEMPTION

Tax exemption for church property is a comparatively late development in the English-speaking world. Henry II, in the twelfth century, taxed the churches. Kings John and Henry III increased the levies. Henry VIII confiscated church lands. The Stuarts taxed all properties that the churches managed to hang on to. Oliver Cromwell did likewise. In the United States tax exemption was not introduced in Kentucky until 1816, in Massachusetts until

1836, in New Hampshire until 1842, in New Jersey until 1851. Missouri taxed church property until 1876.

But even then the tide did not all flow in one direction. In 1850 bills were introduced in both the Senate and the House in Pennsylvania to repeal laws exempting religious real estate. In 1874 a bill to tax church property was introduced in the Iowa State Legislature. In his last State of the Union message on December 7, 1875, President Ulysses S. Grant made the first proposal to amend the Constitution to allow for the federal taxation of church properties. His language was clear as he spoke of "the importance of correcting an evil, . . . the accumulation of the vast amount of untaxed church property." He expressed the view that "the accumulation of so vast a property as here alluded to [church-owned land then stood at $355 million] without taxation may lead to sequestration without constitutional authority." This speech had followed another in Iowa on September 29, 1875, in which he urged that the nation "leave the matter of religion to the family altar, the Church, and the private school, supported entirely by private contributions. Keep the Church and the State forever separate."

In 1876 the Massachusetts House of Representatives debated and voted on a bill to tax all church property over $12,000 in value. On December 7, 1876, President Ulysses S. Grant again proposed an amendment to the Constitution that would tax church property, in order to correct the "evil" of "the accumulation of the vast amount of untaxed church property." William Lloyd Garrison entered the fray in the same year, stating that the state had no right to "exempt church property from taxation." Elizabeth Cady Stanton introduced the argument into the women's suffrage campaign with the following statement:

> If all those magnificent cathedrals with their valuable lands in Boston, Philadelphia and New York were taxed as they should be, the taxes of women who hold property would be proportionately lightened. . . . I cannot see any good reason why wealthy churches and a certain amount of property of the clergy should be exempt from taxation, while every poor widow in the

land, struggling to feed, clothe, and educate a family of children, must be taxed on the narrow lot and humble home.

On July 15, 1877, the U.S. Senate debated the issue of tax exemption for churches in the District of Columbia, and the opposition to exemption was strong. In 1890 the Kentucky State Constitution Convention held a vigorous and extended debate on the issue. The *New York Evening Post* spoke out editorially on the subject:

> The Evening Post *has long been of the opinion that the American theory of a self-supporting church ought to be carried out to its full and legitimate conclusion, and that the separation of church and state ought to be complete. It should include the total discontinuance of contributions of public money, direct or indirect, to the support of any religious establishment. We have never been able to see the slightest difference in principle between the appropriation of a certain sum of money raised by tax to a particular church, and a release of that church from tax on its property to the same amount. The cost of the act, in either case, falls upon the taxpayers generally.*

When exemptions began, they were specific and modest. Initially, the only property exempt from taxation, for example, was "parts of lots upon which such buildings [churches and other houses of worship] are erected" so long as the lots were "in no event more than one acre." But as the churches fought for more exemptions, the limits were gradually broadened. Today the exemptions encompass just about anything so long as its use is allegedly "not for profit" and "if no income is derived therefrom." Even these restrictions are loosely observed or evaded.

THE INTERNAL REVENUE CODE

The current Internal Revenue Code demonstrates that the federal government is out to favor organized religions as much as possible. Section 501(C) of the code exempts from taxation any "church, . . . convention or association of churches," and the Internal Revenue Service maintains a regularly updated list of qualifying organizations, called a "Cumulative List." The Roman Catholic church in the United States has 154 dioceses, in which are located almost 24,000 churches; hundreds of orders of sisters and of brothers; universities; colleges; and over 10,000 elementary and secondary schools. There are also countless other Roman Catholic agencies in the 9,000 parishes of the United States, such as the Catholic charities, hospitals, seminaries, homes for the aged, retreat houses, and Propagation of the Faith offices. In the "Cumulative List" these are all made tax-free by one entry—on page 458—which gives complete freedom from taxation to:

> *Roman Catholic Church in the United States, its Territories and possessions. (All churches and institutions of the Roman Catholic Church in the United States, its Territories and possessions, including archdioceses, dioceses, schools, colleges, universities, orphanages, homes, hospitals, religious orders, etc.)*

On the same page are listed dozens and dozens of similar religious organizations. On page 227 there are twenty "Billy Graham" organizations listed as tax-exempt. There are tens of thousands of organizations listed in the "Cumulative List," all tax-exempt because of religion; and under any single entry, such as the one for the Roman Catholic church, there may be scores, or hundreds, or thousands of affiliated agencies or groups that are not actually listed but are legally subsumed.

Any church or group listed or subsumed is traditionally given a tax-exempt status on any income, be it rents, profits, dividends, interest, gifts, inheritances, royalties, capital gains, and so on. Churches and organized religious groups pay no real estate tax, no inheritance tax, no income tax, no sales tax, no gift tax, no employment tax, and no social security tax; and they are immune, by law, in most states, from damage suits when persons are injured on their property.

For most of the twentieth century the churches have been completely sacrosanct and immune from even the hint of taxation. In 1950, for instance, the federal income tax laws were revised to remove alleged abuses. Among other things, nonprofit organizations were newly required to pay corporate profit taxes on "business income" that was "unrelated" to their nonprofit activities. All nonprofit organizations were required to do so, that is, except organized religions, which were carefully excluded from the new requirement.

By the late 1960s, however, enough glaring publicity had been turned on the churches and their profit-making activities that even the federal government began to take heed. Congressional hearings on church wealth and the possibility of church taxation began in June 1968 in the House Ways and Means Committee. In testimony, the assistant secretary of the treasury said that no reliable estimates exist as to the scope of church business and investment operations, but that they were believed to be growing. He pleaded that the federal government itself was in the dark because religious groups do not even have to file returns or statements on their income and assets. He did assert what should be obvious, however, that most churches are no longer dependent on "charitable contributions or membership fees" to keep them going. With tax exemptions, they have developed funds that multiply through investment, and any investment they make usually "bears no relation to the community's evaluation" of the churches' supposed role in the community. Any church's economic growth in these days, with such favorable tax exemptions, he continued, "is limited only by the financial acumen and commercial skills of its managers." In sum, what the assistant secretary was saying was that organized religion had become organized Big Business, with a corporate management no longer responsive to the needs or desires of the members (the parishioners) since it was no longer dependent upon their contributions for the organization's financial enterprises.

After months of wrangling among church groups and between church groups and the government, a tax study or recommendation had still not come out of the House Ways and Means Committee, when, in February 1969, two major religious organizations jointly offered a proposal to Wilbur Mills, the chairman. The proposal later came to be known

erroneously as "the effort of church groups to get themselves taxed." It was hardly that! The scattered reports from
the wire services, newspapers, and magazines were wildly
confused and inaccurate. What actually happened is that
the United States Catholic Conference (USCC) and the
National Council of Churches of Christ (NCCC) jointly made
a few guarded proposals to Mills.

First, the USCC-NCCC asked that any new law provide
adequate safeguards to prevent governmental involvement
in the internal and financial affairs of churches. In reply,
the Ways and Means Committee agreed to protect churches
from unnecessary tax audits.

Second, the USCC-NCCC asked that any new law
preserve the churches' exemption from taxation upon what
they called "passive" income or "investment" income,
including income from royalties, dividends, interest, rents,
and gains from the disposition of property. The Ways and
Means Committee agreed to these exemptions (except in
the case of "debt financing," noted below).

Third, the USCC-NCCC asked that under any new law
the churches not be taxed on what the churches considered
to be their "traditional functions"—such as the printing and
sale of religious publications, with or without advertising,
and "customary fund-raising activities." The Ways and
Means Committee again bowed to the wishes of the
churches, offering only one exception: advertising would be
taxed if the publications in which it appeared made any
profits.

Fourth, the USCC-NCCC agreed that churches might be
willing to divest themselves of business activities "unrelated" to their traditional functions, but they would like a
five-year tax-free grace period in which to accomplish the
divestiture. The House committee accepted this proposal.

The USCC-NCCC and the Ways and Means Committee
disagreed on the issue of "debt financing." Under this
scheme, a tax-exempt religious organization has custom-
arily been able to purchase a business firm's real estate on
credit, lease the real estate back to the business firm
(usually for five years or less), receive the business firm's
profits as rent, and use this rent to pay the original purchase
price. Under this scheme the churches lose nothing, for

they do not pay even taxes on the deal. The Ways and Means Committee wanted to close this loophole and make all tax-exempt organizations, including churches and religious groups, subject to taxation on rents, dividends, interest, royalties, and capital gains to the extent that such income is derived from debt-financed property. The USCC-NCCC believed that the committee's proposal went "far beyond a cure of the abuse involved" and asked that only debt-financed *rents* be taxed.

The final House bill, with a severely weakened debt-financing proposal, was passed and sent to the Senate. The Senate Finance Committee made only two notable changes. The first was rather absurd or naive: it exempted from the new law any churches with income or assets of $5,000 a year or less. The number of churches with such income or assets is infinitesimal. The second change exempted trades or businesses, such as television or radio stations, which are licensed by a federal regulatory agency and which are operated by religious or educational groups—provided that these groups had owned the businesses or trades before May 27, 1959, and did not, through these trades or businesses, receive more than 10 percent of net income from "unrelated" activities. This second change seemingly came about in order to help station WWL in New Orleans, owned by the Jesuits; the chairman of the Senate Finance Committee was Russell B. Long from Louisiana.

The Tax Reform Act of 1969 was signed by President Nixon on December 30. It had a few useful elements. It had, for example, rules on the acquisition of income-producing property, but, significantly, the rules favored religious groups over other types of nonprofit organizations. For most organizations, the income-producing property must be "in the neighborhood of other property owned by the organization," and the organization must intend to use the property for its tax-exempt purpose within ten years. The income gathered during that ten years would be tax-free. For religious organizations, however, the rules were lighter: "a church or convention or association of churches" had fifteen tax-free years and was not subject to the neighborhood test. The final measure also went comparatively easy on church-owned profit-making businesses.

The law generally applied only to businesses acquired after May 27, 1959. And until 1976 churches could continue to own other profit-making businesses acquired after May 27, 1959, without paying taxes; after 1976, ordinary taxes would have to be paid on them. In the meantime, of course, they could, if they wished, divest themselves of such businesses at a nice tax-free profit. Most importantly, any organized religious group still could invest in corporations quite freely without paying taxes on dividends or interest or capital gains, just so long as it did not gain a controlling interest.

Finally, the new law prescribed that the account books of church groups could be examined by the federal government if there was reason to suspect "unrelated" business income.

Because the government in the past has been too timid to "suspect" and investigate the finances of the churches, however, there is scarcely any immediate hope that the government will do so in the future. Until the government insists that the churches give full and periodic disclosure of their holdings and income, under penalty of fine or imprisonment of its officials for failure to do so, the government really has no precise way of knowing what the churches own and receive and for what they can be taxed or restricted or penalized. Indeed, under the continuing cloak of secrecy, the churches can disregard the new law and invest and wheel and deal as they have always done.

Furthermore, the churches are totally free of any threat that new federal legislation might arise to lessen their tax-free wealth. To quote the July 1974 issue of the Baptist newsletter *Report from the Capital:*

> *There are no bills currently alive in Congress which would abolish either the tax deductibility of gifts to churches, schools and other public charities or the tax-free status of ministers' housing allowances. There are no committees—either the regular standing committees or a "blue ribbon" special committee—which are holding hearings or contemplating holding hearings.*

Indeed, since 1969 there have been no viable congressional efforts of any kind aimed at the churches' tax-free status— and there are no prospects on the horizon.

8 This Land Is Their Land
Church Ownership of Property

In the early part of this century, before the churches protested and Congress ended the practice, the Bureau of the Census of the United States government compiled and issued decennial reports of church holdings. In the report of 1916, the Roman Catholic church was recorded as holding the most real estate, which was valued at over $374 million. Of the 202 denominations listed, 13 owned almost all the property. They were:

Roman Catholic	$ 374,206,895
Methodist	292,186,239
Baptist	194,177,426
Presbyterian	187,707,251
Episcopalian	164,990,150
Lutheran	82,353,436
Congregational	80,842,813
Disciples of Christ	40,327,201
Reformed	39,044,719
Jewish	31,012,576
Unitarian	15,247,349
United Brethren	13,787,579
German Evangelical	13,118,273
Total	$1,529,001,907

With the holdings of the other smaller denominations included, the total rose to $1,676,600,582. This figure, however, covers only the real estate containing edifices "used for worship" and thus does not include the value of parsonages, cemeteries, parochial school buildings, theological seminaries, monasteries, or convents. In fact, 28.7 percent of the churches that reported also indicated ownership of 65,272 parish houses valued at $218,500,000, thereby bringing the overall total value reported to almost $2 billion (exclusive, that is, of other properties).

In ten years the value of the holdings doubled. By 1926 the real estate owned by the churches had increased in extent and value by 115 percent. Now, out of 213 reporting denominations, 10 held most of the property:

Roman Catholic	$837,271,063
Methodist	600,244,638
Presbyterian	405,951,601
Baptist	358,829,541
Episcopalian	314,596,733
Congregational	162,212,522
Disciples of Christ	114,850,211
Lutheran	114,526,248
Jewish	97,401,688
Reformed	83,101,697

The total in this year of 1926 was well over $3.8 billion for the houses of worship alone. Adding on the 77,346 parish houses worth $475.2 million, we come to an overall total of $4.3 billion—which, again, does not include such property as parsonages, cemeteries, and monasteries.

In 1936, during the Great Depression, when all prices fell drastically, there was a considerable drop in the recorded value of church property. Eight major reporting landholders were the following:

Roman Catholic	$787,001,357
Methodist	482,970,087
Presbyterian	323,661,480
Baptist	285,341,768
Episcopalian	267,400,447
Lutheran	183,851,886

Disciples of Christ	88,070,194
United Brethren	27,435,058

The total for the 256 denominations reporting was almost $3.5 billion, for houses of worship alone. There were also 71,235 parish houses worth $344.5 million, bringing the total to $3.8 billion—a drop of a half billion dollars from the prosperity year of 1926. Measured against the general economic decline, however, the churches were generally holding their own and not doing badly at all.

THE GREAT POSTWAR LAND GIVEAWAY

The Second World War intervened to lift the nation economically out of the Depression. Meanwhile, organized religion made no further reports on its property, and the federal government made no survey during the war years.

Toward the end of the war, Congress began to consider the problem of how eventually to dispose of all the extra federal property that had been acquired through the war effort, principally for use by the armed forces. Thus on October 3, 1944, it passed the Surplus Property Act, creating the War Assets Administration to distribute all the excess federal land and buildings to other government entities and to nonprofit institutions. Spelled out in the act were certain objectives:

> (1) (A) *Surplus property that is appropriate for school, classroom, or other educational use may be sold or leased to the States and their political subdivisions and instrumentalities, and tax-supported educational institutions, and to other nonprofit educational institutions which have been held exempt from taxation under section 101 (6) of the Internal Revenue Code.*
>
> (B) *Surplus medical supplies, equipment, and property suitable for use in the protection of public health, including research, may be sold or leased to the States and their political subdivisions and instrumentalities, and to tax-supported medical institutions and to hospitals or other similar institutions*

*not operated for profit which have been held exempt
from taxation under section 101 (6) of the Internal
Revenue Code.*

*(C) In fixing the sale or lease value of property to be
disposed of under subparagraph (A) and subparagraph (B) of this paragraph, the Board shall take
into consideration any benefit which has accrued or
may accrue to the United States from the use of
such property by any such State, political subdivi-
sion, instrumentality, or institution.*

*(2) Surplus property shall be disposed of so as to afford
public and governmental institutions, nonprofit or
tax-supported educational institutions, charitable
eleemosynary institutions, nonprofit or tax-supported hospitals and similar institutions, States, their
political subdivisions and instrumentalities, and
volunteer fire companies, an opportunity to fulfill,
in the public interest, their legitimate needs.*

Though an attorney myself, I cannot find in these words
any intent of Congress to turn over any of the excess
property to organized religion. Indeed, Congress would be
precluded from doing so by the First Amendment. It is true
that the Internal Revenue Code does grant income-tax
exemption to entities "organized and operated exclusively
for religious, charitable, scientific, testing for public safety,
literary, or educational purposes or for the prevention of
cruelty to children or animals." However, it is also emphat-
ically clear from the wording of the Surplus Property Act
that the property, upon distribution, had to be for the
public interest or for the legitimate needs of the United
States representing all its people.

When Japan surrendered in August 1945, the administrator of the War Assets Administration immediately asked
the acting Attorney General to make a ruling on the sale or
disposal of this property. Just nine days later, on August 23,
1945, the ruling was issued, empowering the administrator
to grant price "discounts" to organizations that had been
certified by the Bureau of Internal Revenue as being
nonprofit educational institutions exempt from taxation—
discounts amounting to as much as 100 percent. Such

discounts were considered appropriate in cases "where the benefits to accrue to the United States from the proposed use will exceed the established current market value of the property." There was no indication that the benefits referred to religious purposes.

In the ensuing eighteen months the United States carried out the huge task of demobilizing 12 million members of the armed forces, thereby emptying a large number of military and naval bases, which the War Assets Administration was appointed to dispose of. Soon it became apparent that much of the land was to go to organized religion. The first religious group to move in was the Baptists. On October 23, 1947, the De Land Naval Air Station in Florida, consisting of 120 acres of land and six buildings, was transferred to the Baptist-owned John B. Stetson University. Originally purchased by the government for $704,501, the property was evaluated at only $218,116 for the transfer and then discounted 100 percent in order to give it to the Baptists *for nothing*.

What followed within the next year is incredible. On February 26, 1948, the Pine Acres Niagara Falls project of the Public Housing Authority, consisting of 7.58 acres of land and two buildings in Buffalo, New York, was sold to the Bishop Duffy High School—transfer of title being made to the Roman Catholic Diocese of Buffalo. The property had cost the government $169,076 but was evaluated at $72,076 and then discounted 60 percent for a final price of $28,830.40. That may seem like a steal; but of all the property distributed by the War Assets Administration in 1948 that was the only property for which any money at all was paid!

On April 18, 1948, the 6.36 acres and ten buildings of Fort Oglethorpe, Georgia, originally purchased by the government for $99,876, were given at 100 percent discount to the Roman Catholic Redemptionist Fathers. Eleven days later, Baptist-owned Southern College was freely presented with 121 acres and 110 buildings that had been purchased originally for $1,493,552. Three weeks later, on May 19, 1948, a war plant, Basic Magnesium, Inc., in Nevada, surrendered 12.8 acres of government land and two buildings (original cost $464,741) which were transferred to the

Roman Catholic Sisters of the Third Order of St. Dominic for nothing. On July 20, 1948, 20.3 acres and 20 buildings of the Plattsburgh Rifle Range in Nebraska were given free to the Lutheran Immanuel Deaconess Institute. Two weeks later, on August 4, 1948, the Nitre Depot in Massachusetts, consisting of 7.03 acres of land and two buildings, was given to the Roman Catholic Immaculate Conception Church School. Three weeks later, 273 acres and 47 buildings of the Laurenburg-Macton Army Air Force Base in North Carolina were given to the Presbyterian Junior College.

The largest single gift of real estate came in October, when Camp McQuade, California, surrendered 300 acres of land and 237 buildings to the Monterey Bay Academy run by the Seventh-Day Adventists. The Seventh-Day Adventists are supposed to be "strict constructionists" when it comes to the constitutional separation of church and state. Yet not only did they eagerly accept the government's benefaction in this instance, but over the years they received another 145 gifts.

All in all, from October 1947 to March 1949, organized religion received—free—987.74 acres of land and 484 buildings. Of the 275 denominations in America, 25 have profited from this distribution of real estate since the war.

Although the Roman Catholic church has been the target of much criticism for its share of this government largesse, it has not in fact received a disproportionate amount relative to the other churches. However, neither has it done badly. It has received land and buildings from the government 261 times since 1948, amounting to 16 percent of the land and 26 percent of the buildings disposed of under this scheme.

A careful reading of the *Congressional Record* comprising all the debates concerning the War Assets Administration and its succeeding agencies reveals that the legislators at no time intended to earmark either the land or the buildings for religious use. Indeed, one section noted:

> (f) *The disposal of surplus property under this section to States and political subdivisions and instrumentalities thereof shall be given priority over all other disposals of*

*property provided for in this Act except transfers under
section 12 [to federal agencies].*

Nevertheless, religious organizations were given first priority in this giant giveaway—contrary to the spirit of the law and in defiance of the Constitution.

How the climate has changed from the days of our Founding Fathers! In the early nineteenth century, when Congress randomly attempted to give a parcel of land in the Mississippi territory to the Baptist church, President James Madison vetoed the bill. On returning it to the House of Representatives on February 28, 1811, he said that he had vetoed it because "the bill in reserving a certain parcel of land of the United States for the use of said Baptist Church comprises a principle and precedent for the appropriation of funds of the United States for the use and support of religious societies, contrary to the Constitution."

CALCULATING THE COST

In the early 1960s various newspapers across the nation began trying to discover the true extent of the property owned by the churches. Finally, in 1964, a Protestant organization, Americans United, commissioned a survey in selected cities, the results of which were published throughout the country.

The investigatory method used by Americans United was to examine the assessment rolls for real estate taxation— admittedly an unwieldy source, since different states handle the recording differently. Some states make no assessment of church land. Some states make perfunctory assessments, knowing that the land and buildings yield no taxes and therefore require no accurate or current appraisals. Also, assessment rates vary: in one city the rate may be 40 percent of the property's actual value, in another it may be 30 percent, in others no more than 10 percent. To make matters still more complicated, only eighteen states have compiled tax-exempt inventories—that is, breakdowns of the various types of institutions, religious and otherwise, receiving tax exemptions. In these inventories, categories are not clearly defined, details vary, evaluations are approximate, and compliance with legal requirements are only partially realized. For example, all cemeteries may be listed together, without distinguishing those owned by religious groups. This is important, because cemeteries are traditional moneymakers for organized religion, and in direct competition with commercial cemeteries. The same situation pertains to parochial schools, day-care centers, nursing homes, hospitals, religious colleges and universities, seminaries, monasteries, convents, parsonages, and administrative buildings. When all "charitable organizations" are relegated to a single category, there is simply no way to sort out what is owned by organized religion and what is not so owned.

Anyway, the researchers for Americans United went ahead and attempted to survey Buffalo, New York City Baltimore, the District of Columbia, and Denver. Extrapolating from their results in these pilot cities, they reached the following estimates of the extent and value of religious property in the United States:

	Percent of Private, Tax-exempt Land Wealth Owned by Organized Religion in the United States	Estimated Value
Roman Catholic	55.97	$44.5 billion
Protestant	11.2	28.0 billion
Jewish	8.8	7.0 billion
Total	75.97	$79.5 billion

In 1968 a more detailed survey of the original pilot cities, together with ten more, was carried out by Americans United, with the following results:

	Percent of Private, Tax-exempt Land Wealth Owned by Organized Religion in the United States	Estimated Value
Roman Catholic	31.7	$ 54.2 billion
Protestant	23.7	40.5 billion
Jewish	4.4	7.5 billion
Total	59.8	$102.2 billion

In other words, of all the privately owned land that is tax-exempt, organized religion owned 59.8 percent, worth $102.2 billion. If this land had been taxed in 1968 at the median going rate, the communities involved would have had $2.2 billion more in revenue! *And we are only talking about obvious church real estate and the buildings thereon.* This does not take into consideration church businesses, stocks and bonds, or any other wealth accruing to organized religion from any other sources.

This means that in 1968, on real estate taxes alone, each family of five in the United States paid $55.50 extra so that the more obvious church properties in their communities could be tax-free. Of course, several years have gone by since then, and I can only hazard a guess as to the increase. Organized religion increased its ownership of real estate in the United States from $3.5 billion in 1936 to $102.2 billion in 1968. That is an increase of $3.1 billion a year. Therefore, estimating conservatively, I can say at this writing that its real estate should already have reached $118 billion. At a 4 percent rate of taxation, which is minimal for land, the yield in real estate tax alone would be $2.5 billion.

How did the value of church real estate reach such staggering proportions? Obviously one of the ways was through government gifts after World War II, as shown in this table, which chronicles the rise in the value of property owned by organized religion in the United States:

1850	$ 87,328,801
1860	171,397,932
1870	354,483,581
1890	679,426,489
1906	1,257,575,867
1916	1,676,600,582
1926	3,839,500,610
1936	3,411,875,467
1946	data unavailable ⎱ ⎰ federal government grants
1956	data unavailable ⎰ ⎱ during this time
1964	79,500,000,000 (estimated)
1968	102,413,400,000 (estimated)
1974	118,000,000,000 (estimated)

CHALLENGING THE TAX EXEMPTION

When the value of land owned by organized religion grows at such a rate, it is time for the government to exercise its legal function of inventorying and assessing that real estate so that the public may know the cost of religion to the national community. Because this real estate is tax exempt, all taxpayers share the burden of increased taxation in order to maintain these religious establishments, and therefore we have a right to know the precise extent of the churches' holdings.

In 1963 I myself brought a suit in Baltimore, asking organized religion in that city to pay its fair share of taxes on real estate that it owned. The case was concluded in the Maryland Court of Appeals on February 14, 1966, when the court decided that:

1. Organized religion does gain an economic benefit from tax exemptions and this benefit is at the expense of the general taxpayer.
2. Organized religion needs these benefits, and should have them, because it renders secular "benefits to the community such as aid to the poor and aged, day nurseries, care of the sick and efforts to eliminate racial inequalities."

The court ruled further that the tax exemption was a

valid discretionary political decision of the State legislature. Because houses of worship serve worthy purposes and their exemptions are so hoary in history and widespread in geography, they should be sustained notwithstanding the First Amendment.

An appeal to the Supreme Court was made, but on October 10, 1966, it refused to review the Maryland decision.

A New York citizen then decided to challenge the tax exemption for religious organizations in his state. In this instance, however, the Supreme Court decided in June of 1969 to review the case. The state of New York, like Maryland before it, took the side of the churches and argued that the land should be tax-exempt. Thirty-six other states joined with New York in this plea to the court. One of those states was Texas, where I am a resident. At no time was the question put to the taxpayers of Texas as to whether or not they desired to join this case on behalf of the churches. I doubt very seriously whether taxpayers in the other states were asked if they wished to go on subsidizing organized religion.

Basically, organized religion's argument in the case was that on church property any tax would be a tax "on religion" and would thus infringe on religious liberties. I also entered a brief on the case, and the issue that I emphasized was that if lands were to be taxed for public revenue they should be taxed equally, without regard to ownership. Thus, anyone desiring to own land was on notice that a tax ran with that land no matter to what use he might wish to put it. (Meanwhile, New York City had estimated that religious institutions in that city owned $692 million worth of real estate, which, if taxed, would bring in $36 million annually to New York City alone.)

On May 4, 1970, in a 7-1 decision, the Supreme Court held that organized religion should be tax-exempt on its land. Chief Justice Warren Burger declared, in a memorable phrase, that the role of the state toward religion should be one of "benevolent neutrality." Of course, neutral is neutral —and for the state to be benevolent or malevolent deprives it of its neutrality. But Burger's reasoning got even fuzzier as he went along. He admitted that the religious clauses in the Bill of Rights were intended to ensure that no religion would be supported, favored, commanded, or inhibited, and he also admitted that tax exemption "necessarily operates to afford an indirect economic benefit" to organized religion, but he nonetheless decided that this was not government "sponsorship, financial support and active involvement." He opined, "The grant of a tax exemption is not sponsorship since the government does not transfer part of its revenues to churches but simply abstains from demanding that the church support the state." Burger further argued that the government's taxation of churches would itself be an involvement in religion because the government would need to become involved in "tax valuation of church property, tax liens, tax foreclosures."

On the contrary, it is obvious that any government that gives churches special financial privileges not enjoyed by others is an "active" government getting "involved" with religion. Religion is being treated differently and specially, primarily because it is religion. Most basic of all is the fact that churches are used for religious purposes, and such use is specifically denied government aid by the Constitution!

9 In God We Trust, In Securities We Invest
The Churches' Stake in Private Enterprise

Frequently in the United States there have been efforts to learn how much money organized religion has invested and where and to what purpose the income from the investments has been put. Unfortunately, however, the churches need not report to anyone, anywhere, on any level. No city, county, state, or federal law requires such accounting. All speculation as to how much money organized religion has invested is just that—speculation.

In this chapter, in discussing the churches' income from stocks, bonds, and real estate investments, I will have occasion to mention various denominations' "financial reports" or "financial statements." But one should be careful not to confuse such reports with the financial reports that are legally required of corporations and that are subject to the audits of the Internal Revenue Service, the Securities and Exchange Commission, the Justice Department's antitrust division, or any other agency of government. On the contrary, they are merely voluntary financial statements that are really sales brochures through which denominations advertise the virtues of their missionary activities, Sunday School programs, church building efforts, and the like, with an eye to enticing more gifts from the faithful. The accuracy of the reports thus is questionable. As in the case of the churches' reports of membership, their reports of financial dealings have to be received with a measure of caution and doubt. Nevertheless, we who are involved in keeping an eye on church activities are grateful for even these tiny glimpses of the stratagems of the money changers behind the altar.

Using these reports, inadequate as they may be, many individuals and groups have tried to estimate the churches' total investments. In 1968, for example, the executive secretary of the United Church of Christ's Board of Homeland Ministries estimated that up to $10 billion in stocks, bonds, and mortgages was held by national and state religious agencies. Louis Cassels, religious writer for United Press International, estimated that stocks and bonds held by organized religion were worth $20 billion. This did not include any securities owned by individual parishes, churches, religious orders, or clergymen. A Wall Street brokerage also tried to find out how much organized religion had invested in securities. After reaching the sum of $3 billion, it abandoned the effort as too complicated because of the diversity of names used to conceal church portfolios. Just a sampling of the confusion of names will indicate the problem. St. Mary's Convent Foreign Mission Fund of the Sisters of the Holy Cross in Indiana variously puts its holdings under three different names—Angela & Co., Annunciata & Co., and August & Co. The Roman Catholic Diocese of Vermont is hidden under the names of Bishop & Co. and Trubell & Co. The Roman Catholic St. Louis University uses the name Doikes & Co. The Roman Catholic Fordham University uses the name Joseph T. Keating. The Union Theological Seminary in Virginia lists its holdings under the name Lamore & Co. The Nazareth Convent and Academy Corporation of Concordia, Kansas, uses Nazcon & Co. St. Mary of the Woods Roman Catholic College of Indiana is listed as Mow Co. The First Church of Christ Scientist in Boston is listed as Science & Co. Why do the churches resort to these disguises? I do not know. What do they own? No one knows. Hundreds of accounts handled by banks have code names that would seem to be covers for religious organizations, but even expert investigators have often been frustrated in trying to establish identities.

The churches and other religious groups do not talk about this, but they will defend vociferously their zeal for investing. In August 1972, for instance, in a Lexington, North Carolina, newspaper, the vice-president of the annuity board of the Southern Baptist Convention published his organization's stand in a "Letter to the Editor," which stated that the organization's "funds must be invested to provide retirement benefits for the many thousands of our members throughout our great nation." Also, "were it not for these pension agencies, some governmental body would be compelled to provide such services at great expense in taxes." The statement evaded completely, however, the issue of why these investments must be tax-free for members of his religion, therefore increasing the taxes on others, and why his annuity board must be completely free of the kind of governmental supervision or accountability to which other nonprofit, welfare-motivated pension fund boards are subject.

How large are such tax-free investments? No one knows, but a few small examples might begin to give some idea of the overwhelming nature of church holdings.

AN EXAMPLE OF SALVATION ARMY INVESTMENTS

Most organized religious groups give very fragmented reports on their finances. The Salvation Army is a good example. I had occasion to check on the Salvation Army because I once had a running argument with the Salvation Army hostels. In every city where these hostels exist, their real estate is tax-exempt, and the income from the hostels is free of federal income tax. Yet, if an Atheist is down on his luck and must seek refuge there, the Salvation Army tells him, "No prayer, no supper." If it were just a private matter, they might be correct in forcing this act of faith. But so long as they hold themselves up as a public charity and accept a tax exemption and largesse from the public they should not interfere with the private conscience. But that is another issue.

In 1970 I was able to obtain partial information on Salvation Army investments, and I was surprised to find that every activity of the Salvation Army reported in the Eastern Territorial Headquarters earns a profit and that every activity has a trust fund associated with it. The Men's Social Service Centers, for instance, had annual income from the sale of waste paper, rags, furniture, and clothing, and annual income from meals and lodgings, all totaling $9,470,024. The centers also had an annual income of $46,768 from a trust investment and an annual income of $4,817 from an endowment fund—for a total of $51,585. To earn this $51,585—at, say, a 1970 interest rate of 5 percent—they would have had to have $1,037,000 invested. The Women's Social Service Department had an annual income of $9,165 from trust investments, indicating about $183,300 invested at 5 percent. The Officers' Retirement Fund had an annual income of $446,034 from trust investments and trust endowments, indicating at least $8,920,680 invested. The Legacy, Property and Maintenance Reserves Deposits reported an annual income of $3,592,111, indicating a portfolio worth $71,842,200.

This was just one territorial headquarters of the Salvation Army. The Salvation Army has five territorial headquarters, each with its own trust funds. In other words, the Salvation Army has some enormous investment portfolios.

AN EXAMPLE OF PRESBYTERIAN INVESTMENTS

Because I grew up in the Presbyterian church, I like to check on it from time to time to see what it is doing theologically and otherwise. As of December 31, 1970, it had $42,983,150 to invest. When it sought more money from its supporters, it frankly noted:

We believe that the primary motive for giving to the church is the desire to advance the cause of Christ. Yet every Steward of God's resources recognizes that making

*a gift or bequest to the church involves tax considera-
tions. The laws of our land encourage giving to the
church, and provide a number of different ways to do
so.*

*Areas of possible tax saving are with federal income
tax, state income tax, capital gains tax, estate tax,
inheritance tax and gift tax.*

This statement implies that the United States has given
these exemptions "to advance the cause of Christ," which
is, of course, not permissible under the Constitution.

What did the Presbyterian church do with its nearly $43
million of investment capital? It purchased utility stock
worth $3 million, industrial stock worth $10 million, bank
and insurance stock worth $14 million, and preferred stock
worth $1 million. It also purchased U.S. treasury notes,
federal agency bonds, and federal government bonds worth
$3 million, industrial and finance bonds worth $7 million,
and public utility bonds worth $5 million.

All these are "God's resources," of which the Presbyterian church feels it is a legitimate steward. Many of these
resources have been put into blue chips such as Du Pont,
Dow Chemical, Eastman Kodak, General Motors, Gulf Oil,
B. F. Goodrich, J. C. Penney, IBM, Sears Roebuck, Shell
Oil, Standard Oil of New Jersey, and Texaco. In bonds, the
church favors the Aluminum Company of America, American Airlines, and United Airlines. Finance companies give
good returns, so the church has purchased stock in Commercial Credit Company, General Acceptance Corporation,
and the State Loan and Finance Company.

The Presbyterians, like all other churches, have special
trust funds that are administered and reported separately,
so that one can never really know how much is where or
what the total is. For instance, in 1958 a man placed
$1,459,770 in a bank in Philadelphia and asked the bank to
administer a trust fund for the United Presbyterian church.
In 1970 he added 1,463 shares of Sun Oil stock to this total.
Even if invested only at 5 percent, this brings the church
$75,000 a year, which is not reported to any government
agency.

AN EXAMPLE OF EPISCOPALIAN INVESTMENTS

The Episcopal church has what it calls "trust funds" for its Domestic and Foreign Missionary Society. At the close of 1970 it had 781 of these funds, constituting an investment of $39.2 million, which would bring in a net annual income of $1,901,000 (at 5 percent).

This church prefers a diversified investment portfolio, in which 38.2 percent of its available cash is used to purchase bonds, 2.8 percent to purchase preferred stock, 52.8 percent to purchase common stock, and 6 percent to handle mortgages and real estate. The church invests heavily in public utility bonds such as Alabama Power Company, Appalachian Power Company, Arkansas Power and Light Company, Baltimore Gas and Electric, Boston Gas Company, Central Maine Power Company, Cleveland Electric Illuminating, Consolidated Edison, Georgia Power Company, Florida Power Company, Idaho Power Company, Illinois Power Company, Kentucky Utilities, and Michigan Wisconsin Pipeline. It also likes the bonds of Beneficial Finance, CIT, Commercial Credit Company, and General Acceptance Corporation. And, of course, the blue chips are favored, with investments in U.S. Steel, Standard Oil, Sun Oil, American Airlines, Bethlehem Steel, North American Rockwell, and AT&T.

The Episcopal church also has special funds. One such fund, Trust Fund No. 416, was established in 1928 when a woman in Massachusetts willed $90,000 to the church and designated that the income be used for current expenses in the United States. At 5 percent from 1928 forward, this one trust fund (out of no one knows how many trust funds) has already brought in at least $202,500 in interest to the church. Moreover, if the interest has been added to the capital each year, the sum would have doubled in fifteen years—that is, it would have been $180,000 by 1943—and then again doubled to $360,000 by 1958, and then again doubled to $720,000 by 1973, so that it would be earning $36,000 a year today at a 5 percent rate. It could well be earning double that amount.

AN EXAMPLE OF BAPTIST INVESTMENTS

The 1971 annual report of the Southern Baptist Convention lists "Financial Statements of Agencies" under its jurisdiction. Over twenty such agencies are listed in the report. Let us look at just four of these.

The Baptists' Foreign Mission Board has listed, in addition to permanent funds of $16.7 million and current funds of $36.7 million, the following investments:

Stocks	$ 7,381,399.20
Bonds	11,991,905.89
Miscellaneous	8,802,292.37
Total	$28,175,597.46

The Baptists' Home Mission Board, which purchases bonds from issuing churches and resells them to individuals, had by the end of 1970 resold approximately $2.5 billion worth of church bonds. It also listed $2.2 million in "marketable securities."

The Baptists' Sunday School Board reported these investments:

Corporate stocks	$2,447,832
Mutual fund stocks	845,527
Utility bonds	2,162,017
Corporate bonds	1,494,674
U.S. government bonds	1,266,707
Total	$8,216.767

The Baptists' Annuity Board reported that the total "invested assets" of its Dollar Fund were:

Bonds	$ 27,715,125
Loans (including mortgages)	85,231,767
Equity securities	74,824,525
Real estate	49,020,338
Other invested assets	1,856,796
Total	$236,856,006

Thus at the end of 1970, these four boards alone of the Southern Baptist Convention between them had well over a quarter of a billion dollars in investments.

AN EXAMPLE OF ROMAN CATHOLIC INVESTMENTS

Of all the churches, the Roman Catholic church has been the most determined to keep its financial matters to itself. The National Association of Laymen, hoping to remedy "financial abuses within the Catholic Church," tried to get a complete list of church investments, but the effort fell far short of success. Only 32 out of the 154 Catholic archdioceses are listed in the NAL's second annual report (1972), and the reports from these are incomplete and fragmentary. Some listed their investments but not their income from them, while others listed their income but not their investments. Nonetheless, using a modest 5 percent return on investment as a calculating tool, we can reasonably and conservatively estimate that these thirty-two archdioceses had investments totaling $113.6 million, which yielded an income of $6.5 million.

This estimate, of course, covers only 20 percent of the archdioceses in the country; and not included are most of the big ones—Boston, Brooklyn, Cincinnati, Cleveland, Columbus, Dallas, Detroit, Indianapolis, Los Angeles, Miami, New Orleans, New York, Oakland, Oklahoma City, Philadelphia, Pittsburgh, San Francisco, Savannah, and Toledo. All we can do is guess at their holdings. On the basis of the NAL figures, however, a little simple multiplication would put the value of diocesan investments at about $568 million and the income derived therefrom at $32.5 million.

Remember, we are talking about diocesan investments *only*. This does not include the holdings of the parishes, fraternal orders, religious orders, associations, charities, and so on. In fact, if the situation in Portland, Maine, is representative (of the archdioceses responding to the NAL survey, it was the only one that reported parish holdings) then parish investments alone are *over three times* the diocesan investments. It is easy to see why one stock market expert recently estimated that the total Roman Catholic investments, of all kinds, were probably in the neighborhood of $20 billion.

THE UNKNOWN WEALTH

A trust fund here, a common stock there, corporate bonds, mutual funds, corporate loans—there probably is no form of business ownership or investment in which the churches are not involved and from which they do not derive no one knows how many tens of millions of dollars of tax-free income, at the taxpayer's expense. And until the churches are forced to disclose their holdings, no one will know.

Organized religions point out that other eleemosynary organizations are also tax exempt and also invest in stocks and bonds. True, but the constitutional prohibition is not that "Congress shall make no law respecting an establishment of hospitals or charities." It is "Congress shall make no law respecting an establishment of religion." The principle on which our nation is founded is that religion is a private affair, not a public one and that, therefore, it should not be assisted by government at the expense of the general taxpayer. Moreover, these other eleemosynary organizations—unlike the churches—are required by law to file yearly information returns with the Internal Revenue Service. They must also report to the Securities and Exchange Commission and other regulatory agencies. Organized religion is not placed under any such reporting controls.

THE CHURCHES FLEX THEIR ECONOMIC MUSCLES

An interesting and disturbing aspect of these investments and the vast economic power thus accumulated by the churches is the growing evidence that the churches are beginning to wield that power to exert various types of influence on the businesses in which they invest. The United Church of Christ has actually put out a "how to do it" brochure, describing the means of exerting influence. It speaks in this kind of language:

> *A church organization which holds stock of a large corporation may disapprove certain policies, practices or attitudes of the corporation. To bring about a modification of such policies, practices or attitudes, the stockholder has four basic options. Those options are: to sell the stock; to institute litigation; to participate actively in stockholders' meetings; and to seek in other ways to persuade the management of the corporation to take certain action.*

The United Church of Christ then examines these ways in which business can be influenced by organized religion. With respect to sale of stock, it says:

> *A sale of stock, without first communicating with the management of the corporation, is not likely to influence the management to take action desired by the [religious] organization. Rather, it is the threat of a sale plus the willingness to go through with the threat that must be considered as a possible weapon to influence management. . . .*
>
> *Effective publication of the fact that a respected institution is selling stock of a corporation (or threatening to do so) for clearly defined moral or social reasons can have a clear impact upon corporate management.*

On the question of whether or not to buy stock in an "immoral" company in the first place, the United Church of Christ is rather equivocal. Sometimes a church should refrain from buying such stock, but, on the other hand, it should not pass up a good money-making investment:

> *Churches have traditionally not bought stock in corporations whose products or practices they consider deleterious or harmful. Until recently, this self-conscious non-purchase policy was usually limited to stocks of tobacco and liquor producers. As church concern about other issues and the relation of corporate practices to them has increased, many urge that this policy be extended to apply to other concerns.*

The decision as to whether church investors should seek "social impact" or "purity of holdings" is most crucial. Generally, the [United Church of Christ] believes that investors should seek the best investment opportunities on financial grounds and then work from within to alter corporate practices.

The brochure then talks of the tactic of instituting litigation to get corporate policies changed:

The directors and officers of a corporation have broad discretionary powers to manage the corporation. A stockholder may, however, bring . . . [a legal] action challenging . . . certain acts of the corporation. . . . The stockholder must show that the acts have caused (or threatened) damage to the corporation or its stockholders.

The church concedes that this is a feeble means of pressuring corporate managers when only moral or social—rather than economic—results are sought; moreover, "other means of influencing corporate practices are likely to be more effective and less costly." In other words, do not let moral fervor get too expensive! The brochure then takes up the matter of attending stockholders' meetings:

A church organization should carefully examine the issues involved in any social proposal presented to the stockholders, and make its judgment as to the propriety of the proposal in maximizing social impact. It should consider appearing in person at the stockholders' meeting if the proposal is important.

This appearance at the meeting, the church says, could well be effective without incurring costs to the church. Other means of persuasion are also urged:

As a stockholder of a corporation, a church organization can, through correspondence and personal visits with corporate executives, as well as by public statements, have an important influence on the corporation's policies.

Moreover:

> It is reasonable to expect that most alert, well reasoned managements will welcome expressions of views on the part of persons having a substantial interest in the enterprise.

But the church should be pragmatic:

> The church organization should be selective in deciding what issues should be raised with a corporation's management. Only important issues should be raised. A church organization doesn't have the manpower, and it cannot afford, to delve into matters of minor importance.

The church, in other words, should measure its ethical goals and hesitate to incur litigation costs and costs of moral suasion, particularly when the target is a corporation from which it is deriving stock dividends.

The tactics outlined by the United Church of Christ do not exhaust the possibilities. Most significantly—and most ominously—organized religion is now getting its clergy adopted into the ranks of corporate management. Oral Roberts is now a director of Oklahoma Natural Gas Company. The president of Notre Dame University, Theodore Hesburgh, a Roman Catholic priest, is on Chase Manhattan Bank's board of directors. The Reverend Leon Sullivan of Philadelphia is a General Motors director.

What have been some of the moral and social wrongs that the churches have tried to combat in corporations in which they have invested? On many of the issues, most people would agree with the moral position taken by the churches. Some churches have sponsored stockholder resolutions against companies dealing with racist South Africa and Rhodesia or against companies investing in Angola, Mozambique, and other lands that have struggled against colonial rule. A few churches have rid themselves of stock in companies having war contracts, as in Vietnam (though generally, divestment of such stocks came after the war ended and profits declined). Many churches have sought to have corporations end racial or sex discrimination in hiring and placement and end other social wrongs.

Now, I do not for a moment condemn the churches' moral position in these instances. I certainly hold no brief for militarism, racism, or colonialism; and I am delighted to see the churches belatedly developing a social conscience about such things. However, I do object to the methods that the churches have chosen to use. I do object to the United Church of Christ's guidelines.

The basic premise of democracy is that all the people of the nation should share in the decision-making process. In all these social issues, the various churches have decided that they can shortcut the democratic process and coerce independent companies into an acceptance of the churches' moral or political position. Unfortunately, the churches' positions are as apt to be for the suppression of individual freedom as for the support of it.

Whenever the churches move to influence a business, the implication is that they do so with the taxpayer's and the government's approval, for the tax-exempt position of the churches is a government mandate for their continued operations, and the increased burdens on the taxpayer as a result of these exemptions makes the taxpayer a party to all the church schemes to foster its own moralistic stance.

10 In My Father's House Are Many Mansions
The Churches as Money Brokers

This chapter deals only in summary fashion with a few methods used by religious organizations to acquire still more money and property. Because it is impossible to obtain complete information about church businesses and financial dealings, our information is necessarily simplified and shadowy. Whether it be leaseback operations (which will be placed under some legal restrictions in 1976), insurance plans, or religious bond sales, every financial device serves to add to the wealth of the churches and to remove property or business profits from conscientious taxpayers. Ultimately, every device employed by church financiers robs taxpaying citizens of more dollars and furthers organized religion's political and other commercial activities.

The business deals referred to in this chapter are obviously more complex than I can possibly describe here and still make them clear. In many cases it is their complexity which helps to disguise their basic character. As the laws change, moreover, the character of the deals change, for the churches are as skilled at finding loopholes and shifting tax burdens as are the financial wizards who earn millions of dollars a year and pay few or no taxes. Indeed, the churches can often lay claim to greater financial skill, for they earn hundreds of millions and pay scarcely any taxes.

Organized religion's investments in American business and industry go far beyond the purchase of stocks and bonds, discussed in the previous chapter. Its relation to business has become even more direct. It owns profit-making businesses and business properties outright or holds them through complicated leasing arrangements. Most important, all the profits gathered by the churches under these schemes have been wholly tax-free.

Given all the churches' complicated holdings and dealings, it is impossible to estimate precisely the consequent tax loss to the government, but most responsible sources estimate that the loss from all companies owned outright by the churches or involved in so-called leasebacks is *$6.5 billion a year*. Governor George Wallace's estimate of the size of this tax loss is revealed in his statement calling for "the levying of taxes upon the estimated $150 billion worth of church commercial property now in competition with business and industries in our free enterprise system."

LEASEBACKS

One of the most notable examples of the churches' "charitable" mission has been their willingness to share their tax exemptions with private enterprise. Giving tax shelter to "needy" businesses has been made possible—and profitable—by an ingenious scheme known as leaseback (which, incidentally, was held to be within the law by the U.S. Supreme Court in its 1965 Clay Brown decision). This is how it works: Say a business earns $200,000 a year before taxes; the federal tax rate is overall 50 percent, or about $100,000, and the remaining $100,000 is profit. Let us say that the owner agrees to sell the business to a church or religious organization for $2 million (probably an inflated price). The church, however, actually pays nothing, for the deal calls for the church to pay the prior owner 80 percent of the profits each year until $2 million is paid.

As noted, the business earns $200,000 yearly before taxes. Of this the prior owner gets 80 percent, or $160,000 a year, and the church gets $40,000. This former owner probably continues to manage the business under a management contract. On the $160,000 a year that he gets from the church he pays a 25 percent capital gains tax of $40,000. He therefore has a net profit of $120,000 a year, whereas formerly he had only $100,000, while the church gets $40,000 a year tax-free on the deal. The taxpayers then have to make up the $60,000 a year that the government formerly got but no longer receives under the new arrangement. The church and the businessman have successfully avoided $60,000 a year in taxes.

There are variations on this theme. Frequently the business is an older one and involves a building such as a factory or a hotel. For every businessman, building depreciation is a major financial consideration, since this is deductible as a business loss. If he has listed the factory or hotel as worth $1 million, for instance, he may possibly be able to deduct $50,000 a year (at 5 percent a year) as depreciation. At this rate, however, after twenty years the depreciation is exhausted (20 times $50,000 is $1 million, the total original value of the building); he can qualify for a depreciation no longer. So he sells the building to a religious organization, perhaps for an inflated price—$1 million or more—and then leases back the building for some yearly rent. Again, the church pays nothing; the rent is applied to the purchase price of $1 million so that the owner gets free rent for many years; and the church, after the bill is paid, gets a free building.

When foundations or colleges and universities engage in such transactions with private business, they have to report each year to the Internal Revenue Service on the income derived from the transactions and its use; only by doing so can they retain their tax-exempt status. Organized religion is totally immune from any such scrutiny. It need not report any transaction to anyone. It can buy, sell, operate, or lease, without any tax payment or disclosure. Naturally, then, the businessman who desires to engage in a leaseback turns more and more to a church or religious organization, where there is less scrutiny by the tax man.

Who loses in this arrangement? The government loses a source of tax revenue, and all taxpayers lose by having to pay higher taxes to cover the revenue that the government would otherwise have received.

In leaseback deals, organized religion invests no money, no skills, no managerial expertise. A religious organization simply lends its tax exemption to businesses and, unlike all other tax-exempt organizations, is allowed to own these competitive, money-making businesses, unrelated to its religious purposes, without paying one cent of tax on its income or disclosing its income. The Clay Brown decision in 1965 authorized this unique tax shelter for businesses, and the religious organizations of the country have been quick to come forward to assist businessmen who desire to avoid taxation.

To find out the full extent of business-religious lease-backs is impossible. I have approached many business establishments and many church groups over the years and most of them reply, in essence, that it is none of my business. Borden Milk Company has been the most frank and honest with me. It wrote:

> First, any arrangements that Borden may have with religious or educational institutions on the use of property is strictly on a business basis, and is undertaken with the objective of using our funds as efficiently as possible. This is in the stockholders' interest, and it is entirely legal.
>
> Let me be specific. There are four pieces of property which appear to come within the area of activity which you question. Three of these are in Texas and one is in California. In each case, the land and buildings from which we operate are owned by the Southern Baptist Convention. . . . The church is our landlord, and we have negotiated leases with them which are favorable to us from the standpoint of making these operations profitable.

Again, I stress the fact that so far as we are concerned it is strictly a business deal.

For both religion and business, it is business as usual; and, as usual, the taxpayer gets the business.

In 1970 the annuity board of the Southern Baptist Convention listed among its assets the sum of $47,163,592 as "properties under liquidating leases." There is indication that $2,532,377 of this sum was derived from leasebacks and involved, besides Borden Milk, such companies as Bemis Bags, Burlington Mills, Burroughs, Dunlop, Firestone, Fruehauf, Hertz, Hutrig, Mack Trucks, Mobil Oil, Newberry, Rath, Reynolds Metals, Textron, and Westinghouse. Yet the vice-president of the annuity board, when approached by a newspaper reporter in 1971, denied knowledge of any such holdings.

The churches are very touchy indeed about their leaseback arrangements. The Southern Baptist Convention insists that the Borden Milk deal should not be associated with the Southern Baptist Convention itself, but with "the Annuity Board"—which of course is officially a part of the Southern Baptist Convention. The Roman Catholic church does not want leasebacks involving the Knights of Columbus to be discussed in terms of church ownership. There is at every turn an attempt by the churches to disclaim involvement in such deals, which is curious if these business ventures are as aboveboard as they are proclaimed to be. Of course the Internal Revenue Service has occasionally sought to have such ventures outlawed—which may account for the touchiness of the churches.

The churches are not the only ones who are touchy, however. I once wrote to the former director of the Internal Revenue Service, asking him to clarify the following information that he had given to Congress:

One church, for example, has become a wholesale distributor of popular phonograph records, another has acquired at least seven sportswear and clothing manufacturing businesses. A third manufactures mobile homes and operates a drilling business. Others conduct real-estate development businesses, provide petroleum storage facilities and carry on a broad variety of manufacturing enterprises.

I wanted to know the names of the businesses and churches, and I wanted to know whether any of the arrangements had involved leasebacks or church ownership of the businesses. His reply was that I should check with CBS television, which had done a program on the subject. The program, however, turned out to be vague and uninformative; and CBS, in any case, refused me permission to quote from the program. This was a typically futile runaround.

A 1969 U.S. Senate committee dug up a number of items like the following:

A foundation set up by [Roman Catholic] Loyola University of Los Angeles bought twenty-four separate businesses during a nine-year period. Among its tax-sheltered enterprises were three dairies, a plastic factory, a hotel, a foundry, a printing company and businesses producing oil burners, rubber treads and locks. The Tax Court upheld the foundation's tax exemption last January, finding its activities entirely consistent with present law.

Unfortunately, however, although the Senate committee compiled voluminous evidence on church-owned businesses, it never discovered which ones involved leasebacks. That there were quite a number is suggested by a solicitation letter, circulated by a church, which was submitted to the committee. It read in part: "The church has made and will continue to make acquisitions of companies by paying to the sellers *a more attractive selling price than a commercial buyer will pay.*" The italics appeared in the original and would certainly seem to refer to leasebacks.

As one observer noted at the time:

The school you attend,
the hospital that treats you,
the hotel that houses you,
the clothing that covers you,

the insurance that protects you,
the nursing home that shelters you,
the funeral home that prepares you for
the cemetery in which you are buried,

may all be connected with, sponsored or owned by a church, without your even knowing it.

Occasionally we get glimpses of previously hidden leaseback deals almost by accident. In 1954, for example, Illinois Wesleyan University, a Methodist school, purchased two Hull hotels in California, the Roosevelt in Hollywood and the El Rancho in Sacramento, for $10 million. The university paid $200,000 cash and assumed mortgages and then leased the hotels back to the Emme Corporation, which continued to operate them. Within five years the university had its cash investment back, plus tax-free profits. Then on August 5, 1959, the Chicago *Daily News* carried a story that the university had sold the two hotels to St. Andrew's of the Roman Catholic Archdiocese of Chicago. Thomas E. Hull, in a newspaper interview, said that he would continue to manage the hotels for the new owner and that they would continue to be known as Hull hotels. The Monsignor of St. Andrew's promptly denied that his parish had ever owned a hotel, and the Archdiocese of Chicago said nothing.

In another instance, it was reported that three churches of Bloomington, Illinois—the First Christian, the First Baptist, and the Second Presbyterian—owned the Biltmore Hotel in Dayton, Ohio. The minister of the First Christian church, when contacted, however, insisted that the hotel had never been owned by the churches. He said that the hotel was held by some lay trustees of Illinois Wesleyan University in a trust fund to aid the university, the three churches, and the local YMCA. The income from the trust was being used to retire the church building debts, according to this minister, and his church "has not received anything from it in years." This, too, sounds very much like a leaseback. Illinois Wesleyan University says nothing. Meanwhile, I have seen several stories in which the three Bloomington churches are charged with the ownership of the two hotels in California. An opening of the financial records of either Illinois Wesleyan University or the hotels in question could settle this matter and would allow the taxpayer to know just what it is that he is supporting: a Methodist university, a Roman Catholic church, a Baptist church, a Presbyterian church, or whatever.

INSURANCE SCHEMES

Never ones to pass up a good money-making opportunity, many American churches and related organizations have gone into the insurance business. I have a letter from the Lutheran Council in the United States informing me that the Association for Lutherans Insurance is a fraternal insurance company which does not pay any income tax. In its annual report for 1971, the Ozite Company of Libertyville reported that its facilities there had been sold to the Lutherans' association in September of that year, presumably on a leaseback basis. Yet this insurance company competes with commercial ones in offering retirement income, programming, mortgage insurance, education insurance, and guaranteed insurability for Lutherans. The Ohio Knights of Columbus offer hospital insurance that pays the insured $1,800 per month while hospitalized if he is Roman Catholic.

The quasi-religious insurance business is very obscure. We know only that the Lutherans have well over $3 billion in life insurance policies in force. The Knights of Columbus have over $1.5 billion. Of the other thirteen such religious-sponsored insurance companies of which I am aware, there is little or nothing known, but certain facts can be derived from the skimpy evidence available. I asked my insurance representative what the return on $4.5 billion in life insurance policies would be to an ordinary tax-paying insurance company, and he gave me the annual reports for the Benjamin Franklin Life Insurance Company for the past eight years. In 1971 this company had $8.25 billion worth of insurance in force. Its premium income from this was $166.5 million, and its investment income was $63.5 million. The $3 billion in policies handled by the Lutherans and the $1.5 billion handled by the Knights of Columbus are probably producing proportionately similar returns. On its $8.25 billion in insurance, Benjamin Franklin Life Insurance Company paid $11.5 million in taxes. The equivalent tax on the Lutherans and the Knights of Columbus would have been about $5.5 million. By now, it will come as no surprise to the reader to find out that they did not pay it.

The taxpayers make up for all this. You cannot even purchase this tax-exempt insurance if you are not a Lutheran or a Roman Catholic, yet you must pay increased taxes so that the Lutherans and Roman Catholics can enjoy this benefit!

RELIGIOUS BONDS

Organized religion also receives substantial income from the sale of "religious bonds." A religious bond is a first mortgage, a serial, or a sinking-fund bond issued on a church, college, hospital, or other religious institution to secure money for building. Through these bonds, the church or institution borrows directly from individual investors. On my desk are prospectuses from a number of different churches and religious organizations offering interest returns of from 6 to 8.5 percent on such bonds. On each, in fine print, the following notice appears:

These securities have not been registered with the Securities and Exchange Commission, being exempt securities under Section 3(a)(4) of the Securities Act of 1933, as amended.

On one of these prospectuses, a note has been added saying that their generous terms have been made possible by a "Federal Government Interest Grant." The prospectus is from the Roman Catholic Loyola University in New Orleans, and it is for a new law school building. The note explains:

The Corporation has received an annual interest grant from the U.S. Department of Health, Education and Welfare by the terms of which the Federal Government *has agreed to pay all interest in excess of 3% on Notes being issued up to 85% of eligible project costs. The Corporation has been awarded an annual grant of $113,800 which is subject to final review of eligible costs and interest after completion of the project.*

In other words, the 6 to 8.5 percent interest that this religious group offers as an inducement to people to purchase these bonds, and hence assist the church in building, comes not so much from the religious group as from the government, which pays all interest in excess of 3 percent up to 85 percent of the project costs. In addition, although backed up by government money, there is not even the security of registration of the bonds with the Securities and Exchange Commission.

The fact that church bonds are not subject to the same scrutiny as those of business corporations leaves the general public open to the possibility of fraud. In July 1970, for instance, the *Wall Street Journal,* carried out an extensive investigation of the Baptist Foundation of America, Inc. The foundation had been set up by six Baptist ministers as a nonprofit organization to operate hospitals, retirement centers, and community centers, but from its inception it had consistently been involved in dubious transactions. Not only had it dealt with a swindler and a bad-check artist, but its assets were highly questionable. Notes worth millions of dollars were issued and sold on the basis of an alleged $20 million worth of assets. In one deal, the foundation agreed to buy an inn in California and backed up the notes by assets supposed to include 54,729 acres of land in Tennessee. The Cumberland County tax assessor said, however, "It's an impossibility for that land to be here"; the county had just finished an extensive property remapping, and all its land was accounted for. The Baptist Foundation of America has never appeared as an owner and has never been on the tax rolls.

Nor does the foundation appear as a property owner in Marion County, Tennessee, where it purports to own 6,000 acres, or in nearby Warren County, where it claims another 5,000. Another asset is a California mining property worth

$7.5 million, though the county tax assessor's office conveniently lists the property at a "fair market price" of only $1,600. The mine's last recorded production, in 1966, amounted to thirteen tons of antimony ore worth $17,000.

The notes of the Baptist Foundation of America were still around in 1970, and attempts to use them as collateral for hefty bank loans were made in New York, Rhode Island, New Jersey, and Florida. Over $600,000 of them showed up in the inflated assets of the Community National Life Insurance Company of Tulsa, Oklahoma. Several executives of that company were indicted by a federal grand jury in New York for allegedly conspiring to bilk banks and other lending institutions through the fraudulent use of life insurance policies as collateral for loans. A bank in Toledo, Ohio, gave four $90,000 loans to the Baptist Foundation of America, all of which were in default at the time of the *Wall Street Journal* investigation. Late in 1970, the head of the foundation was indicted on charges of grand theft, passing bad checks, and giving kickbacks to a loan officer. Since that time the foundation has disappeared from the news.

In 1967 the largest Baptist church in New Orleans was accused by the Securities and Exchange Commission of defrauding the public with the sale of more than $12 million in church bonds from 1956 to 1967. In selling the bonds, according to the lawsuit, the church misled investors by telling them that certain bonds would be used to build a high-rise office and apartment building, that it had sufficient income to pay the bondholders interest and pay back the principal as due, that it would make weekly sinking-fund deposits, that there was no danger of losing one's money by investing in church bonds, and that the church bonds were comparable to U.S. savings bonds. Instead, it has failed to inform investors that since 1963 the church's revenue has been insufficient to meet projected bond repayment schedules, that it has no prospects for completing the high-rise building, and that sinking-fund payments have been made by using proceeds from the sale of bonds to meet interest commitments.

11 Cradle-to-Grave Profits
*Church Day-Care Centers, Hospitals,
and Retirement Homes*

The sweeping social legislation of the 1960s and 1970s has provided organized religion with extraordinary new opportunities to fund their sectarian activities with coin from the public purse.

DAY-CARE CENTERS

I worked for seventeen years in the slums of this country as a probation officer, a psychiatric social worker, a social welfare investigator, and a counselor for neglected children. Perhaps the most heartbreaking aspect of that work was to see the need for child-care centers. The children of working mothers in impoverished communities particularly need learning opportunities in an environment that will assist in their personality development. Therefore, in all directions and at all times, we social workers pleaded with community leaders for assistance. I personally felt that it was a shame that so many church buildings were empty six days a week, but approaching the ministers to help proved to be a fruitless endeavor.

Then in the early 1960s came federal funds, and the churches immediately became interested. The Economic Opportunity Act of 1964, Title I of the Elementary and Secondary Education Act of 1965, and the Comprehensive Head Start Child Development Act of 1970 turned out to be bonanzas for organized religion.

For many years there have been independent child-care centers operated by private enterprise. In most states they must be licensed and meet certain community criteria. Usually they are continually inspected and subject to loss of license and punitive sanctions if they are not operated in compliance with rules promulgated for the safety and well-being of the children. All such centers are subject to real estate taxes and taxes upon profits. The average day-care center enrolls about sixty-five children, serves at least one hot meal, has qualified instructors and staff, attempts some kind of creative play and learning program, and has a well-equipped playground and playrooms as well as facilities for rest.

Several years ago, because the demand for such independent centers began to outrun the supply, there developed centers organized as industrial franchises. Under this scheme, an individual enterpriser purchases a franchise from a central agency that has an established name and mode of operation, including an organized learning program and an organized curriculum. The individual sets up and manages the center and employs the necessary trained teachers. For a fee averaging about $25 per child per week, the center could have an annual profit of about $16,500 after taxes.

Another form of day-care center is that operated by businesses or industry for their working mothers. The Avco Corporation in Boston, for instance, provides centers for preschoolers from three months to six years of age and has even opened the centers to children of nonemployees as well as employees. The rate is $15 a week for up to two children, and $10 a week for each additional child, with a small additional fee for meals and snacks. Avco paid the initial cost of starting the center and pays 44 percent of all operating costs. A food subsidy is provided by the federal school lunch program. Many other companies have similar centers.

Labor organizations also have day-care facilities for children of their members. The Amalgamated Clothing Workers, for instance, has centers in Illinois, Virginia, and Pennsylvania that are funded partly by union subsidies and partly by small fees charged the parents of each child enrolled. Typically, the children are provided with trained teachers and two hot meals a day.

In sum, private enterprise has thus demonstrated that it can set up and operate day-care centers, pay taxes, and provide services acceptable to upper-middle class parents for about $25 a week per child. Parents who use the nonprofit facilities provided by employers or labor organizations can usually obtain care for even less—about $15 a week per child.

When the federal government began to make funds available for day-care centers, the churches began offering their services and facilities and the per-child cost increased alarmingly. In 1970, for example, the Unitarian Universalist church of Garden City, New York, inaugurated a day-care center for thirty-one underprivileged children, using church facilities that otherwise would have been used only for about 1 1/2 hours each week for Sunday school. The projected budget (requested by the state of New York and the federal government) was $97,000 for the first year of operation—or, $60.17 of taxpayers' money each week for each of the thirty-one disadvantaged children. (The Federal Lunch Program, by the way, paid for the children's food.) This is a far cry from $25 a week.

The Unitarian Universalist church refused to disclose any financial information or to elaborate on how the proposed $97,000 of taxpayers' money would be spent. In a public meeting the minister of this church stated that the operation of the day-care center would be "fulfilling a religious purpose" of the church. Now, in order for the government to permit organized religion's participation in such programs, it has structured the funding in such a way that the church itself theoretically will not receive the funds. However, the following question-and-answer exchanges with the minister at that public meeting will illustrate the extent to which this principle of church-state separation is observed:

> Q: *You expressed in your speech here tonight that this will be an entirely separate and independent corporation which is to run this day-care center?*
>
> A: *I didn't say it would be an independent corporation. It will be a separate corporation, three-fifths of the board from the Unitarian Universalist Church. . . . It is a separate corporation to maintain separation of Church and State.*
>
> Q: *If that is the case then your congregation, as a congregation, cannot direct what this separate corporation shall do.*
>
> A: *We can direct three-fifths of the board members to vote, as to how to vote, and we will. . . . [Currently] 87 percent of the Unitarian Universalist churches in the State of New York operate day-care centers or nursery schools. This is a church function. It is religiously motivated. . . . I think you will find few leaders of American Christianity and Judaism who will not agree it is a church function.*
>
> Q: *May I ask how many of the 87 percent of the churches that adopted or opened day-care centers or nursery schools operated with public funds?*
>
> A: *I know the Freeport one operates largely out of public funds, but these are paid to the mothers on welfare as a supplement to their checks and then paid to the Day-Center Corporation.*

THE ANTIPOVERTY PROGRAMS

The disbursement of government funds to religious organizations for their charitable or education efforts is a matter so contrary to our Constitution that President James Madison dealt with it in a veto message to Congress on February 11, 1811, after Congress had passed a bill to incorporate the Protestant Episcopal Church in Alexandria, Virginia. Among other reasons, all basically upholding the separation of church and state, he noted:

Because the bill vests in the said incorporated church an authority to provide for the support of the poor and the education of poor children of the same, an authority which, being altogether superfluous if the provision is to be the result of pious charity, would be a precedent for giving to religious societies as such a legal agency in carrying into effect a public and civic duty.

The Economic Opportunity Act of 1964 went directly counter to this premise. Its effect was to widen government subsidies to programs advanced and administrated by organized religion. Two provisions of the law were especially unfortunate in this respect, sections 203 and 113. The former authorized grants of tax funds to "private nonpublic organizations," and the latter provided both funds and people for use "for local projects sponsored by private nonprofit organizations." It is true that a "sectarian disclaimer" was added, barring funds for "the construction, operation or maintenance of any facility used or to be used for sectarian instruction or as a place of worship." And it is also true that section 6 of the "Conditions Applicable to the Use of Grants for Activities to Be Conducted by a Church or Church Related Organization" stipulated that "Facilities renovated or rented for programs financed in whole or in part by this grant shall be devoid of sectarian or religious symbols, decorations, or other sectarian identification." However, the *Washington Post* editorialized:

No amount of covering up of religious symbols can avoid making the religious institution itself seem the source of benefactions financed out of public funds. For all the good intentions and good will entailed, we believe there is more a danger than welfare in this partnership between church and state.

Under this antipoverty program, organized religion expended tax funds, raised through compulsion from everyone, and administered those funds as it saw fit on programs that it initiated. One immediate benefit of the program was the income to the churches from rental of their facilities. A small but amusing example of this is provided by a church in Pascagoula, Mississippi, which received a monthly check from the Head Start program in respect of the following items:

> $100 a month for the use of the toilet
> $120 a month for the use of the refrigerator
> $110 a month for the use of the stove
> $120 a month for the use of the sink
> $10 a month for the use of the garbage can
> $92 a month for the use of the carpet

More seriously, the *Wall Street Journal* revealed in a series of articles that the federal money often went to pay off church mortgages, because of the loopholes in the law.

The real effect of the program was candidly summed up by R. Sargent Shriver, the head of the Office of Economic Opportunity (OEO), in remarks presented at the "Diamond Jubilee" banquet of the Sisters of the Blessed Sacrament. In delivering a government check for $7.5 million to the Roman Catholic diocese of Natchez-Hattiesburg, Mississippi, Shriver said:

> Three or four years ago it was impossible for a federal agency to give a direct grant to a religious group. Today, we are giving hundreds of grants without violating the principle of separation of Church and State.

In one year alone OEO gave $90 million to church groups for the "war on poverty."

In addition, a shift of personnel began to take place from pulpits to government payrolls. Thousands of ministers, priests, and nuns left their positions with the churches to become administators of the antipoverty programs. R. Sargent Shriver himself remarked that the initials OEO had come to stand for "Office of Ecclesiastical Outcasts." A common joke was that no one could be hired by OEO if a ministerial background was lacking. This caused friction. Taxpayers' funds went to pay the salaries of church personnel supposedly working full-time on OEO programs, when in fact they were actually working for the church or the religious organization. One example will suffice. In Evansville, Indiana, during the school year from September 1964 to June 1965, 183 persons received employment from OEO, and, of these, 138 were posted in parochial schools. The diocesan superintendent was ecstatic, explaining that only two of the parochial schools had been able to afford a secretary on the staff prior to the federal programming.

Squabbles erupted as the different religious groups vied for OEO funds. In Philadelphia, the Roman Catholic Archdiocese augmented the personnel of its parochial schools and church-related colleges with OEO tax funds to such an extent that protests arose from the Greater Philadelphia Council of Churches, the Episcopal Diocese of Pennsylvania, the American Civil Liberties Union, the Philadelphia Teachers Association, the Philadelphia Home and School Council, several Jewish organizations, and leaders of the Lutheran, Methodist, Baptist, and United Church of Christ denominations.

Where one church was very powerful, it carried the field. The *New York Times* of May 24, 1965, deplored the fact that the New York and Brooklyn Roman Catholic dioceses had together managed to obtain $440,000 when the entire New York Board of Education received only $2.6 million. Thus was established another precedent leading to the further erosion of the church-state wall. In this connection, it is helpful to remember the words of Madison's "Memorial and Remonstrance against Religious Assessments":

> *It is proper to take alarm at the first experiment on our liberties. We hold this prudent jealously to be the first duty of citizens and one of the noblest characteristics of the late Revolution. The freemen of America did not wait till usurped power had strengthened itself by exercise, and entangled the question in precedents. They saw all the consequences in the principle, and they avoided the consequences by denying the principle.*
>
> *Who does not see that the same authority which can establish Christianity, in exclusion of all other Religions, may establish with the same ease any particular Sect of Christians, in exclusion of all other Sects.*

We see this happening already throughout the nation. The Lutherans are strong in Minnesota, the Baptists in the South, the Mormons in Utah and adjacent states, the

Roman Catholics in Maryland, Massachusetts, Pennsylvania, Michigan, Illinois, and other very populous states. Sectionally, the situation that Madison feared seems now in existence.

Of course one of the goals of the churches in the Head Start program was proselytizing. The Methodist *Gazette and Daily* of August 15,1972, reported, for instance, that one Methodist church ladies' auxiliary operating a Head Start program in its church as "its missionary project" for the year wound up with the conversion of "several families of the children." The holding of neighborhood programs in churches made it mandatory for parents to send their children into churches or church buildings if they wished to participate in the tax-funded programs, whether or not the churches represented the faith of the family. With this there was always, as one minister expressed it, "the possibility of getting parents some day to attend our church."

No test case has yet come up in the courts in the matter of day-care centers. However, with the United States government committing $500 million in tax funds to day-care centers in 1970-1971, $600 million in 1971-1972, and $700 million each year since, it's about time that this issue was put to the judicial test.

CHURCH HOSPITALS

Since World War II the federal government has provided grants totaling billions of dollars for the construction of hospitals, clinics, and other medical facilities such as nursing homes, diagnostic centers, treatment centers, rehabilitation centers, and chronic disease sanatoriums. Frequently the grants have covered one-third to two-thirds of such construction.

Organized religion has profited by the arrangement. Under just one authorization, the Hill-Burton Act, a total of $168 million was earmarked for Roman Catholic institutions, $59 million for Protestant institutions, and $9 million for Jewish institutions from 1947 to 1958. The yearly garner is impressive. Under various authorizations from 1947 to 1958, for example, the Roman Catholic church received an average of $14 million a year or about $40,000 every day of taxpayers' money from government funds for the construction of Catholic hospitals. And from 1961 to 1966 the yearly take more than doubled to $30.5 million, or about $83,500 every day. The amount is now much greater, for according to the Roman Catholic Hospital Association, their hospitals have a current value in excess of $1.5 billion—and of that the American taxpayer donated at least one-third.

Are the hospitals and other medical facilities owned and operated by organized religion and built partly at the taxpayer's expense really nonprofit institutions? We cannot know, for there is no agency of government, at any level, that requires any of the church institutions to show whether they are making a profit or taking a loss. We never get a look at their balance sheets. Nevertheless, the federal government gives them millions of dollars each month of every year.

Although figures on profits may never come to light, occasionally by accident we do get a glimpse of the funds being shuffled about by one religious group or another. In 1967, for instance, the Poor Sisters of St. Francis Seraph of Perpetual Adoration, operating mainly in the Midwest, found themselves victims in an investment scandal, whereby they were bilked of some $2 million. In the course of the exposé and its aftermath, some of the financial worth of the Poor Sisters was revealed. By their own statement, the Poor Sisters' net worth was put at $86 million. In the postwar years up to 1967, nine of their thirteen hospitals had drawn over $11.6 million in federal construction funds:

Hospital	Location	No. of Sisters	No. of Beds	Federal Funds
St. James	Chicago Heights, Ill.	16	250	$ 1,593,000
St. Francis	Evanston, Ill.	30	401	197,259
St. Margaret	Hammond, Ind.	23	393	2,339,268
St. Elizabeth	Lafayette, Ind.	28	448	850,640
St. Joseph's	Logansport, Ind.	18	132	400,000
St. Anthony's	Michigan City, Ind.	13	100	2,163,332
St. Anthony's	Terre Haute, Ind.	16	285	841,952
St. Anthony's	Louisville, Ky.	19	244	2,554,481
St. Jude	Memphis, Tenn.	?	?	697,102
Total				$11,667,634

These figures show that nine hospitals belonging to one Roman Catholic religious order obtained $11.6 million from the federal government—*one* order, that is, out of the 539 Roman Catholic religious orders currently operating in the United States. If all 788 Roman Catholic hospitals have been federally subsidized to the same extent as those of the Poor Sisters—and there is no reason to doubt that they have—the Catholic church must have received hospital grants totaling more than $1 billion.

The scandal involving the Poor Sisters, by the way, makes interesting reading. A self-advertised Texas oil tycoon named Ernest Medders promised the Poor Sisters a substantial part of his $500 million oil fortune if they would only assist him financially until he came into his "fortune." The Poor Sisters responded by giving Mr. Medders the generous sum of $40,000 a month in cash for four years— nearly $2 million in all. These grants, of course, were just loans or, put more euphemistically, an investment on the part of the Poor Sisters. When Mr. Medders came into his fortune, he would repay them many times over. Alas, the payoff never came. It so happened that there were no oil wells; indeed, there was no fortune of any kind, except that which the Poor Sisters had so willingly provided. And, of course, the funds advanced to Mr. Medders by the Poor Sisters all disappeared.

The scandal is especially damning when one considers that it is quite conceivable that some of the federal moneys given to the Poor Sisters and earmarked for the building of hospitals and related equipment may have ended up being used to finance Medders' scheme. Since religious groups like the Poor Sisters never have to report how they use their government funds, we can never know all the ins and outs of all such chicaneries.

The picture of the churches drawing on public funds, possibly using them even for profit, is made worse when one considers that not only federal funds are involved. They also seek additional tax funds from their local communities. In 1964, for example, the Jersey City Medical Center, built at a cost of $40 million to the taxpayers, was leased to Seton Hall University, a Roman Catholic institution. Neither the church nor the university, however, ever paid the rent, so the medical center became a giveaway by default. Then, after nine years of operating the hospital, the church decided it wanted more funds and demanded $6 million a year from Jersey City to operate the hospital. Or take another example. In Irvine, Kentucky, $95,000 in city funds and $90,000 in county funds (in addition to $200,000 in federal funds) were used to build a hospital subsequently leased to the Roman Catholic Benedictine Sisters for $1.00 a year for 99 years.

Many other communities, under similar arrangements, have given away public hospitals free to the Roman Catholic church—notably in Baudette, Minnesota; Ketchikan, Alaska; West Allis, Wisconsin; Opelousas, Louisiana; New Castle, Wyoming; South St. Paul, Minnesota; Jeannette, Pennsylvania; and New Iberia, Louisiana.

A grave issue can be raised with regard to the care available at such Catholic-run, publicly financed hospitals. There have been many cases in which a hospital of this sort was the only one in a particular community and it refused to perform legal operations—specifically, abortions—because performing an abortion was against the convictions of the people administering and working in the hospital.

CHURCH RETIREMENT HOMES

In the 1960s the Department of Housing and Urban Development and the Federal Housing Administration ruled that private, nonprofit organizations were eligible for participation in low- and moderate-income housing programs. The Community Facilities Division of the Department of Housing and Urban Development provided funds for loans, and section 236 of the National Housing Act provided interest subsidies for those who wished to invest. By 1966 the Federal Rent Subsidy Act was also providing funds for tenants.

Organized religion moved in. Faced with the constitutional question of separation of church and state, the government had to develop a rationale to permit organized religion's participation in these programs. The system thus worked out was that under these programs the church group would not be the actual recipient of federal assistance.

Rather, a nonprofit mortgagor would own and operate the housing project and would receive assistance on behalf of the occupants. Church organizations, it was decreed, could participate as "sponsors" under these programs. Mortgagors, however, were forbidden to discriminate in the selection of tenants because of race, religion, or national origin.

In the matter of retirement homes, a few examples will show just how the "nondiscriminatory" system operates in actual practice. The Oblate Fathers, a Roman Catholic order, operates several apartment communities for the elderly. A brochure sent out for the Apartment Community of Our Lady of the Snows tells the story of one such home located in Belleville, Illinois. "Membership fees" start at $8,900 for a single person in a one-room apartment. For two people, a one-room unit costs $11,500. A one-bedroom unit costs $16,500, and a two-bedroom unit $24,000. This "membership fee" permits a person or couple to move in. But there is also included a monthly "life care fee," which varies from $300 a month for single occupancy of the one-room apartment to $480 a month for single occupancy of the two-bedroom unit and $680 a month for double occupancy. Persons are eligible to enter at age sixty-two.

Occupants have no equity in this community, which is owned by the Oblate Fathers. The "membership fee" provides for the lifetime rent of the apartments only. The monthly "life care fee" provides for food, a change of linens once a week, and a "hospital and nursing plan." This latter plan provides little benefit, since it merely organizes or supplements a person's private health insurance and hospital benefit plans, as well as his social security benefits.

Although the community is advertised as nonsectarian, it is on the land of the National Shrine of Our Lady of the Snows, a Roman Catholic institution. The brochures even assure you that the shrine is "your front yard." The resident chapel features "a huge mosaic of the Resurrection of Christ" and a "large free standing mosaic of the Risen Christ." An Oblate father is resident chaplain. It is doubtful that a Jew or even a Protestant would feel very comfortable in these surroundings. Under such religious circumstances we may reasonably assume that many of the retirees would contribute their weekly tithe to the church in chapel attendance and might well make the church, or the retirement community, or the shrine, a beneficiary in their wills. Wills have been a very fruitful source of income for organized religion, and this is no small consideration in inducing the aged to assemble in a religious retirement home or community. And on top of all this, one must remember that religious retirement communities like this are tax-free and financed with federal and local funds.

Another example is that of Christ's Church of the Golden Rule, which paid $1 million in cash in 1962 for 16,400 acres of land in Mendocino County, California, to start up a community of its own. The church now owns and operates there a $500,000 motel, a restaurant, a gift shop, a service station, a sawmill, and a cattle business. No one, however, allegedly "earns" any money, and thus there is no income tax to be paid or any social security contributions to be made. In this instance, residents of the community had to give everything they owned to the church and then apply for public assistance from the county welfare department— even though they might be living in homes valued as high as $100,000. Forty-two of the 125 members of the group living at the cattle ranch drew $125 a month from the Mendocino County Welfare Department. Thirty-five of these were sixty-five years of age or older, and seven were disabled. The county gave $5,250 a month to this tax-exempt venture. The setup was exposed in the news media when the Mendocino County supervisors trimmed $47,000 from the welfare budget in 1968-1969 by cutting back on the cost of aid for dependent children, while continuing to pay $63,000 a year to the religious community.

The Christian and Missionary Alliance Foundation in Florida operates on a smaller but nevertheless profitable scale. On a 75-acre site near Ft. Myers, it has been building a 600-apartment facility around a 2,000-seat "Bible Conference" auditorium, all called Shell Point Village. The complex is described as a "Christian Fellowship" center, so a Muslim, Jew, or humanist is obviously not welcome at the village.

In a question-and-answer brochure, the situation is frankly described:

Q: Are Shell Point Village apartments for rent or are they sold as condominiums?

A: Neither. You can obtain lifetime residency for you or for your companion in a Shell Point apartment by giving a "Founder's Gift" to the Christian and Missionary Alliance Foundation, paying a membership fee, and paying a monthly fee. . . .

For example, two persons can share a studio apartment for their lifetime, after age sixty-five, for a gift of $10,400 plus two memberships at $1,000 each.

Q: Do I actually own my apartment?

A: No. You are entitled to lifetime occupancy. You have no worries about taxes, upkeep, repairs.

It is important to reiterate that the average elderly American who lives in his home and tries to maintain it must pay taxes on the land. Every person in these religious retirement homes is completely exempt from taxation of any sort.

A six-page application form for Shell Point Village inquires closely into income, assets, and health. A picture is also required (this being a device often used by institutions to exclude those not white and gentile). The inquiry into finances seeks specifics on social security, pension, dividends, interest, rental income, mortgage income, trust income, and the amount of money that the retired person has in cash, savings accounts, checking accounts, stocks, bonds, life insurance, and real estate. The confidential report required of a physician includes the results of a rigorous examination report and full medical history and asks the physician for ages at which members of the family have died.

An added feature of this plan is that there is a Life Income Fund Endowment available. This can best be explained by quoting from the brochure again:

LIFE (Life Income Fund Endowment) Trusts are irrevocable gifts to a religious and charitable organization from which the donor retains the income from the gift principal for as long as he lives. As such, LIFE Trusts are not subject to probate.

Q: Is investment in LIFE the same as buying bonds?

A: No. When you participate in the LIFE program you actually make a gift to the Christian and Missionary Alliance Foundation and have assurance of 8 1/2 percent per annum interest for as long as you live. The principal amount is not returned.

Q: Is the LIFE program available to everyone?

A: No, LIFE Trusts are only offered to men and women over sixty-five. A LIFE Trust can be prepared by husband and wife if both are sixty-eight or older with earnings paid to the survivor for as long as he lives. A $10,000 LIFE Trust Agreement will pay you $850 per year FOR AS LONG AS YOU LIVE!

What is not pointed out here is that the religious organization has the $10,000 to invest, tax-free, and takes little risk in giving an 8 1/2 percent return, especially since the entire venture is tax-exempt. No business or bank could compete with these return rates on stocks, bonds, or savings accounts. Ultimately, once again, the burden falls on the taxpayer.

And so it goes on. Sunshine Villas, Golden Age Village, Harbor House, Madonna Tower, Beach Manor, Cathedral Plaza—the contructions are endless. In California alone, assessed valuation of retirement homes almost doubled in just two years, 1964 to 1966, which was when federal funds for these ventures became available in large amounts. Only infrequently does the taxpayer get any credit, and that is when a phrase slips into a newspaper story saying, "a federal loan was approved yesterday for . . . ." Always organized religion takes the credit for what the people support by taxes.

PUBLIC HOUSING

It is not only the aged who are used as bait to attract federal money. The poor are often involved also. When St. Patrick's Catholic Church of San Francisco obtained a 1 percent loan through the U.S. Department of Housing and Urban Development in order to sponsor a 206-unit low-rent project, the church got all the credit and the taxpayer got the bills. And one group called Urban America, Inc., was formed in June 1966 to use seed money to release "millions of dollars in government funds" for low-income housing developments. Participating in this group were the United Church of Christ, the United Presbyterians, the Protestant Episcopal church, the Methodist church, and the American Baptist Convention. The churches noted that under the Housing Act of 1961 federal funds were available to assist them and that the Rent Subsidy Act of 1966 would provide funds to the families who would be renting. Thus organized religion enriches its reputation by "sponsoring" housing that enriches the churches at the expense of the taxpayer.

CHALLENGE TO THE SYSTEM

Fortunately, in some communities tax assessors are growing bold. In August 1971, for example, a real estate tax assessment was placed upon the Temple Beth Sholom Summer Day Camp in Nassau, Long Island, New York. The temple, managing its own camp, provides for 400 children during the summer with daily sessions of arts, crafts, swimming, dancing, music, and other activities. The tax assessor asserted that the day camp "is but part and parcel of the total religious program" and must pay tax on its land. Since that time, more and more New York tax assessors are looking at section 420 of the Real Property Tax Law of New York. This provides that, although real property owned and used exclusively for religious purposes shall be exempt from taxation, any portion that is leased for other purposes shall be subject to taxation. Even if the rental income is used for religious purposes, the property can be taxed, as has been indicated in several recent court decisions. The basis of these new rulings appears to be that such activities constitute unfair competition with private enterprises, which do not have the advantage of operating on tax-exempt property.

In the case of Temple Beth Sholom, the camp had been leased to a private operator who ran it for a profit. In 1969 the New York Supreme Court ruled that the camp was a commercial venture and approved the partial taxation of the temple, which owned the land. In 1971 the temple opened the camp itself, declared that it was a religious camp and that its purpose was to teach children Jewish religious and cultural life. In addition the rabbi declared that any profits would be used for the temple's religious purposes. The reply of the tax assessor was to declare the land to be valued at $61,730 and to order it put on the tax rolls.

The United Church Homes, Inc. lost its tax exemption on Calhoun Beach Homes in California in 1967. The Madonna Towers of the Oblate Fathers in Rochester, Minnesota, had its tax exemption challenged in 1966. In California, the State Assembly Committee on Revenue and Taxation reported in 1968: "A tax exemption for a retirement spa for the wealthy aged violates all the principles of tax policy. . . . Living accommodations including all the latest modern conveniences, heated swimming pools, spacious landscaped grounds and extensive maid service cannot conceivably be classed as charities." One irate California newspaper editor opined, "That's enough for us. We say cut 'em off and cut 'em off now. If the program is legal, and obviously it is, then the laws should be changed." He concluded, "I don't object to their experiment but I don't believe taxpayers should help pay for it."

12   **It Is More Blessed to Receive**
The Churches' Income from Gifts and Games

Besides drawing income from a wide variety of investments, profit-making businesses and government sources, and of course from the sabbath collection plate, the churches have avidly sought out gifts of money and property from various sources and by various means. Because of the tax breaks enjoyed by both the giver and the receiver, such gifts have flowed as if from a horn of plenty.

INDIVIDUAL GIFTS

Let us start off with the example of gift annuities, which to most people seem too good to be true. One reads in newspaper advertisements that earnings of 10 percent or more are possible on the gifts, a far higher return than one gets from investments in most blue-chip stocks. In addition, there are tax savings. Some advertisements stress that gift annuities are for people who have a lot of property and money and want to avoid taxes, whereas others emphasize that they are really for people who could not otherwise afford to give to charity.

The idea of gift annuities is especially appealing to people who own stocks or bonds that they feel do not yield enough income. My sons had this problem for a long time. I had acquired some life insurance stock for each of them in order to pay for their educations, and we despaired over the years at the very small return on this stock. Moreover, like most stock, although it increased in value over the years, selling it at its increased value would have meant our having to pay capital gains tax. What do people do who want high income yield and low tax liability?

Organized religion has the answer—or the answers. There are Christ for the Nations annuities, Oblate Fathers annuities, Maryknoll Fathers annuities, the Society for the Propagation of the Faith annuities, American Bible Society "Life Income Agreements," Lutheran Church-Missouri Synod "Life Income Gift" plans, Catholic Charities annuities, Salvation Army private pension annuities, Florida Baptist Institute and Seminary annuities, Cathedral of Tomorrow "Charitable Trust" annuities. These annuity plans usually offer the same irresistible advantages:

1. An increase in the return on the investment
2. A reduction in income taxes, capital gains taxes, and estate taxes
3. An increase in spendable income

How do they do it? Well, say Mrs. A. at age seventy wants to make a gift to her religion but needs an income also. She has $20,000 in cash to invest. She chooses to invest this sum in an annuity program sponsored by the Salvation Army, since she saves a large amount on taxes and therefore in effect gets a better return. The Salvation Army guarantees her an annual return of 6.5 percent or an annual income of $1,300 until her death. From the date that the gift is made, the principal of $20,000 becomes the irrevocable property of the Salvation Army.

Because a certain amount of Mrs. A's investment in the annuity is considered by the government to be a gift to a religious organization, she can deduct that amount (up to about 50 percent of gross income) on her income tax as a charitable contribution that very first year. In the succeeding five years, she can get additional gift deductions on portions of that very same $20,000—so much so that, depending on her other income and gifts, she may eventually achieve a deduction for the full amount.

What about the $1,300 annual return on her investment? As much as 70 percent can be tax-free. This tax reduction, combined with the several reductions for the charitable contribution, will give Mrs. A more spendable income each year. (Her return, in effect, is more than the quoted 6.5 percent; it approaches 8 to 9 percent.) Finally, when Mrs. A dies, the trust assets of $20,000 will not be subject to estate taxes because the Salvation Army already owns them, nor will her estate be saddled with probate costs.

(The income from gift annuities, by the way, varies with age. If Mrs. A is thirty-five, she receives only a 4 percent return; but if she makes her gift when she is older, the rates rise dramatically—to 5.9 percent from age sixty-five, 7.5 percent from age seventy-five, and 9.8 percent from age eighty-five.)

Where does the money come from to pay these interest rates? The answer is simple. The money that the churches receive is invested in stocks, bonds, and mortgages, the income from which is absolutely tax-free. So if the church earns 8 percent on mortgages, for example, it can well afford to pay Mrs. A her 6.5 percent, or it can even take a small loss by paying her 9.8 percent from age eighty-five, since the obligation to pay anything terminates at her death, and the church is left with full control of both the principal and all the income that it produces.

There is possibly no better example of the special privileges enjoyed under the tax laws than that which comes out in the story of Katherine Drexel, a member of the rich and famous Bouvier family, who became a nun in 1887 when she was twenty-nine years of age. When her father, Anthony Drexel, a partner of J. P. Morgan, died six years later, he left her a $14-million trust, which paid her an income of $800,000 a year in return. From this income she was able to give away about $40 million from 1893 to 1953 (without ever touching the $14 million principal). Because of her family and its powerful connections, a revenue act was passed in 1924 that included a so-called nun's law, which stated that if for eight out of ten years a person's donations are on such a scale that, with tax, they account for at least 90 percent of his or her income, he or she may thereafter take an unlimited deduction. It was the answer to religious prayers. In this case, it brought the Roman Catholic church over $40 million in income—which, of course, was untaxed—and it paved the way for other donors to use the exemption. For instance, until the Revenue Act of 1969, about 100 persons in the United States were using this unlimited charitable deduction to excuse them from paying any income tax. These were usually people, such as John D. Rockefeller III, who had incomes well in excess of $1 million a year.

The Revenue Act of 1969 changed things—but not all for the better. The act did begin to phase out the "nun's law" and thus would eventually make the enormously rich subject to taxes again. But it enabled people with lesser incomes to give more substantial sums to religious organizations tax-free. Previously the average person making a charitable contribution could get a deduction of only 30 percent on his income. The new act permits him to deduct 50 percent. Thus, under the new law, the churches are not suffering, for the increase from 30 to 50 percent across the board will more than offset reduction of contributions from people in a position to give their entire income.

Now we come to the question of how many millions of dollars are involved in these individual gifts to religious institutions. We do have some solid information because the Internal Revenue Service analyzes tax returns. Each year about 33 million to 35 million tax returns contain itemized deductions for gifts to charity. Of the largest twenty-two individual gifts given in 1971, for example, six went to religious institutions, for a total of $18.9 million. The largest was $6.8 million given to the Episcopal Church Foundation by Harvey S. Firestone, Jr., and Raymond Firestone. Mr. and Mrs. Henry J. Gaisman gave $2.25 million to the Roman Catholic Archdiocese of New York. Generally, the public is unaware of the extent of such donations unless the person making the gift happens to be famous. We are aware of

Danny Thomas's funding of a Roman Catholic hospital since he is a television personality. We know that Bing and Kathy Crosby gave $1 million to the Roman Catholic Immaculate Heart College in California. Sometimes if the gift itself is spectacular it may receive media coverage, such as the time in 1970 when a Jewish couple in Beverly Hills gave the Mormon Church in California 1,386 acres of land worth $5 million. It was also newsworthy when the mayor-elect of San Francisco gave $500,000 worth of land to St. Mary's College.

However, the little gifts add up, too. In 1968, of over $12.5 billion given to charity, organized religion received over $7.5 billion, or 60 percent. By 1970, donations had increased to almost $14.5 billion, and of this organized religion received $8.3 billion, or about 57 percent. The flaw in such figures is that they do not tell the entire story. The IRS can check on only what is reported. In 1971, for example, 76,842,000 tax returns were filed by individuals and fiduciaries. Of these, 35,457,000 itemized gifts to charity; the remaining 41,385,000 took the standard deduction. Now, if each of these 41,385,000 had given just one dollar to a religious organization, the result would be over $41 million that would not show up in any budget anywhere. The IRS would have no way of knowing that the money was given to religion. Yet it is from such sources that a tremendous amount of the churches' money comes. No one knows how much.

BEQUESTS

Related to gifts are bequests in wills or testaments— another way in which people are encouraged to contribute to organized religion. Although the Internal Revenue Service reports that 149,000 estate tax returns were filed in 1971, these do not cover the millions of persons who have died under circumstances in which estate taxes did not apply. When, for example, a devout spinster dies and leaves her twenty shares of General Motors stock to her church, no tax is paid because the bequest is made to a tax-exempt organization. It has often been noted that the churches own tremendous numbers of slum houses in the more heavily populated areas of the cities. This is probably the result of many such bequests. Living alone, and without any children, old people often bequeath their homes to the church.

I have attempted a number of times to go into probate offices throughout the country to survey recorded wills for specific periods of time in order to make a systematic analysis of bequests to organized religion. I have been particularly interested in obtaining records for the years 1750, 1800, 1850, 1900, and 1950 in certain areas so that I can analyze the demographic trends of religious land and wealth accumulation. Unfortunately, in seeking this information, I have run into hostility and obstruction at every turn, and therefore no systematic study has ever been made. The churches do not report on bequests. Neither does the United States government in respect to the religious bodies or organized religion. It is one area in which virtually nothing is known. We cannot even make a respectable guess as to the amount of land and wealth the churches have accumulated through bequests.

FUND-RAISING DRIVES

Some church organizations maintain a separate agency or department for soliciting funds from the general public, as distinguished from soliciting funds from their own members or special donors; but there are no controls by any agency representing the public. As in the case of individual gifts, no one really knows how much money organized religion receives from fund-raising drives. But we do know in many instances what individual denominations expect to receive from the general public in specific fund-raising activities. In Chicago, for instance, on one single day in 1972, Catholic Charities expected to raise $22 million. In Cleveland in 1973, the goal was $2.3 million, with 20,000 volunteers combing the city to raise the funds. Not only are Roman Catholics expected to support such drives, but so is the general public. Free newspaper, television, and radio publicity are always given to these drives, and usually various city officials and dignitaries preside at the "kickoff."

The Protestants have similar fund drives. In Chicago, for example, Bob Hope presided at a $100-a-plate dinner for 1,100 business leaders to raise half a million dollars for the Protestant Foundation of Greater Chicago. There are drives for Renewal Funds, Cooperative Program Funds, Community Program Funds, Building Funds, Helping Hand Funds, Action Funds. The charity appeals are unending, as apparently are the funds raised. Of course we cannot know exactly how much is raised because no church or religious organization needs to report to anyone, anywhere, on how much money it has, how much money it receives, or how it chooses to spend it. Moreover, since any gift to these drives is tax deductible, there is no relief for the taxpayer: he is made to support the religious agencies as well as the public agencies.

Organized religion also does very well each year out of funds raised for general charity—that is, funds raised for all charities, not only the specifically church-related charities. For instance, the Tribune Charities in Chicago raises money annually through the College All-Star Football Game, the Golden Gloves, and a six-day Charities Racing Meet at Arlington Park racetrack. In January 1969 a reported $470,000 was raised and distributed to worthy organizations in Chicago, among them:

Catholic Charities of Chicago (Crusade of Mercy division)
Jewish Federation of Chicago
YMCA Central Group
Salvation Army of Chicago
Lutheran Charities Foundation
Lutheran Council of Greater Chicago
Helpers of the Holy Souls
YWCA of Chicago
St. Theresa Chinese Mission
Chicago Missionary Society, Inc.
Gospel League Home
St. Anthony's Inn
Chicago Christian Industrial League
Catholic Youth Organization

St. Vincent's Infant Hospital
St. Mary's of Providence Institute
Episcopal Charities
Young Men's Jewish Council
St. Andrew's Boy Club

The Massachusetts Bay United Fund in Boston collected almost $14 million in 1971; of this, 23 percent went to organizations with obvious religious affiliation. Included were the Catholic Charitable Bureau of Boston and the Combined Jewish Philanthropies of Greater Boston.

FOUNDATION GRANTS

Another very reliable and generous source of income for organized religion is the private foundation. In 1963, for example, the Ford Foundation awarded grants of $25 million to liberal arts colleges, of which $15.3 million—61 percent—went to religious schools. Of these, three were Presbyterian, two were Methodist, two were Baptist, one was Roman Catholic, and one was Church of Christ. The grants went for various kinds of academic research, teacher education, international training and research, linguistics, and population studies. The Roman Catholic—and therefore antipill and antiabortion—Georgetown University got $150,000 to study the rhythm method of contraception. The Church of Christ got money to set up "Seminars for Clergy on Urban Problems."

The Ford Foundation is certainly not the only tax-exempt entity assisting organized religion. There are many, many others. And in years past, what have all the established foundations in America spent in religious grants? Well, let us examine the totals reported from 1968 to 1971:

	Religion	Education
1968	$71 million	$308 million
1969	41 million	202 million
1970	51 million	281 million
1971	73 million	343 million

Now, before we accept these figures at face value, we should remember that the Ford Foundation reported in 1963 that it had given a total of $27 million for "education," when in fact $15.3 million of that went to religious schools. It is probably safe to assume, therefore, that corrected figures for the "religion" and "education" grants for the four years from 1968 through 1971 might more accurately be reflected in this table:

1968	Religion	$ 71 million
	Religious schools	172 million
	Total for religion	$243 million
	Secular education	$136 million
1969	Religion	$ 41 million
	Religious schools	113 million
	Total for religion	$154 million
	Secular education	$ 89 million
1970	Religion	$ 51 million
	Religious schools	157 million
	Total for religion	$208 million
	Secular education	$124 million
1971	Religion	$ 73 million
	Religious schools	192 million
	Total for religion	$265 million
	Secular education	$151 million

Even these may be underestimates, for the Danforth Foundation, for instance, reported assistance to "secular schools" when grants were given to the College of William and Mary to establish a chaplaincy, to Vanderbilt University to establish a chaplaincy, to the University of Colorado to assist its United Protestant Center in a summer program, to Oberlin College to aid campus religious programs, and to Pennsylvania State University to expand the curriculum of its Department of Religious Studies.

The most crucial thing to remember is that foundations are tax-exempt at taxpayer expense and that funds from the foundations flow freely to organized religion. What cannot be done directly by government (in direct tax funds to religion) is done indirectly through the device of foundation grants. Had the government given $2,889,800 to Roman Catholic schools and hospitals in the Archdiocese of St. Louis, it would have been a blatantly unconstitutional exercise. However, when it provided tax breaks and incentives for the Ford Foundation to give this amount in 1955, the transaction was somehow palatable, probably because few taxpayers were aware of what they were supporting.

GAMBLING AND GAMES OF CHANCE

Organized religion has another source of funds in gambling and games of chance. Again, it is extremely difficult to estimate accurately the total sums involved, but we can make an educated guess.

Bingo was legalized in New Jersey in 1954 and in the last twenty years has produced gross proceeds of $890 million. In a typical recent fiscal year, ending June 30, 1972, 11.5 million people attended 53,266 sessions of bingo, from which the organizations conducting the games realized $75.5 million in gross proceeds. Registered with the Legalized Games of Chance Control Commission of New Jersey are 5,761 of these organizations including 802 churches, 99 synagogues, and 1,000 other "religious organizations" —32 percent of the total. If these religious groups were to receive 32 percent of the income, they would gross over $24 million a year. The commission reports, however, that the religious groups rank first in order of income, so that their total revenues are actually much higher.

New York is the state most involved in this type of fund raising. There bingo was legalized, on a local-option basis, in 1959 and is now regulated by the State Bingo Commission. Professional operators are barred, a license must be secured, and financial records must be kept. In the fiscal year ending June 1969, there were 1,853 sponsoring organizations achieving a total gross income of $111.4 million, of which $33.4 million was profit. Unfortunately, I have figures only for the Roman Catholic church, but it is known that local chapters of the Knights of Columbus and

750 Catholic parish groups accounted for over 50 percent of the total gross proceeds. The churches' net proceeds were proportionately even higher, since they save on such overhead costs as taxes, rent, wages, and so on. The local parish groups raised $13.4 million net in the fiscal year July 1968 to June 1969, and the Knights of Columbus groups raised $3.6 million net—a total of $17 million clear profit.

In the one decade of 1959-1969, the Roman Catholic organizations in New York realized about $90 million from bingo. Figures from controlling agencies of twelve other states where bingo is legal suggest that the total annual revenue of the Roman Catholic church from this source may be at least $90 million.

Where bingo is not legal, another situation prevails. In December 1970 a reporter for the *Boston Sunday Globe* reported that "There are a dozen BLITZ or BEANO games going openly in Massachusetts each week in violation of the state's lottery laws. Catholic churches in particular find them excellent ways to raise much-needed funds to support their schools. Police and city officials in 'Beano towns' discreetly turn their heads in another direction." That this is a somewhat charitable view of the situation is revealed in another report from the *Cleveland Plain Dealer*. It appeared on April 14, 1967, under the by-line of Allen Wiggins and deserves to be quoted in great part, with a couple of names deleted:

> The good will of Geauga County parishioners at St. Anselm Catholic Church in Chesterland apparently does not extend to a Plain Dealer *staffer taking pictures of their bingo operation.*
>
> About eight men held me locked in a cloakroom more than a half hour trying to get me to hand over a roll of exposed film. I was finally let go on advice from the Chester Township Police Chief. . . .
>
> As they let me out of the door, one of the eight, a short, stocky man in his late 40s, gave me this Christian admonition: "If I had my way, we'd work you over."
>
> The police did not arrest me, nor did they look into the auditorium where, by their own words, they knew perfectly well a bingo game was going on.

Police Chief —— said he did not bother the bingo operation in the church, and would not unless complaints were made. "It's common knowledge that bingo exists in the Catholic churches in the county," he said. "But it's our position, on advice from the County Prosecutor, that until somebody files a complaint, we'll let things go as they are."

But even though it is common knowledge, Msgr ——, pastor of St. Anselm's does not seem to know about it. At least he flatly denied that bingo was played at St. Anselm's, when I asked him on the afternoon before going to the game.

It was in fact his denial that led me to attend. Others in the county had not been reticent about bingo. Typically, the Rev. pastor of St. Helen Catholic Church in Newbury freely said his church runs a weekly game that draws about 150 persons for a jackpot of $100.

So I had to go to St. Anselm Church to see for myself. The operation was impressive. More than 600 persons filled the auditorium. Accessories provided for their pleasure included a concession stand and an electric tote board that registered numbers as they were called off.

But the biggest draw, of course, was for the prizes. Besides the jackpot, one lucky winner was to take home a console color television set.

It would obviously be impossible, given circumstances such as these, to estimate what income is derived from bingo and beano and other games of chance by all participating churches of organized religion throughout the thirty-nine states where gambling is illegal.

A related source of revenue for organized religious groups is one with which everyone must be familiar from his or her own experience. Churches and synagogues are great believers in raffles, lotteries, and bazaars through which additional hundreds of thousands of dollars are raised to maintain their activities. In many cases these profitable games are not neighborhood projects put on to finance a new stained-glass window in the rectory. They are big business. The Church of the Nativity in New York City, for instance, has a national monthly raffle by mail in both Spanish and English. Like everyone else these days who gets put on mailing lists, I have been the recipient of many such enticements from religious organizations to gamble on winning—for a price—a wide variety of raffle merchandise, such as automobiles, color TV sets, cameras, and even a "Weekend Frolic" in New York City sponsored by the Sisters of St. Dominic in Blauvelt, New York. No one can hazard a guess as to how much money this profitable sideline brings to the sponsoring religious groups, nor is there any way of discovering whether or not the money that is raised is used for the purpose for which it is solicited.

PILGRIMAGES

Before concluding our sampling of the various ways in which churches solicit gifts and other moneys, we should note briefly organized religion's ventures into the travel business, extracting dollars from the eager pilgrim.

It becomes immediately apparent from the reading of any Roman Catholic newspaper that "pilgrimages" are extremely important to that church to give the members a sense of its far-flung empire and of the importance of one's being associated with it. To a lesser degree Protestant publications also advertise pilgrimages, particularly to the Holy Land. The Evangelicals blare out the opportunities.

Actually, the pilgrimages are quite secular and ordinary vacation trips, arranged like ordinary travel agency package deals that include transportation, hotels, meals, and other incidentals. A priest or a minister is usually included in the packet. Recently I noticed that on all the ads for a certain trip—no matter whether Father Murphy led the group, or Father Slominski, or Father Winters, and whether the ads appeared in Illinois, New Jersey, or Minnesota newspapers—there appeared this very secular exhortation:

> No hurry, no worry; just the most relaxing three weeks you can imagine with a small group of congenial people like you.

All the destinations were the same; all the language was the same; and even the promise of an audience with the Pope was consistently there. The prices ranged from $933 to $1,058, depending on the season.

I thought little of this until I began to make arrangements to take a group of American Atheists to India for the World Atheist Meet and found that we could spend three weeks, as a group, seeing both Europe and India for $750 per person, with hotel accommodations and meals. Also I found that all chartered flights and group rates were closely controlled by the Federal Aviation Agency—except, of course, those sponsored by religious organizations. In any event, the package flights look like another source of funds for religion.

To his credit, one Roman Catholic layman became angry about these "pilgrimages" and struck out against, not the money involved, but the hypocrisy.

It is deceiving and exploiting us, stamping a secular pursuit with the seal of the Church and persuading countless good camera-toting American Catholics that their trip to Fatima or Glacier National Park is a response to Christ's call for penance.

If the mold of organized religion is true to pattern, there is a profit for the sect in every one of these ventures, providing a steady, year-round income, while performing also the function of tying the committed even closer to the church.

13 Render Unto Caesar
The Tax-the-Church Debate
and the Movement for Reform

In the previous pages I have suggested only a portion of the vast numbers of enterprises into which organized religion has spread its investments and from which it has drawn its wealth. Its total range of investments, financial holdings, and other sources of income, we know, however, is almost limitless, reaching into mining, electronics, construction industries, steel, oil, plastics, clothing, cosmetics, hotels and motels, apartment houses, office buildings, parking lots, dairies, ranches, farms, orchards, food processing, department stores, discount houses, schools and universities, restaurants, theaters and auditoriums, insurance companies, loan companies, newspapers, radio and television stations, wineries, mills, quarries, fisheries, cemeteries, warehouses, shiplines, airlines, and telephone and power companies. To these business-related sources of income must be added the moneys derived from individual gifts, corporate gifts, foundation grants, rents, interest, wills, bequests, gambling and lotteries, charity appeals and community drives, royalties, capital gains, property sales, hospitals, retirement homes, summer camps, day-care centers, retreats, and a multitude of federal, state, and local subsidies provided under health, education, and welfare legislation. The kinds of enterprises and sources of income enumerated here, as well as many, many more, are known. Because of the grand secrecy of their financial dealings, however, the full extent of the churches' economic imperialisms must be left to the imagination.

One thing is abundantly clear about all this wealth. To the extent that the churches do not pay taxes on their colossal income and property, the average taxpayer must surrender increased sums to make up the difference. Thus, over the years, taxpayers are burdened with paying extra billions of dollars in taxes in order to further the economic strength and power of organized religion.

THE CHURCHES' ARGUMENTS

Churches try to justify this evasion of taxes by arguing that the public receives great benefits from church-sponsored activities and that taxing the churches would curtail and cripple these activities. The question, of course, is whether this argument, as well as others put forward by organized religion, is truly valid. I should like to examine the arguments briefly one by one.

ARGUMENT: *If religious organizations were taxed, they would be forced to cut or end their charitable and welfare services that are of general benefit to the public. The exemption from taxes allows them to perform these services.*

To the degree that any religious organization actually engages in such eleemosynary activities as health, education, and welfare, there is no reason why it should not qualify for prorated exemptions under existing tax laws. The existing laws exempt other nonprofit organizations that perform identical services in every state of our nation.

The basic problem is that we truly do not know the extent or quality of the churches' eleemosynary activities — apart from their advertised claims, which always picture holy men as gentle do-gooders. Without full public disclosure of the size of church wealth and of the way in which it is spent, no one can know how much of organized religion's money is actually being used to support private sectarian activities and how much is going to charitable activities supposedly benefiting the entire community.

A few years ago the vice-president of a California bank, who was also a prominent member of the Seventh-Day Adventists, challenged his own church over its annual Christmas "ingathering" drive, which features colorful pots and bell ringing in shopping centers. He noted:

> The impact of the literature and appeals and the emotionalism surrounding the solicitation is giving the public an erroneous concept that the major share is used for foreign health and welfare. This is misleading because more than 50 percent of the funds are used in the United States for the erection of church buildings, purchase of land and equipment for church facilities, an extensive parochial school system and other institutional activities.

The banker then asked the Los Angeles City Social Services Department for external audit of the denomination's "ingathering" funds. Thus, it was learned that the Seventh-Day Adventists, having set a goal of $836,000 for North America during the Christmas season of 1968, actually came up with over $6.6 million, about eight times what had been anticipated. Of this sum, 40 percent was retained by the General Conference and 60 percent was distributed to regional and local conferences. Moreover, although the Adventists' promotional material had declared that the proceeds would aid disaster victims and the poor, the funds did not go to disaster victims or the poor. They went to two Adventist summer camps, to Adventist hospitals and parochial schools, to Adventist churches for miscellaneous expenses, to Adventist students in need of tuition assistance, to construction of Adventist welfare centers, and to capital improvement projects at Adventist schools. The banker complained:

If we are to continue soliciting funds from the public, we have an obligation to give the normal assurances to which the contributor is entitled, fully itemized disclosure of fund disbursement, external audits and no commingling of funds.

No matter how much money churches collect in fund drives and gifts or how much they may claim to aid "the poor, the hungry, and the homeless," the public still relies on local, state, and federal governments to take care of the vast majority of people requiring welfare aid and relief. Social security covers the totally disabled and aged workers with dependent children. States assist the mentally ill with hospitals and clinics and the blind and deaf with schools and homes. The parentless child goes to county and city foster homes or child-care centers. Delinquents are treated in state and county homes and institutions. Narcotics addicts receive care in local or federally funded hospitals. The unemployed are compensated at the state level and the industrially disabled through workmen's compensation laws, in part federally supported. Veterans get special help for education, for land, for home and business loans, and for hospital care and old-age benefits, all with federal money. Universal education for children comes from the state, with local controls and with some federal funding. Heart ailments, muscular dystrophy, arthritis, and other diseases are researched by private foundations, and health programs are supported by public campaigns and by the federal government. Public hospitals and clinics, federally subsidized or supported by state, county, or city, provide the full range of health care. The Red Cross, the National Guard, and the Coast Guard help in disasters. Goodwill Industries and other organizations hire and train the handicapped. Many private secular agencies supported by community fund raising, provide care for unwed mothers, adoption for children, and marriage and other personal counseling.

What is left for the churches to do? What *do* they do?

What they seem to do, they do not do for free. Catholic Charities, as well as other denominational counseling services, charges for counseling on a graduated scale of ability to pay. When a child must be placed in a foster home, the church organization seeks welfare grants from the city or county to cover the expenses if the parents are unable to pay. If a child is entitled to social security, the church agency is quick to make applications for payments. As a social worker for seventeen years, I personally arranged for payment to many Roman Catholic, Protestant, and Jewish agencies for child care. Every church agency makes certain that it receives all the public welfare, social security, and other government benefits available to the children, the aged, and the disabled in its care.

A clear example is needed here. Outside Omaha, Nebraska, there is a particular Roman Catholic institution that almost everyone knows. This is Boys Town, founded in 1918 by Father Edward Flanagan to house homeless boys. Boys Town's prinicpal fund raising used to be conducted via nationwide appeals mailed out across the nation each year at Christmas and Easter. Generally the impression was given that Boys Town was struggling and could survive only through donations from the public.

Then in 1972 it was revealed that Boys Town was anything but impoverished. It had a 1,300-acre campus with plant valued at $15 million. The money appeals were bringing in close to $20 million a year for the care of about 700 boys. In fact, its fund raising had been so successful that Boys Town had an investment portfolio of about $209 million. This money, invested in stocks and bonds, was yielding an income of $8.1 million annually—tax-free, of course. In addition, Boys Town received public funds amounting to $200,000 a year from two state programs and two federal programs.

Although Father Flanagan had originally dreamed of providing a home for 1,000 boys, the population of Boys Town has never exceeded about 800. In 1972, when the financial exposé occurred, there were less than 700 boys there, while about 1,500 were being turned away each year. Yet, from the yield of the investment portfolio alone, the home had an annual income of almost $12,000 per boy. The fund-raising appeals provided an extra $25,000 a year per boy. That was $37,000 a year for every boy in Boys Town!

Two years later, in July 1974, it was reported that the enrollment had dropped to 510 boys, making the situation even more shocking.

Despite this, and despite the fact that the venture is completely tax-exempt, and as such imposes a burden on the Nebraska taxpayers, Boys Town has not seen fit to have a regularly scheduled program to enable underprivileged boys from the Omaha area to use its splendid facilities, even for a summer vacation.

In the 1971 Christmas appeal two boys were depicted mailing stacks of letters. One of the fund raisers at Boys Town explained: "We want people to think the boys send out the mail." The letters, sent to 34 million families across the country, said, "There will be no joyous Christmas season this year for many homeless and forgotten boys." It was certainly a true statement, but it was unrelated to the boys at Boys Town.

Meanwhile, Boys Town's fund raisers continue to spend about $3 million a year on such appeals, which includes the salaries of the 100 women who work on the campaigns in a five-story office building in downtown Omaha. (The office building is also owned by Boys Town.)

Indeed, when newsmen asked if the home would stop asking for public help in view of the disclosure about its finances, the priest who heads Boys Town rejected the suggestion out of hand. "We want to keep Boys Town in the hearts and minds of the country," he said. "If we quit making appeals, people will begin to wonder if there is something wrong with our operation."

Finally, with regard to the churches' claim that taxes would restrict their aid to the public, I may simply ask how they define "public." The public at large? Of course not. It is quite evident that most community services provided by churches and other religious organizations are not truly public but are directed mainly toward their own members and their members' families. The services are aimed more at tying members closer to the church than at benefiting the general public. Under such circumstances, it is at least debatable whether private religious groups function as competently or perform services as fairly and equitably as do nonsectarian private and government agencies.

ARGUMENT: *So long as the tax exemptions are offered equally to all religions, everyone benefits equally. There is no discrimination.*

The obvious defect in this argument lies in its assumption that everyone is associated with organized religion and benefits from it. The argument completely ignores those who do not attend church or do not wish to be associated with a church or other religious organization. Atheists and agnostics, among others, receive no tax benefits.

Nevertheless, let us in turn ask a more serious question —whether churchgoers themselves benefit equally, regardless of their faiths. The answer is that they do not. Religious exemptions from taxation are geared to the size of a church's wealth, not to the size of its membership. Property tax exemptions, for example, fall most beneficently upon the largest landowners, and thus the richer denominations have a clear advantage over the poorer ones. In fact, each member of the poorer congregations is put in the position of contributing to the support of the richer denominations by an increased rate of taxation upon his own individual property. The tax rate on the Baptist homeowner in Utah, for instance, is increased considerably because the Mormon church, owning tremendous amounts of land in the state, is tax-exempt. The Baptist subsidizes the Mormon church through increased taxes on his property, whether he desires to do so or not. Conversely, in the predominantly Baptist state of Alabama, the Mormon homeowner pays an increased tax because of the exemptions given to the Baptist church in that state. The Mormon subsidizes the Baptist church through increased taxes on his property, whether he desires to do so or not.

If organized religion's landholdings were taxed, the churchgoer as well as the nonchurchgoer would have a tax reduction. The churchgoer could then give the money he saves to the church of his choice rather than see a larger benefit accrue to the biggest landholding church in his area.

ARGUMENT: *Taxing religious organizations would place a financial hardship on them, at least on the poorer and younger religions.*

No one is out to bring down any religion through taxation. Hardship cases can always be reckoned with through special provisions. If a religious organization claiming hardship would come forward to put its complete financial situation on public record, then an objective appraisal could be made regarding the effect of taxation. Indeed, for such an appraisal, the public has a clear need to know all the financial benefits that all the churches are currently receiving and to know whether or not the benefits are really needed and are not simply frosting on a rich cake.

There is another way to look at this argument. In this argument the religious organizations seem to be saying that they cannot depend on member support and must ask for a public subsidy. To quote Benjamin Franklin:

> *When a religion is good, I conceive it will support itself; and when it does not support itself, and God does not take care to support it—so that its professors are obliged to call for help of the civil power—it is a sign, I apprehend, of its being a bad one.*

ARGUMENT: *Taxing churches would amount to a double tax on individual churchgoers—a tax on their personal income and a tax on their contributions that the churches have converted into real estate or other investments.*

All personal donations to organized religion can be deducted from one's gross taxable income, so that no "double" taxation can exist. Members of organized religion would suffer no more than members of any other taxpaying institution. Indeed, because church contributions are deductible from personal income taxes, church members fare better than members of other private organizations who are denied such deductions. The members of any organization, I believe, are responsible for its financial health. It is not the responsibility of the general public or the government.

ARGUMENT: *The Constitution guarantees that there shall be no laws "prohibiting the free exercise" of religion. Ending tax exemptions for organized religion would hamper the free exercise of religion by church members.*

The "free exercise" clause of the First Amendment protects the rights to prayer, mass, sermons, sacraments, and other such practices and credos. A real estate tax, on the other hand, is a nondiscriminatory levy placed alike *on all who desire to hold land,* irrespective of the landowners' beliefs. It is a major part of the budget of every local community and usually supports a number of public services. Such a tax aims neither at the promotion nor at the restriction of religious belief. The First Amendment also protects freedom of speech, but it does not relieve printers or publishers from taxes on their land.

In every community in America where churches receive the benefits of such public services as fire protection, mail service, police protection, traffic control, street paving, water and sewer lines, and assistance in times of natural catastrophe, they should at least pay their fair share of the cost of providing the services. To require the general populace to pay for these services to the church is inequitable.

The First Amendment says that Congress should make no laws *prohibiting* the free exercise of religion; it says nothing about *favoring* religion. Indeed, it says that Congress shall do nothing toward "establishment of religion." The state, then, must with equal care protect the rights of those who choose not to attend church. Going to or staying away from church, seeking membership or not seeking membership in a religious organization—these are matters of private decision. The state cannot burden the non-churchgoer with taxes in order to subsidize churches. Anyone interested in assisting religious organizations can do so simply by attending churches and contributing to them. At present there is discrimination against the non-churchgoer. Government compulsion is used to extract higher taxes from him. This is an indirect means of obtaining from the general taxpayer money that he would not donate of his own volition.

Religious tax exemptions indeed are a direct violation of the constitutional doctrine of the separation of church and state. The principal effect of the laws granting tax exemptions to organized religion is to advance religion by giving it a preferred status. Basically, the state and federal governments have actually gone into the business of supporting religion, because they are doing indirectly through tax exemptions that which they are forbidden by the Constitution to do directly; governments are indirectly subsidizing churches.

ARGUMENT: *Churches, as the community arms of organized religion, are worthy missionary institutions and deserve government support so that they can take their programs and views to the people.*

The programs and views of the different churches are conflicting, and the public should not be asked to finance a debate. Many beliefs and practices of one church or sect are repugnant to other churches or sects. The religious community, for instance, is split over questions of birth control, legalized abortion, liberalized divorce laws, freedom of speech with respect to obscenity, and tax support for parochial schools. What is considered "good" by one religious sect may be anathema to another, but the taxpayers must pay for all of them whether they agree or disagree with any of the religious or theological arguments.

Each and every week the churches—in all their lobbying for parochial aid and more tax breaks, in all their lobbying against abortion or birth control, in all their attempts at suppressing freedom of speech and other freedoms—are being financed essentially out of funds withheld from the public coffers, funds granted them by government through the tax giveaway and augmented by boundless investments. Whether he likes it or not, the average taxpayer is thus in effect paying for organized religion's lobbying and finagling. He may vigorously oppose the ideas of the antiabortionists, but willy-nilly he helps pay for their propagandizing. He may fight against aid to parochial schools, but the taxes that he pays—and the churches do not—give the churches the financial power to fight in favor of parochial aid. In short, the taxpayer pays for the churches' political imperialisms as well as their financial empires.

SIGNS OF REFORM

The real problem, of course, is that organized religion in this country wields so much political power. Elected officials are afraid of losing the religious vote. So long as religious leaders can claim to influence their flocks in one direction or another, elected officials will heed what these religious leaders say. After thousands of appearances all over the United States for well over a decade, however, I can see that those of us concerned with the inequity of the tax burden on persons not affiliated with organized religion are finally beginning to win our fight in a number of cities and states.

For one thing, the states are tightening up their laws. American cities have traditionally relied on real estate taxes to support city services, especially the local schools, police and fire departments, traffic controls, and snow removal units. This source of revenue, however, has been eroded over the past several decades by the granting of tax exemptions on property. The total amount of tax-exempt land varies from city to city, but it can range from 33 percent in New York, San Francisco, Pittsburgh, St. Paul, and St. Louis up to 40 or 45 percent in Harrisburg, Niagara Falls, Buffalo, and Newark. It is difficult to say how much of this tax-exempt property is owned by organized religion, but the following percentages are as accurate as reporting procedures will allow them to be:

Washington, D.C.	5.0 %	Portland (Oregon)	22.0 %
St. Louis	8.0	Minneapolis	23.7
Denver	8.2	Cleveland	24.0
Boston	13.0	Richmond	24.5
Buffalo	18.4	Baltimore	25.0
Providence	18.7	Hartford	28.3
Pittsburgh	20.0	St. Paul	29.9

A number of state and local governments have begun to try to reverse the trend. As early as 1967, the states of Oklahoma and Rhode Island had begun considering taxation of religious property. In 1968 the mayor and city council finance committee of Washington, D.C., began such consideration. By 1969 various states were setting up commissions to begin the study of exemptions. In Minnesota a two-year study was authorized by the Minnesota Legislature. The language of the bill authorizing the study was pointed enough:

> *Because of the change in circumstances through passage of time, or because of the need for increased revenue for state and local governments, such exemptions should be discontinued.*

Idaho, Vermont, Pennsylvania, New Jersey, and Wisconsin all moved in the same direction. In Utah only a voice vote killed a bill to inventory all exempt property. In 1970 California announced that "houses of worship" filing late annual applications for exemptions would need to pay a penalty of 10 percent of the exemption. In 1971 Washington's Pierce County put land and buildings of the Church of Jesus Christ of Latter Day Saints (Mormons), worth $1,351,980, on the tax rolls because church authorities had not proven that this property was supported entirely by donations. The church replied that "such disclosures would constitute a breach of confidence between church members" and started to appeal the decision. In Titusville, Florida, in 1973 the tax assessor announced that he would put 90 churches, assessed at $15 million, on the tax rolls because those churches had not bothered to file for their exemptions. In Michigan in 1972, a bill that would have required churches to disclose their worth was killed by only one vote in the Senate. A New Hampshire legislative committee began considering a bill that would tax parsonages, rectories, convents, and other living quarters. Oregon, after struggling since 1963 to pass a bill assessing organized religion at one-third of the valuation of its real properties, tried to pass a bill for taxation at one-fourth; the bill was approved by the House in April 1969 but killed in a Senate committee. In the state of Washington a bill was introduced to reduce the real estate tax exemption by requiring payment of the assessed value of the land but not of the buildings; this failed to clear committee.

In some states, nevertheless, some laws were passed. In Kansas the law granting tax exemptions on parsonages and dwellings for ministers was repealed. Colorado decided to tax church-owned property not used specifically for religion. In Arizona, Maricopa County, which includes Phoenix, put all church parsonages on the tax rolls. California began taxing rectories, halls, and other structures that were not strictly religious in function. In 1968, for example, the Roman Catholic Archdiocese of Los Angeles paid $1,657,697 in property taxes.

Charges for "municipal services" began to appear by 1969. On January 1, 1970, Milwaukee began charging a sewer fee of $8.78 per $1,000 of assessment. New York started charging the churches for service in that year. By 1972 a dozen cities in Colorado were asking for "partial taxes" to cover the cost of fire, water, police, sanitation, and other essential community services. In March 1972, Portland, Oregon, put the administrative buildings of nine denominations on the property tax rolls. In 1973 Binghamton, New York, pioneered a new technique when it began sending out "courtesy bills" to churches detailing the cost of providing city services to church properties. Ross Memorial Presbyterian Church was given a bill of $2,988.69 and made a partial payment of $154.81 early in the year. The Congregation of Jehovah's Witnesses paid $126.25 on account.

Politicians are becoming aware of people's disapproval of existing practices. In 1970 the mayor of Boston proposed a "service charge" on churches for community services of police, fire, traffic control, parking, and snow removal. In 1971 a candidate for public office in Salt Lake City ran on a platform that included a promise to tax churches a "service fee" on land.

Courts and attorneys general in various states are now restricting organized religion's landholdings. Rulings have gone against the Evangelical United Brethren church in Ohio, which wanted tax exemption on its three-story office building in Dayton, and in Kansas, where it wanted exemptions on its parking lots and bookstores. In Idaho, the attorney general's opinion was that the farms of the Mormons were commercial and revenue-earning and therefore taxable. The same decision was handed down in Arizona. In Kentucky the attorney general has said that property purchased for future expansion is not exempt and that church-owned buses are subject to a personal property tax. In Nashville, the taxing body revoked the tax exemption of the Baptist Sunday School Board, the Methodist Publishing House, the Methodist Board of Evangelism, the Seventh-Day Adventists' Southern Publications Association, the National Baptist Publishing Board, and the offices of the National Baptist Convention of the U.S.A.

The courts are upholding the tax assessors. In one case, the Baptist Sunday School Board claimed that the ultimate use of the profit, not the actual use of the property, determines its tax exemption. The court, however, ruled that even if the profit does ultimately go to a church cause, this is not sufficient to save the property from taxation if the property is being used immediately for nonreligious purposes. It then ordered the Baptists to pay a real estate tax on that part of the land and buildings not used for "purely religious activity."

Finally, a Dallas tax assessor has been brave enough to say, "If it produces income, it is taxable." The moment of truth, it seems, may be approaching.

PRESSURE FOR GREATER DISCLOSURE OF HOLDINGS

Private citizens, newspapers, and various groups are beginning to seek fuller disclosures of church holdings. In 1967 a Roman Catholic group calling itself the National Association of Laymen began to press the Roman Catholic church for a disclosure of its finances. In its first annual report, issued in November 1970, the association had persuaded 23 of the 154 archdioceses in the nation to offer some sort of report. Here is what some of them disclosed with regard to the value of their land, buildings, and equipment:

Baltimore	$29.2 million
St. Louis	33.1 million
Detroit	5.5 million
Joliet (Illinois)	4.1 million
Amarillo	2.7 million
Oklahoma City	7.34 million
Duluth	6.0 million
Rochester	.52 million
St. Paul	14.78 million

These disclosures were so obviously incomplete that the National Association of Laymen issued caustic statements criticizing all twenty-three reporting dioceses. Their second annual report, issued in January 1972, was more comprehensive, and all 154 dioceses were rated on a scale for adequacy of disclosures. Seventy of these did not report at all. As a result of the NAL's efforts, however, the giant Archdiocese of New York for the first time issued a financial statement. It reported assets of $643 million, of which 90 percent was in "land, buildings and equipment." That marked a beginning.

In 1971 the *Pittsburgh Press* published a very thorough ward-by-ward disclosure of all tax-exempt property in Pittsburgh, accompanied by an explanation of the revenue loss involved. It was a remarkable public service. In Pinellas County, Florida, the *Evening Independent* did a series of eleven articles exposing "church wealth."

In 1969 *The Episcopalian* magazine prophetically stated that "'Should the churches be taxed?' is no longer an issue. The issue now becomes 'What kind of taxes should the churches pay?'" In the same year the United Presbyterian church's New Jersey synod accepted a recommendation that its 400 churches consider paying municipalities for services. (At the time, however, this same church was in its fourth year of litigation in order to escape taxes on its retirement village at Hightstown, New Jersey.) In 1968 the American Lutheran church declared that it was "sound public policy" to levy upon churches "nondiscriminatory charges for municipal services such as water, sewage, police and fire protection." A study commission of the United Methodist church urged all religious bodies to consider it their "responsibility to make appropriate contributions in lieu of taxes for essential services provided by the government." A policy statement adopted in 1969 by the National Council of Churches of Christ declared that "churches should be willing to pay their just share of the cost of municipal services they receive, such as fire, police, and sanitation services." Unfortunately, however, despite the fine rhetoric, I can find no evidence that these churches have ever voluntarily paid a penny for such services in any city in the United States since 1968.

There can be no solution to all these problems until first we know the scope of the problem. Private groups and newspapers simply do not have the resources to discover the full extent of the churches' tax-exempt ownership of property nor the size of its income from other sources. The federal government does. It is time for it to get on with the job.

The Challenge

The question is always: If the laws granting organized religion special advantages are unconstitutional, why are they passed by our legislatures? and how?

That the religious community of the United States lobbies in Congress is an open fact of life. During the early summer of 1974, for instance, religious representatives spent days in the halls of Congress giving testimony on the proposed "Right to Life" or antiabortion amendment to the Constitution. Most major churches have lobbying offices in Washington, D.C., and in the state capitals to make their needs and ideas and predilections known to the legislatures. I have myself been present when the Texas Legislature was packed with nuns during a political battle over aid to parochial schools and colleges. By and large, the secular community, the world of the average citizen, is outside the communication of such legislative events, and the average citizen does not even know that such legislative maneuvering is occurring.

The churches, however, are very politically aware and have internal communications systems that alert them to legislation that may affect their position. Their lobbyists are constantly in contact with the legislators who write the bills and with the legislators who process them through legislative committees. The churches are then in an excellent position for a follow-up, and they have the grass roots organizations to see to it that the legislators are recipients of mail, telephone calls, and in-person visits that will influence the passing of the bill. Although the average citizen cannot take time off from his employment to talk to his legislator, the minister considers it a part of his duty to take the time. Whereas the citizen may be able to discuss the matter only with his family or friends, the minister can —and does—ask his congregation to write letters to the legislators. Whereas the citizen must rely on his own financial resources, the churches and their ministers have many tax benefits and moneys to finance their campaigns. It is a battle between David and Goliath, except of course that the citizen-taxpayer, as David, is even denied the sling.

Challenging the laws that corrupt the principle of church-state separation is a lengthy and costly procedure. The effort to wage the battle in the courts and legislatures of our land may even draw penalties from the government: one formerly tax-exempt organization—Americans United— lost its tax-exempt status because of its dedication to the principle of church-state separation, when the Internal Revenue Service ruled that it was attempting to influence legislation by its litigation. It is true that the Internal Revenue Code expressly denies exemption to any organization that is substantially engaged in "carrying out propaganda or otherwise attempting to influence legislation." Nevertheless, no religious groups have ever lost their exemptions even though they are constantly deep in the battle to influence legislation. Indeed, their counsel is frequently sought out by Congress and state legislatures prior to formulating new laws.

Extraordinarily, in many cases the very organization— government—that should support an individual suit turns out to be on the opposing side. I myself was involved in a suit against the city of Baltimore and the Roman Catholic church when I attempted to make the churches in that city pay their fair share of the real-estate tax burden. The municipality, instead of helping to guard the principle and the taxpayer, leagued with the church and added its power, money, and prestige to fight the citizen and taxpayer.

But challenges can and will go on. If there are no challenges, the unjust laws continue until the principle of church-state separation is lost. In many ways, we are now well on the way to the loss of the principle. The scarcity of challenges does not mean that the laws are constitutional or morally justifiable; it means simply that average citizens are restrained by the great expense, difficulty, and time required to engage in the battle. The challenges are beyond an average citizen's capabilities. Organizations must be formed, funded, and encouraged to do the job. Currently there are only two such organizations in the United States: Americans United, composed of religious minorities, predominantly Baptist, and based in Washington, D.C.; and the Society of Separationists, Inc., composed of nonreligious persons and based in Austin, Texas. Hopefully, there will soon be more.

There is one organization in the United States that is committed to the struggle for **absolute and complete** separation of church and state.

If you feel, after reading this book, that you should be helping, you can send a contribution (which is tax deductible for you) to that organization.

The Society of Separationists, Inc., is an educational, nonpolitical, nonprofit, tax-exempt organization and can be reached by writing to Post Office Box 2117, Austin, Texas 78767.

An introductory and information packet is available for $1.00.

Index